Imagining the Possibilities

Creative Approaches
to Orientation and Mobility Instruction
for Persons Who Are Visually Impaired

Diane L. Fazzi
Barbara A. Petersmeyer

AFB

PRESS

NEW YORK

Printed in the United States of America

Library of Congress Cataloging-in-Publication Data

Fazzi, Diane L.
   Imagining the possibilities: creative approaches to orientation and mobility instruction for persons who are visually impaired / Diane L. Fazzi, Barbara A. Petersmeyer.
      p.   cm.
   Includes bibliographical references and index.
   ISBN 0-89128-382-X (alk. paper)
      1. Blind—Orientation and Mobility—Study and teaching.   2. Visually handicapped—Orientation and mobility—Study and teaching.   3. Orientation and mobility instructors—Handbooks, manuals, etc.   I. Petersmeyer, Barbara A. II. Title

HV1758.F39 2001
362.4'18—dc21   2001023986

Credits:
Photographs: Tom and Barbara A. Petersmeyer
Illustrations: Terry Fields, pp. 61, 222; Patty Patchrint, pp. 204, 237, 244, 247, 253, 254, 256, 257, 313; Barbara A. Petersmeyer, pp. 40, 272, 279.

The American Foundation for the Blind—the organization to which Helen Keller devoted more than 40 years of her life—is a national nonprofit whose mission is to eliminate the inequities faced by the 10 million Americans who are blind or visually impaired. Headquartered in New York City, AFB maintains offices in Atlanta, Chicago, Dallas, San Francisco, and a governmental relations office in Washington, DC.

Contents

Acknowledgments   v

Introduction   vii

About the Authors   xi

1 Preparing for Teaching: Comprehensive Assessment   1

2 Laying the Groundwork for Creative Instruction: O&M Plan Basics   32

3 Making Learning Meaningful and Fun: Elements of Innovative Instruction   65

4 Teaching Concepts Creatively: Theory and Best Practices   91

5 Integrating Individual Teaching and Learning Styles: Motivating O&M Instruction   132

6 Selecting Training Environments: Sites for Different Students   231

7 Choosing Teaching Materials: Maps, Models, Manipulatives, and More   261

8 Working with Others: Collaboration, Professional Development, and Public Relations   327

References   345

Sources of Products   347

Index of Activities   351

Index   357

Acknowledgments

When two people decide to write together, the journey always seems to take longer than expected. What started as a sharing of ideas between a creative student teacher and a supportive master teacher evolved into an instructional strategies seminar, guest lectures, workshops, and this book.

Each of the students with whom we have worked gave us opportunities to learn more about teaching and to expand our creative approaches. We are very thankful to the staff and students from the Visually Impaired Program of the Los Angeles Unified School District and the faculty, staff, master teachers, mentors, and students from the Orientation & Mobility Specialist Training Program at California State University, Los Angeles for their contributions and support.

We are also indebted to the staff at AFB Press and our peer reviewers for their thoughtful guidance. They provided essential feedback that helped us to organize the book in a meaningful way.

Our families were our greatest source of encouragement. We especially have to thank Vince for cooking dinner every Tuesday (our longstanding "book night") and Tom for ice cream delivery. Kathryn, who was born halfway through this project, had lots of opportunity to practice patience while she waited for Mommy and Barbara to put away the manuscript and read books more interesting to a toddler.

While we are both excited about the completion of this project, we have by no means finished imagining the possibilities.

Imagining the Possibilities: Creative Approaches to Orientation and Mobility Instruction for Persons Who Are Visually Impaired is designed to be a hands-on teaching resource for pre-service and practicing orientation and mobility (O&M) specialists. Although there are ample resources that O&M specialists rely on for the basics in content and techniques of *what* to teach individuals who are visually impaired, this book explores approaches for *how* to teach independent travel skills creatively to a wide range of students who are blind or visually impaired, including those with multiple disabilities. O&M specialists who can develop a repertoire of creative teaching approaches will be most effective in delivering meaningful instruction to students of all ages and ability levels.

There are a variety of publications on the curriculum for and theory of O&M instruction (Blasch, Wiener, & Welsh, 1997; Hill & Ponder, 1976; Jacobson, 1993; LaGrow & Weessies, 1994; Pogrund et al., 1993). Some resources present the curriculum in sequential outline form, others incorporate the use of behavioral objectives, and still others provide expanded narrative descriptions. Furthermore, the actual descriptions of skills and techniques vary by author.

In preparing this instructional strategies book, the authors assumed that readers would already know the curriculum to be taught. The preservice O&M specialist will need to have completed an introductory course (including sleepshade-blindfold training) in the skills and techniques of O&M before he or she uses the book. Terms and techniques basic to the O&M curriculum are not defined because the emphasis is on teaching approaches, not on replicating existing curricular resources.

The authors also assume that only professionally trained O&M instructors will be performing the strategies and activities in this book. Others should be discouraged from attempting these techniques without the special training required.

The preparation of O&M specialists may be under the auspices of a special education or rehabilitation department, depending on the university where a particular training program is housed. Requirements for course work in general teaching methods and the level of prior teaching experience of students in O&M training programs vary. This book attempts to present teaching methods within the context of O&M training and present instructional strategies that are most applicable to the profession. It can be used as a complement to O&M methodology seminars and in preparation for or as a supplement to the supervised teaching experience. The book should be especially helpful for planning lessons and creative learning units for individual students. Practicing O&M specialists may use it as a source of new teaching ideas and approaches.

Teachers of students with visual impairments may find this book to be a useful teaching resource as well. Attention to overlaps in the curricula of education and O&M, such as concept development, should promote the sharing of ideas and successful approaches that can improve the overall quality of education for students who are blind or visually impaired.

Imagining the Possibilities was conceptualized as a hands-on resource that could have immediate applications for day-to-day teaching. The eight chapters are intended to be used sequentially, since key components of earlier chapters provide a foundation for later chapters. General ideas developed in Chapters 1, 2, and 3 are built upon and integrated in Chapters 4 and 5, and Chapters 6, 7, and 8 present concrete suggestions for handling the "nuts and bolts" of teaching O&M. Each chapter includes specific examples and strategies for assessment or instruction in O&M, idea boxes with teaching tips, and sample lesson plans. Appendixes to each chapter give samples of forms and lists of activities that O&M specialists can use or adapt in assessment or teaching.

In Chapter 1, the importance of preparation for teaching O&M is stressed and strategies for planning and implementing O&M assessments are given. The appendix provides a list of assessment tools and sample interview questions. Lesson planning basics are highlighted in Chapter 2. The use of instructional units is suggested as an effective format for planning and a means for integrating skills and concepts that are essential to independent travel. Chapter 3 presents creative strategies for motivating students and making learning fun and meaningful. In Chapter 4, concept development theory is reviewed, including the development of concepts in students who are blind or visually impaired, best practices in concept instruction, and why formalized approaches to concept development are important. Strategies for concept development are also provided. The appendixes to Chapters 2, 3, and 4 include samples of lesson plans and instructional units that the O&M teacher can use as models. Chapter 5 uses Howard Gardner's theory of multiple intelligences as a framework for individualizing teaching approaches. Specific ideas on how to integrate teaching and learning styles to optimize instructional planning are provided, and the appendix contains many additional ideas for teaching activities that are suited to different styles of teaching and learning. Chapter 6 presents an in-depth approach to selecting motivating training environments and expanding the usage of areas that have been chosen. Practical step-by-step guides for scouting lesson locations and ways of organizing different environments for students are given. The thoughtful use of instructional materials is discussed in Chapter 7. The appendix includes a number of "recipes" for inexpensive, easy-to-make, easy-to-find materials, emphasizing the positive outcomes of student-generated materials and resources that are developed jointly by the O&M specialist and the student or students. The book closes with Chapter 8, on collaboration and professional development, which also deals with the need to develop professional networks and provides suggestions on ways to avoid O&M specialists' burnout.

It is hoped that the contents of *Imagining the Possibilities* will help preservice and practicing O&M specialists explore a variety of instructional approaches that may be used with individual students. The most effective teaching is always a combination of art and science. Although there is no exact O&M cookbook to follow and no resource can provde all of the answers, *Imagining the Possibilities* should jump-start the creative juices and help to generate many other innovative teaching ideas that can be passed along from one professional to another.

About the Authors

Diane L. Fazzi, Ph.D., COMS, is Associate Professor of Special Education at California State University, Los Angeles and coordinator of the Orientation & Mobility Specialist Training Program. Prior to joining the faculty of California State, she was an orientation and mobility specialist and teacher of the visually impaired in public school districts in Southern California, as well as at the Royal Victorian Institute for the Blind in Melbourne, Australia. Dr. Fazzi is a peer reviewer for the *Journal of Visual Impairment & Blindness*, a member of the Research Committee of the Blind Childrens Center in Los Angeles, and is active in both state and national professional organizations. She is the co-author of *Early Focus: Working with Young Blind and Visually Impaired Children and Their Families* and the author of numerous book chapters, journal articles, and conference presentations on working with young children who are visually impaired.

Barbara A. Petersmeyer, M.A., M.F.A., COMS, is an orientation and mobility specialist in the Visually Impaired Program of the Los Angeles Unified School District in Los Angeles, California. She has made many conference presentations on orientation and mobility and creative teaching strategies, taught numerous in-service workshops, and is active in statewide professional organizations. She has been a master teacher for the California State University, Los Angeles, Orientation & Mobility Specialist Training Program and is a graduate of that program. Ms. Petersmeyer has more than 20 years' experience as a dance educator, performer, and choreographer in Wisconsin, California, Korea, and Japan.

1

Preparing for Teaching:
Comprehensive Assessment

CHAPTER PREVIEW

Knowing the Curriculum
  O&M Skills and Techniques
  Requisite O&M Concepts

Knowing the Student: Assessment
  Avoiding Assumptions
  Planning for the Assessment
  Conducting the Assessment
  Ongoing Assessment

Knowing the Environment
  Physical Characteristics of the Travel Environment
  Social Aspects of the Travel Environment

Appendixes
  1.A   Sample O&M Assessment Interview Questions
  1.B   Bibliography of O&M Assessment Tools
  1.C   O&M Assessment Plan Form

THIS BOOK is about exploring creative teaching approaches and ideas for making orientation and mobility (O&M) instruction both enjoyable and meaningful for students. As with any teaching field, however, before O&M instructors can begin to improvise and imagine possibilities for creative instruction, they must first learn the basic subject matter or content that they will be teaching. In addition, today's O&M specialists are often called upon to teach the O&M curriculum to a wide range of students who are blind or visually impaired. Techniques and skills for independent and semi-independent travel must be adapted to meet the needs of a wide variety of students—from young children to older adults, students with multiple disabilities and additional health impairments, and individuals from culturally and linguistically diverse backgrounds. Thus, O&M instruction is individualized to a large degree. Consequently, even more than in most fields, assessment is crucial for planning instruction for a student because O&M specialists must understand the abilities, experiences, and interests of the students they will be teaching. From this dual foundation of mastery and assessment, O&M specialists can begin to plan instruction and consider a range of teaching strategies.

In addition to individualizing teaching strategies for a wide range of students, another important aspect of O&M instruction is the use of a variety of teaching environments, rather than a single classroom. Thus, in preparing to teach, O&M specialists must know the curriculum, assess their students' current abilities and learning styles, and become familiar with potential travel environments.

Teaching the skills, techniques, and concepts related to travel for individuals who are blind or visually impaired is a dynamic process. Unlike some aspects of classroom teaching that can be planned by using a teacher's manual for a specific curriculum, O&M lessons take place in a variety of changing environments that require a different kind of lesson preparation. There is no teaching manual from which to draw homework assignments and worksheets to be completed in the classroom.

KNOWING THE CURRICULUM

As with all fields of teaching, teachers must first know the curriculum or content of what they will be teaching before they can begin to impart the information to their students. For example, a math teacher masters mathematical skills and information and then learns how to teach students these skills and information. Likewise, the O&M specialist needs to master the skills and concepts that are relevant to purposeful movement for students who are blind or visually impaired.

O&M Skills and Techniques

Before O&M specialists plan and implement individualized O&M programs, it is imperative that they are fully familiar with the curriculum that they will be required to teach. Thus, student teachers in O&M may need to review the textbook and/or notes that were used during the introductory course in skills and techniques for independent travel. Beginning O&M specialists must be confident with the terminology, application of skills in the travel environment, appropriate teaching sequence, and rationale for using each technique. Without this confidence, they will find it challenging to consider and decide on teaching adaptations and particular strategies that may be the most effective with specific students.

Experienced O&M specialists must also be knowledgeable about the O&M curriculum to be effective teachers. Those who have not previously taught a particular part of the curriculum or who will be working in a different training area with a new population of students may need to take a refresher course or otherwise review the specific content area. For example, if an O&M specialist had previously worked only in a suburban area and was going to instruct a client from a rural area for the first time, he or she might have to review aspects of the curriculum that relate to rural travel. Such reviews of information are also necessary when accepted techniques and skills have changed—either as a result of new research findings or because of the demands of new features in the environment or new technology—for example, dealing with the reduced sounds of electric cars or learning techniques for using a tactile pedestrian adapter to cross a street with a traffic light. (A tactile pedestrian adapter is a device that can be installed at pedestrian push buttons to provide a tactile signal that the pedestrian signal is indicating "walk.") Reading professional journals and new textbooks, attending relevant O&M conferences, networking with other O&M specialists, and supervising O&M student teachers are all possible avenues for keeping up to date on the O&M curriculum (see Keeping Current with the Content of the O&M Curriculum).

For a review of O&M skills and techniques, the specialist has many sources to draw from (Hill & Ponder, 1976; Jacobson, 1993; LaGrow & Weessies, 1994; Pogrund et. al, 1993). While there are a variety of ways to organize units within a traditional O&M curriculum, Table 1.1 presents one possible traditional unit organization. It includes a list of the units included in the traditional sequence of the O&M curriculum, along with a sample of the skills and techniques that are taught in each unit. (For a complete review of the O&M curriculum, including the skills and techniques taught in each unit, consult one of the sources just cited.)

Table 1.1 Examples of Skills and Concepts Taught in Traditional O&M Curricular Units

O&M Unit	Examples of O&M Skills	Examples of O&M Concepts
Basic skills	Sighted (human) guide Hand trailing Protective technique Squaring off	Next to Behind Forearm Shoulder width
Indoor travel/cane skills	Diagonal cane technique Two-point touch technique Selective trailing Stair travel	Arc width In front Diagonal Midline Landmark Route shapes
Residential travel	Sidewalk travel Simple street crossings Recovery from veer Use of the sun for orientation purposes Constant-contact cane technique	Slope Intersecting sidewalks Block Alley Sidewalk strip
Light business travel	Midblock travel Traffic light-controlled crossings Information gathering Use of the address system	Street furniture Building line Traffic surge Intersection Median strip
Use of public transportation	Bus travel Route planning Soliciting public assistance Telephone skills	Bus route Schedule Cardinal directions Platform Fare
Metropolitan/urban travel	Complex/large street crossings Use of revolving doors	Subway Plaza Skyscraper Traffic jam Revolving door
Special areas/circumstances	Rural travel Snow travel Night travel Mall travel	Snowbank Escalator Dirt road Parking lot Food court

KEEPING CURRENT WITH THE CONTENT OF THE O&M CURRICULUM

- Read texts, books, and journal articles to keep abreast of current research and practices in the field of visual impairment.

- Attend professional conferences, when possible, to hear colleagues' presentations, to network with other professionals, and to visit exhibits of new technologies and instructional materials.

- Volunteer to supervise a student teacher and learn through observation and sharing what new things are being taught at the O&M university training programs.

- Serve as a mentor teacher for new O&M specialists in your district or agency.

- Network with other professionals to share ideas on the curriculum, skills, and techniques.

- Participate in O&M e-mail discussion groups to learn about regional differences in travel skills and techniques that are taught and used.

- Utilize public transportation for personal travel occasionally to remain aware of the challenges your students may face.

- Become acquainted with the local city or county traffic engineer to discuss the safe use of traffic hardware and intersection configurations by pedestrians.

Requisite O&M Concepts

Another important aspect of knowing the curriculum is to be familiar with the requisite concepts that are needed for successful independent and semi-independent travel. Each travel skill has related concepts that are important for learning and applying the skill appropriately. For example, to learn the cane technique known as *constant contact*, a person would benefit from understanding body concepts related to the proper arm position and wrist movement used in the technique and what is meant by the term *arc width.* Once the technique is mastered, the individual must also have the conceptual understanding necessary to know when to apply the particular skill. For example, if the person is going to use the constant-contact cane technique to detect the curb at the end of each block, he or she needs to understand the many environmental concepts related to anticipating one's approach to a curb (including slope and parallel and perpendicular traffic patterns). Table 1.1 also provides examples of concepts that may need to be addressed with students who are blind or visually impaired as a basis for the O&M skills taught in each curricular unit.

In some cases, the concepts that are integral to independent travel are obvious, but in other cases, concepts may be overlooked or glossed over quickly. When conducting a training unit on bus travel, most O&M specialists recognize that novice bus travelers may need to become familiar with the interior layout of a public bus and that they will benefit from understanding cardinal directions when asking for information about bus stops and transferring from one bus to another. However, novice bus travelers also need to understand the concept of bus routes. Knowing how bus routes are established and why (for example, that there may be only one or two buses on a remote route and many more buses on a heavily used route) helps the traveler to understand why the pickup timing may be different. Understanding that many bus routes form a loop can help novice travelers figure out what to do when they have missed the desired bus stop.

Adults who are adventitiously blind or visually impaired (that is, who lost their vision in childhood or adulthood) may already have much of the conceptual knowledge necessary to learn the skills they will apply. However, it cannot be assumed that they know all the concepts in the O&M curriculum. That is why individualized assessments are so important in O&M. During the assessment process, the O&M specialist gleans which concepts need to be introduced and which concepts need to be reintroduced so they can be perceived from an auditory or tactile format and be successfully applied to appropriate travel situations. For example, an adventitiously visually impaired adult may fully understand the concept of intersection from a former driver's point of view, but may benefit from further work on aspects of the concepts, such as those involved in crossing streets safely, that apply to pedestrians. Furthermore, the person will need to relearn these concepts on the basis of appropriate visual or auditory cues. Therefore, instruction in these concepts would probably incorporate auditory and tactile formats as appropriate.

When assessment results indicate that persons who are congenitally blind or visually impaired (that is, who were born blind or visually impaired or became so shortly after birth) require intense instruction in concept development, O&M specialists need to take more time to consider which concepts are needed so as to present the O&M curriculum effectively. For an in-depth discussion of concept development related to independent travel, see Chapter 4.

Once O&M specialists are thoroughly familiar with the curriculum they are to teach, they have a greater opportunity to think about creative ways to teach the curriculum to individual students. To design lessons that make learning fun and meaningful, O&M specialists have to get to know each student as an individual.

KNOWING THE STUDENT: ASSESSMENT

There are many advantages to working with blind or visually impaired students on a one-to-one basis. However, those advantages are accompanied by the increased accountability to individualize instruction appropriately. An important key to planning an O&M program is to get to know the student.

The population of individuals who are blind or visually impaired is extremely heterogeneous. This diversity requires the O&M specialist to consider many factors in tailoring an individualized O&M program that may have an impact on the learning of independent travel skills, including the following:

- The age appropriateness of approaches and activities needs to be considered when assessing and designing O&M lessons (O&M specialists may provide services to infants, toddlers, children, youths, working-age adults, and older adults).

- Some students are congenitally blind or visually impaired, whereas others are adventitiously blind or visually impaired.

- Students may have various degrees of visual functioning that will influence the type of instruction that is provided.

- Although visual impairment may be the sole disability for some students, many students have additional disabilities or health impairments that need to be addressed in planning their programs.

- The cultural and linguistic background of the student is another important factor that can affect teaching and learning in O&M.

Avoiding Assumptions

It is important to avoid making assumptions when getting to know students. One common assumption that is often made by student teachers in O&M and new O&M specialists is that all students on their O&M caseloads are eager to learn travel skills. For a variety of reasons, this may not be the case. For example, a person with low vision (that is, whose vision is severe enough to interfere with daily functioning but who retains some useful vision) who enters a state rehabilitation center with the primary goal of receiving low vision devices and services may be told that he or she will also receive O&M training. If the individual has not requested or expected the O&M services, he or she may be hesitant to begin instruction. Other students, including older adults, may not want to travel unaccompanied. Students may also express fear or anxiety related to independent travel, causing them to be initially resistant to instruction. This resistance may be reinforced by some family members who are fearful of their visually impaired relative's attempts to be independent. School-age students, especially those who may benefit from using a long cane or monocular on campus, may resist O&M services if the services identify them as being visually impaired or make them feel different from their peers. However, many students with visual impairments are eager to begin O&M instruction and are enthusiastic about increasing their independence. Many students become more interested in O&M as they gain confidence in their abilities and trust in their O&M specialist during the instructional process.

Given the many factors that influence O&M instruction of individual students, the assessment process is an important part of the O&M specialist's job. Many of the skills needed to conduct high-quality assessments develop over time with the expertise gained from assessing visually impaired students; however, there are a few basic steps that will help O&M specialists better prepare for the formal assessment.

Planning for the Assessment

Although a great deal can be learned informally from working with a specific student over time, the formal O&M assessment is the appropriate starting point from which to design an O&M program. Both instructors and students benefit from understanding the purposes of the assessment, including these:

- to gather information on the individual's current level of performance in independent travel and conceptual development so that an appropriate O&M program plan can be developed;

- to gather information on the student's physical, sensory, cognitive, and emotional ability and motivation to learn new skills and concepts;

- to assess the environmental travel demands in the home, school, work, or community areas to determine which skills will be most relevant for the individual student; and

- to provide an opportunity for the student and O&M specialist to learn about each other's learning and teaching styles.

An assessment generally involves the following six steps:

1. conducting interviews

2. reviewing records and files

3. selecting appropriate assessment tools

4. observing the student during natural routines

5. selecting assessment environments

6. planning appropriate assessment activities

A planning sheet can help the O&M specialist to organize and prepare for individualized assessments. By selecting ahead of time the tool, environment, and activity that will be used for each particular area related to O&M, the O&M specialist can conduct an assessment that is both efficient and effective. Readers can follow the sample assessment plan of an eighth-grade student who is functionally blind and has no additional disabilities in Figure 1.1 as each step in the assessment process is discussed. (A blank planning form for the reader's use appears in Appendix 1.C at the end of this chapter.) The O&M instructor in this example used a combination of self-made interview questions and the school district's O&M assessment tool. This form can be adapted by expanding the assessment areas, methods, and activities as appropriate.

Conducting Interviews

It is important to take time to establish a working rapport with the student who will be assessed. An informal interview to discover O&M

O&M Assessment Plan

Student's Name _Dylan James_   Instructor _Michell_   Date _01-12-01_

Assessment Domain	Assessment Tool	Assessment Areas	Method	Description of Assessment Activities
Personal	Self-made list of interview questions	School life Home life Friends Interests/hobbies General travel	Interview student Interview family Review records	Review last year's files. Ask student preplanned questions about interests and prior O&M experiences. Ask father preplanned questions about priorities.
Visual Functioning	N/A	N/A	N/A	N/A
Mobility	"Azusa Unified School District Priority Goals Checklist" (Grade 8)	Campus travel Cane skills Residential block travel Residential street crossings	Campus observation Travel route in residential area	Observe student travel between classes. Do residential L-shaped route with two plus-shaped intersection crossings.
Orientation	"Azusa Unified School District Priority Goals Checklist" (Grade 8)	Cardinal directions Route reversals Landmarking	Campus observation observation Travel route in residential area	Ask student to identify landmarks and then travel two campus routes. Use Chang Kit (see Chapter 4) to assess cardinal directions. Ask student to problem-solve and reverse L-shaped route.
Conceptual	"Azusa Unified School District Priority Goals Checklist" (Grade 8)	Parallel and perpendicular two-way versus four-way stops on a residential block	In-class activity Travel route in residential area	Use tactile model to assess intersection concepts. Ask student to identify and explain traffic controls in residential area. Have student locate and describe function of specific residential block concepts.
Other				

Key: Assessment Tool—e.g., Azusa Unified School District
Assessment Area—e.g., cane skills and residential street crossings
Method—e.g., observation, interview, travel, game
Description of Activities—e.g., residential L-shaped route with two plus-shaped intersection crossings

Figure 1.1

Sample Completed O&M Assessment Plan

This sample assessment planning form was prepared for an eighth grade student who is functionally blind and has no additional disabilities. A combination of self-made interview questions and the school district's O&M assessment tool were used. Assessment areas, methods, and activity descriptions can be expanded as appropriate.

goals, prior experiences, and attitudes toward training will help solidify the domains that are most crucial to assess.

For example, the O&M specialist may ask elementary-age students to describe their home neighborhoods, activities or hobbies that they are involved with at home, or their favorite O&M lessons when they worked with their previous instructor. Junior high school and high school students can be asked to describe travel in their home area in greater detail, including traffic flow (for example, a heavy flow or number of cars versus a light flow or number of cars and cars moving through the area at a high speed versus a low speed) and traffic controls (such as a stop sign versus a traffic light) in the neighborhood. They can also be asked to identify specific units or O&M skills that were addressed during the previous year. Adults with adventitious visual impairment may be asked about their immediate and long-term goals for independent travel and which transportation options for nondrivers they are aware of or with which they are familiar. In Figure 1.1, the O&M specialist prepared interview questions to find out about this eighth grader's interests, hobbies, and prior O&M training.

The interview may also give the O&M specialist an idea of strategies and approaches (including communication style or vocabulary level) that may be effective for getting the maximum information from the student during the actual assessment. When the student does not speak English and a bilingual O&M specialist is unavailable, an interpreter needs to be used.

In some cases, the O&M specialist will want to interview significant people in the person's life—including family members, the teachers of students with visual impairments, classroom teachers (general education and special education), teaching assistants, the adapted physical education specialist, the speech and language specialist, the occupational or physical therapist, the optometrist, the rehabilitation teacher, or the rehabilitation counselor—about the individual's travel skills and goals. Whenever a referral for an O&M assessment is made by a family member or professional, it is important to discuss the original concerns that were the impetus for the referral. Simply asking an open-ended question, such as "What are your mobility concerns for Dylan?" can start the discussion rolling. The information can then be used to design an appropriate assessment that will address areas of concern.

Other professionals can discuss their expectations for the person's independent or assisted travel within the school or work environment (as appropriate) and describe how the person gets from one class or work area to another. Family members can describe how the individual navigates the house, yard, and surrounding neighborhood and provide information on his or her daily habits, possible hobbies, and any other changes in activity level that may be due to the vision loss. (For a list of sample interview questions that can be used with adults, school-age students, and family members, see Appendix 1.A at the end of this chapter.)

Reviewing Records or Files

Medical, rehabilitation, and/or educational records and files can be reviewed to extrapolate additional useful information about the student, such as his or her visual functioning, use of low vision devices, other disabilities or health impairments, and present level of academic achievement or adaptive functioning.

Visual Functioning

Information on visual functioning (including acuity, visual fields, diagnosis, and prognosis) can be used to plan assessments and to individualize instruction. For example, the O&M specialist would want to include night travel in the O&M assessment of a young adult who has retinitis pigmentosa, anticipating possible night blindness. In assessing the visual functioning of a preschool child with cortical visual impairment, the O&M specialist may want to incorporate the color yellow and moving targets. Yellow has been found to be the preferred color, and moving targets help to activate the peripheral vision that is typically functioning well in many of these children.

Use of Low Vision Devices

Whenever it is noted that low vision devices have been prescribed, the use of these devices should be included in the assessment process. Appropriate viewing targets and scanning tasks can be part of the functional vision assessment. Lessons that incorporate these devices in travel experiences will motivate students to learn to use them daily.

The Presence of Other Disabilities or Health Impairments

Information about the presence of additional disabilities or health impairments can be used to prepare for the assessment and eventually to help interpret the assessment results. By knowing the physical capabilities (such as stamina, strength, and balance) of the individual, the O&M specialist can select the appropriate assessment area and length of the route. Information on the individual's cognitive capabilities (for instance, information processing, recall, and problem solving) can help the O&M specialist determine how much detail to include in an activity or route or how many segments to give the student.

The presence of additional disabilities may also need to be considered when interpreting the results of an assessment. The causes (visual impairment and/or other disability) of some O&M difficulties may need to be teased apart. For example, if an older adult, who previously had a stroke, has difficulty completing a three-part orientation task, it must be determined whether the difficulty is a result of disorientation owing to blindness or short-term memory loss from the stroke. Similarly, if a student with mild cerebral palsy is unable to demonstrate accurate street-crossing timing at simple traffic light controlled intersections, it must be determined whether the student is able to recognize the appropriate time to cross or if the late timing is caused by a slow motor-processing and response time.

Levels of Academic Achievement and Adaptive Functioning

Present levels of academic achievement are relevant to O&M assessment as they relate to a student's ability to travel independently. For example, information on the current reading level of a student with low vision can help the O&M specialist select appropriate signs for the student to locate and read during the assessment. Math skills are relevant to assessing number concepts used in the address system, and money skills are important in evaluating a student's ability to make purchases and use public transportation.

The files on adults who are visually impaired may describe the adults' current levels of adaptive functioning (as for cooking, personal hygiene, O&M, and use of adaptive technology). This information can be useful in planning appropriate assessments that are relevant to an individual's daily life. For example, if a file indicates that an adult is currently semi-independent in using his or her home kitchen to prepare simple meals and the person is highly motivated to work on this area, part of the O&M functional vision assessment can be conducted in his or her local grocery store.

The sheer volume of papers that may be found in an individual's file often overwhelms beginning O&M specialists. To save time, the specialists can start by locating the most current medical reports and check earlier reports only if questions about the individual's medical history arise. In addition to medical reports, other useful files and reports are likely to be those completed by previous O&M specialists. These summary reports and the goals in the Individualized Educational Program (IEP) or Individualized Written Rehabilitation Program (IWRP) reflect the areas in which the student has already received instruction. A close review of the reports may indicate previously effective instructional approaches and the relative pace at which the student has been able to grasp the O&M curriculum as well. The reports of other specialists, including school psychologists, teachers, social workers, and rehabilitation teachers and counselors, may give O&M specialists a glimpse of the bigger picture that is often helpful in developing an individually tailored O&M program. However, all reports should be reviewed with caution because some may contain a degree of bias. The reports and files should form a framework from which to start, but it is incumbent upon O&M specialists to make their own assessments of students' potential for learning independent travel skills.

Selecting Appropriate Assessment Tools

Choosing an appropriate O&M assessment tool is another important aspect of preparing for a formal assessment. Among the commercially available tools, several are specific to young or school-age children (Anthony, 1992; Brown & Bour, 1986; Dodson-Burk & Hill, 1989; Hill, 1981) and consist primarily of checklists for skill or concept development. Teaching Age-Appropriate Purposeful Skills (TAPS) (Pogrund et al., 1995) provides a companion assessment tool with its curriculum that includes functional mobility tasks that can be assessed in given environments. Individual or small groups of O&M specialists commonly develop their own assessment tools that are then used by a given school district or agency (Fazzi, 1998). Some O&M assessment tools that are designed for use with a range of age groups are listed in Appendix 1.B at the end of this chapter. It is the responsibility of the O&M specialist to select the most appropriate tool for an individual student. The O&M specialist in the example given in Figure 1.1 used the school district's checklist to determine goals for the student in each O&M domain.

When selecting or designing an appropriate assessment tool, an O&M specialist must consider the student's age, visual abilities, level of skills, additional disabilities, travel environments, and the student's and family's priorities with regard to goals. The tool should be simple to follow, and data should be easy to record. All relevant O&M domains (personal-social, motor, sensory, conceptual, orientation skills, and mobility skills) should be included in the tool. Most important, the results of the assessment should paint a full and realistic picture of the individual's current abilities and provide clear and relevant information that can be used to formulate appropriate O&M goals.

Observing during Natural Routines

After the O&M specialist has identified the domains and skill areas to be assessed and has selected or designed an appropriate tool, it is helpful to find time to observe the visually impaired individual in his or her natural environment. Observing individuals as they move about at home and in school or work environments during daily routines may reveal their typical habits and patterns of movement (see Conducting Natural Observations as Part of the O&M Assessment Process). For example, the O&M specialist in Figure 1.1 planned to observe the student in the natural environment of the school campus and then later use a planned assessment route in a residential area that matched the student's current level of skills.

Since individuals sometimes perform differently (either better or worse) during an assessment than at other times, a naturalistic observation can give the O&M specialist a better idea of their actual daily functioning. The O&M specialist can easily spend time at school to observe students as they move about classrooms and cafeterias and travel routes between classes. These types of observations may be less practical for adults at home or work, but they also yield information that is useful to the assessment process.

Selecting Assessment Environments

To select an appropriate environment in which to complete the assessment, O&M specialists need to preview activities and assessment routes based on the student's age, visual abilities, mobility experience, and other characteristics, as well as the domains to be assessed. Each assessment should contain age-appropriate activities, and the duration of the assessment should be determined according to the student's attention span and stamina.

For example, an assessment route for a person who is functionally blind who has had no previous training will be different from one for an experienced traveler who has low vision. The assessment activity for the functionally blind individual may give the student opportunities to demonstrate basic O&M skills in relatively quiet surroundings. Without

CONDUCTING NATURAL OBSERVATIONS AS PART OF THE O&M ASSESSMENT PROCESS.

- Observe young children in their homes and yards (if applicable) to see how they move (or are moved) from room to room or one area to another and how they get to familiar toys and people.

- Observe preschool-age children both at home and at school to see how they move about in each environment, how they play with toys and other children and adults, and whether they are encouraged to move independently.

- Observe similar-age children who are sighted to see the kinds of things they do and places they go independently in a typical daily routine.

- Observe elementary school-age children as they move about in their classrooms and to other locations at school (such as the rest room, office, and cafeteria) during the actual times they do so.

- Observe elementary school-age children on the playground to see how their O&M skills are used during free-play time.

- Observe the patterns of teachers and assistants to determine how much travel assistance is typically given in a day or in specific circumstances.

- Observe high school-age students complete routes between classes and to and from the bus.

- Observe adults move about their homes during a first home visit when they offer to get you a cup of coffee or drink of water.

- Observe older adults who reside in assisted care facilities or nursing homes, move between key areas in the facility, including the type of assistance provided by others.

prior O&M training or experience, it would be unreasonable to plan an advanced travel route that requires the student to use an assortment of cane skills. In contrast, the experienced traveler with low vision could complete a more complex assessment route that incorporates a variety of obstacles, changes in levels, signage, varied lighting and contrast areas, street crossings, and orientation challenges. The activities planned for a 3 year old (for example, two or three 15–30-minute assessments that incorporate the use of play) would look different from those planned for a 15 year old (for instance, a combination of functional tasks that last an hour or more). The student in Figure 1.1 had previous O&M training. Based on a review of student files, the residential assessment route chosen would enable the O&M specialist to determine how well the student applies skills and concepts in this area.

The cultural and linguistic background of the individual also needs to be considered when selecting an assessment area or activity. For example, a student with low vision whose primary language is Vietnamese may be better able to demonstrate his or her skills in locating and reading signage in his or her home neighborhood where signs are in both Vietnamese and English. Food markets are often full of things that can be used as part of an assessment. If an adult typically shops at a local specialty Vietnamese market, perhaps part of the assessment could be conducted there. It would be an excellent opportunity to observe the individual's daily functioning and allow him or her to share some interesting things about the culture. Planning culturally relevant assessment activities demonstrates that the O&M specialist respects the individual and is interested in learning about the person's culture.

Conducting the Assessment

During the assessment, the O&M specialist needs to gather as much useful information as possible in a limited time. In general, the assessment should begin in an environment in which the individual would be expected to be able to do some form of independent or semi-independent travel. Starting with simple skills and concepts to ensure some sense of success, the assessment can then move on to more challenging tasks. When the tasks become difficult or overly frustrating, the O&M specialist may want to return to a few simpler tasks and then end the assessment on a positive note. Activities planned for the assessment in Figure 1.1 (residential travel and use of tactile model to initially assess concepts) would be familiar tasks for this student and instill confidence prior to examining more challenging skills.

The planned activities or routes should require the student to demonstrate a range of skills for the O&M specialist to observe, but a series of effective questions will help to fill the gaps in information. Table 1.2 categorizes the various levels of questions that can be asked. This classification is based on Bloom's taxonomy of learning (Bloom, Englehart, Furst, Hill, & Krathwohl, 1956), which identifies six levels of learning in the cognitive domain, from the simplest level of recall of information through increasingly more complex intellectual activities. The verb or phrase listed in the second column for each level of cognitive activity describes the type of activity an individual may be required to do to answer questions at that level, and the last column provides examples of O&M questions for each level.

Thus, questions can be carefully chosen to yield accurate information and avoid frustrating a student. Questions that test the simple recall of information (like, How many blocks is it from your house to the bus stop?) are limiting in the amount of information that is gained. Yes–no questions (such as, Is this a four-way stop-sign controlled intersection?) may lead some students to guess the answer and hence yield inaccurate information. Recall and yes–no questions can be followed by open-ended questions (for example, Why do you think it is necessary to have a four-way stop sign at this particular intersection?) to gain additional information. Higher-level questions that require the student to make comparisons, apply information to new situations, and engage in problem solving will help to increase the quantity and quality of responses during assessments. Sidebar 1.1 lists some common traps that

Table 1.2 Levels of Questions

Level of Learning	Cognitive Activity	Sample Question
Knowledge	Recall	*"What bus number are you supposed to take?"*
Comprehension	Interpret, translate, summarize	*"How do you know this intersection has a four-way stop?"*
Application	Use information in a new situation	*"Which lining-up technique would you use at this crossing?"*
Analysis	Separate the whole into parts until the relationship between them is clear	*"What category of intersections does this one fall into?"*
Synthesis	Combine elements to form a new entity	*"What is an alternate route to locate your classroom from the bus stop?"*
Evaluation	Act of decision making, judging	*"What is the most appropriate technique to use at this crossing, and <u>why</u> would you use that one?"*

Source: Based on Bloom's taxonomy of learning. See B. Bloom, M. Englehart, E. Furst, W. Hill, & D. Krathwohl, *Taxonomy of Educational Objectives. Handbook 1: Cognitive Domain* (New York: David McKay, 1956).

Sidebar 1.1 Common Questioning Traps to Avoid

"Yes Man," "No Man" Questions

The constant use of yes-and-no questions does little to obtain in-depth information during the assessment process. The overreliance on these questions can also lead to inaccuracies associated with self-reports. Yes-and-no questions do not facilitate critical thinking when they are overused during instruction.

Questioning Trap	Preferred Approach
"Do you know your way around campus?"	"Which campus routes are the most challenging for you?"
"Can you see the traffic light across the street?"	"Describe the location of the traffic light across the street."

"50–50 Chance" Questions

The use of 50–50 chance questions encourages students to guess during the assessment process and yields little in the way of accurate information about the student's abilities. When these questions are used, remember to vary the order of the correct choice.

Questioning Trap	Preferred Approach
"Do you cross with the parallel or perpendicular surge?"	"What is the appropriate traffic to use to time your crossing?"
"Is the landmark for this route the drinking fountain or the elevator?"	"Which landmark do you use for this route?"

"Once Is Never Enough" Questions

It is common to repeat a question when a student does not give an answer. When this happens frequently, a pattern may develop in which a student does not attempt to answer until the second or third time. When students learn that instructors will continue to repeat unanswered questions, they may become less responsive—confident that nothing more will be expected of them. Any question is likely to be repeated if a student does not answer. It is best to illustrate a typical question and how it might be repeated.

Questioning Trap	Preferred Approach
"Sasha, have you finished your route?"	"When you have reached your destination,
"Are you at the ending point of your route?"	describe the route that you followed."

O&M specialists can fall into when questioning their students and offers some alternative approaches to help avoid them.

Students with low vision may be easily frustrated if asked a series of "Can you see . . . .?" questions. Instead, the O&M specialist can ask them to let him or her know when they first see a given target. In assessing an elementary-age student with low vision, the O&M specialist could select a residential route that contains two fire hydrants along one side of a block. While in close proximity to the first hydrant, the O&M specialist could say, "I spy something yellow" (or "red," as the case may be) to assess the student's ability to spot the target. A series of questions, such as the following, could assess related environmental concepts like form, label, function, and location:

1. How would you describe the object—shape, size, material, and so on? (form)

2. What is it? (label)

3. What does it do? (function)

4. Where can you usually find it? (location)

The student is then asked to look around, guess what it is, and then point to the object. The student could then be asked to travel farther and stop when he or she first spots the next fire hydrant, so the O&M specialist could observe the student's scanning strategies.

For young children and some students with multiple disabilities, it may be useful to enlist the assistance of a teacher, parent, caregiver, or other individual who is familiar to the student in conducting the actual assessment. Assistance may be needed in special cases in which a student uses an alternative communication system (such as a communication board or sign language). The goal is to get as much accurate information as possible. When the student is not proficient in English, a bilingual specialist or interpreter should be used.

The O&M specialist must be careful to avoid making positive and negative comments during the assessment. For example, persons with low vision may get the mistaken notion that they have done a "good job" only when they are able to see something if the O&M specialist praises them each time they are able to see a target. Instead, the O&M specialist should simply accept a student's responses to assessment questions with a casual "OK" or "uh-huh." In general, the assessment is not the appropriate time to begin addressing inaccuracies or areas of concern. It is often helpful to remind the student frequently that the goal of the assessment is to find the appropriate starting place for instruction, so an individualized O&M program can be planned that will meet his or her needs.

Ongoing Assessment

Following a well-planned and executed formal assessment, the O&M specialist will know a great deal more about the person's abilities and interests. But the end of the formal assessment does not mean the end of the assessment process. Assessment is an ongoing part of teaching. During each lesson, the O&M specialist learns a great deal more about the student's travel abilities, including the student's functioning in a variety of environments, daily fluctuations in the student's visual functioning and energy levels, and the overall effectiveness of various instructional approaches.

Once the instructional process has begun, the O&M specialist will have more opportunities to see the student function in a greater variety of environments, levels of illumination, and changes in weather and to observe daily fluctuations in the student's visual functioning and energy levels that may not have been noted during the initial assessment. Furthermore, over time, O&M specialists and students typically develop a greater rapport and sense of trust. With greater comfort, students may be more likely to provide honest self-reports about their visual functioning than during initial assessments. They may also feel freer to disclose their anxieties or concerns regarding travel opportunities.

The effectiveness of specific instructional strategies can also be evaluated on an ongoing basis. The O&M specialist learns how to phrase things in a way that the student best understands. For example, one student may respond well to the request, "Widen your cane arc," while another may respond better to the request, "Sweep your cane to clear a path for your feet." Proper phrasing may also help the O&M specialist gain additional assessment information. Two O&M specialists may obtain different assessment results on the same student because of the way they phrased questions. For example, asking a particular student if it is safer to cross intersections clockwise or counterclockwise may evoke some confusion, but rephrasing the question to ask if it is safer to cross when the parallel traffic is on your left or right side may yield the correct answer. The effectiveness of other teaching approaches, such as the use of auditory versus tactile teaching materials, can be assessed with individual students from lesson to lesson. The ongoing assessment allows the O&M specialist to make appropriate teaching adjustments and to select travel environments for instruction that provide meaningful learning experiences.

KNOWING THE ENVIRONMENT

Once the O&M specialist knows the student's needs, abilities, and interests, it is imperative to become equally familiar with the travel environments that will be used for instruction so that appropriate lessons can be prepared. Either the O&M specialist selects the travel environment or it is dictated by the student's particular needs. In either case, it is the specialist's responsibility to preview the areas so that they become familiar. (For specific strategies for becoming familiar with travel areas, see Chapter 6.) Both the physical characteristics and the social aspects of the travel environment have an impact on the development of independent travel skills.

Physical Characteristics of the Travel Environment

The O&M specialist must know the physical layout of the indoor and outdoor training areas that will be used. Characteristics of the physical environment that may be important to O&M instruction include these:

- possible shapes of routes;
- illumination, color, and contrast generally found in the area;
- landmarks;
- obstacles and hazards;
- variety in texture, terrain, slope, and open areas; and
- volume and type of pedestrian and vehicular traffic.

An important part of knowing the environment is becoming familiar with travel conditions at specific times of the day. Physical characteristics of the environment that change according to the time of day, such as natural and artificial lighting, can affect travelers who have low vision. For example, in a light business area at dusk, natural lighting is reduced, which makes some landmarks and signage more difficult to see. A light business area has intersections that are predominantly controlled by traffic lights, smaller streets, and less vehicular and pedestrian traffic than downtown or major metropolitan areas. At the same time, artificial lighting may increase from streetlights and headlights, which can create a visual glare or halo effect for some individuals that may make changes in the terrain difficult to anticipate. Thus, the O&M specialist must consider possible changes in lighting that may occur when a student is actually traveling.

Another aspect of the physical environment that often changes according to the time of day is the volume and pattern of pedestrian and/or vehicular traffic in a given area. Without knowing the environment at specific times of the day, an O&M specialist could select and plan for a seemingly simple travel route on a high school campus for a beginning student, for example. This route, which seemed simple at 10:00 A.M., may be difficult to navigate during changes of class periods. The sheer number of students moving from class to class may make tactile landmarks (such as a drinking fountain near the students' lockers) inaccessible and overall orientation challenging because of the increased noise and congestion. Similarly, the volume of vehicular traffic at intersections must also be carefully observed and routes and crossings planned according to specific times of the day. One intersection that seems appropriate for teaching alignment with parallel traffic at 8:00 A.M., when the O&M specialist visited the intersection and planned the lesson, may not have enough traffic for alignment at the time of the lesson at 11:00 A.M. Likewise, an apparently quiet residential intersection may become a crossing nightmare when a nearby elementary school lets out for the day. Such information will save a great deal of time and energy when planning effective O&M lessons.

Social Aspects of the Travel Environment

In addition to learning about the physical travel environment, it is prudent to find out about the "social" aspects of the individual's travel environments. The people whom individuals with visual impairments live with, work with, learn from, and play and socialize with can have a tremendous impact on how independent travel skills may or may not develop. They can either encourage or discourage independence; they can be "enablers" or provide opportunities for success. An enabler is a person who contributes to another person's dependence by always doing things that the person might be capable of doing for himself or herself. Social aspects of the travel environment for individuals with visual impairments may include the attitudes of peers, teachers, colleagues, and family members toward independent travel; expectations for independent travel by the individual and significant others; how people socially move through a given environment (that is, in groups or alone); and the presence or absence of social reinforcers for independent travel.

Each social element can have a great impact (positive or negative) on the ultimate success of O&M training. For example, numerous O&M lessons could be devoted to learning independent travel routes at a middle school campus, but if teachers and peers are quick to provide assistance, the student may never get the opportunity to practice the routes during the school day. If an adult is not expected by other family members to be an independent traveler, time spent working on residential street crossings may be fruitless. In a work setting, most adults typically move about independently, so it would be appropriate for the person with a visual impairment to do the same. However, in a preschool, groups of children may walk places hand in hand, so it would be socially awkward to insist on the young child with a visual impairment traveling alone, behind or in front of the group. In cases in which there are many social reinforcers (such as play with peers following independent travel to the playground), students with visual impairments may be more likely to meet or exceed our expectations for progress in learning travel skills.

Knowledge of the curriculum, the student, and the travel environment are all important for successful instruction. Each component and piece of information helps the O&M specialist plan lessons that will be effective and meet the needs of individual students. Time devoted to preparation is well spent and is the starting point for the O&M plan.

Sample O&M Assessment Interview Questions

INTERVIEW QUESTIONS FOR SCHOOL-AGE STUDENTS

1. Where do you live?

2. Describe your home neighborhood.

3. What is your understanding of O&M training?

4. What can you tell me about your visual impairment?

5. Describe how you see.

6. Have you had any previous O&M training? If yes, describe.

7. What would you like to learn during O&M training?

8. When moving or traveling, are there situations that you are concerned about?

9. How do you travel indoors? Outdoors?

10. Are there any places that you would like to be able to go independently?

11. Do you see differently in the day and in the night?

12. Where do you travel independently now?

13. (If age appropriate) Do you travel independently by bus?

14. Do you have any concerns or fears about travel? About taking O&M?

15. Do you use any low vision devices or adapted mobility devices?

INTERVIEW QUESTIONS FOR FAMILY MEMBERS

1. Where do you live?

2. Describe your home neighborhood.

3. What is your understanding of O&M training?

4. What can you tell me about your child's visual impairment?

5. Describe how your child sees.

6. Has your child had any previous O&M training? If yes, describe.

7. What would you like your child to learn during O&M training?

8. When your child is moving or traveling, are there situations or environments that may cause you to be concerned for your child's safety?

9. How does your child travel indoors? Outdoors?

10. Are there any places that you would like your child to be able to go independently?

11. Does your child see differently in the day and in the night?

12. Where does your child travel independently now?

13. (If age appropriate) Does your child travel independently by bus?

14. Do you have any concerns or fears about your child's travel? About your child taking O&M?

15. Does your child use any low vision devices or adapted mobility devices?

Source: Taken from R. Pogrund, G. Healy, K. Jones, N. Levack, S. Martin-Curry, C. Martinez, J. Marz, B. Robersen-Smith & A. Vrba. *Teaching Age-Appropriate Purposeful Skills (TAPS): An Orientation and Mobility Curriculum for Students with Visual Impairments: Comprehensive Assessment and On-Going Evaluation* (Austin: Texas School for the Blind and Visually Impaired, 1995).

INTERVIEW QUESTIONS FOR ADULT CLIENTS WITH ACQUIRED VISION LOSS

1. Have you had previous O&M training?

2. If so, what was the extent of your training?

3. Describe your previous travel experiences.

4. Have you ever driven a car?

5. What type of mobility devices do you use?

6. Describe your home neighborhood.

7. Is there public transportation within walking distance of your home?

8. Have you ever used the following:

   a. public bus?

   b. metro rail or subway?

   c. paratransit services?

   d. taxi?

9. Where do you travel independently now?

10. Where do you travel with assistance now?

11. When you are traveling, are there any situations that concern you?

12. What is your daily routine?

13. Has your routine changed since the onset of your visual impairment?

14. How do you do grocery shopping or banking?

15. What recreational activities do you participate in?

16. Do you have any hobbies?

17. What do you enjoy doing when you have free time?

18. What is your educational background?

19. Are you currently employed?

20. If yes, what type of job?

21. How do you get to and from work?

22. Do you have any employment or work goals?

23. Do you feel that you need O&M training?

24. If yes, what would you like to learn during O&M training?

25. Are there any places that you would like to be able to go independently?

ADDITIONAL QUESTIONS FOR CLIENTS WHO ARE DIABETIC

1. What type of diabetes do you have, and for how long have you had it?

2. Do you test your own blood sugar? If so, how often?

3. What symptoms do you display if you are having an insulin reaction?

4. What is your preferred method of treatment if you are having an insulin reaction?

5. Do you always carry a source of glucose for treatment of insulin reactions?

6. What is the best time of the day for you to participate in O&M activities?

7. What is your doctor's recommended length of time for physical activities?

8. Do you carry medical identification with you at all times?

ADDITIONAL QUESTIONS FOR CLIENTS WHO HAVE ADDITIONAL PHYSICAL/SENSORY DISABILITIES

1. Do you use any ambulatory devices (such as a support cane, walker, scooter, or wheelchair)?

2. If you use a wheelchair

   a. do you use a manual or motorized wheelchair?

   b. do you use your wheelchair independently?

    c. do you experience any difficulty with inclines?

    d. are you able to enter or exit a bus?

3. Do you have any physical or health restrictions on your travel?

4. Do you use a hearing aid at any time?

5. Can you tell me about any medications that you are taking?

Source: Adapted from S. Stetcher, "Orientation and Mobility Skills Assessment for Adults" (Marin, CA: Marin County Office of Education, 1996).

Bibliography of O&M Assessment Tools

Anderson, S., Boigon, S., & Davis, K. (1986). *The Oregon Project for Visually Impaired and Blind Preschool Children* (5th ed.). Medford, OR: Jackson Education Service District.

Anthony, T. (1992). *Inventory of Purposeful Movement Behaviors.* (Available from Colorado Department of Education, Special Education Services Unit, 201 East Colfax, Denver, CO 80203)

Azusa Unified School District—Program in Visual Impairment. (1983). *Priority Goals Checklist (preschool, grades 3rd, 6th, 8th, and 12th—Versions for students who are totally blind and low vision).* Azusa, CA: Author.

Brown, D., Simmons, V., Methvin, J., Anderson, S., Boignon, S., & Davis, K. (1991). *Oregon Project for Visually Impaired and Blind Preschoolers.* Medford, OR: Jackson County Education Service District.

Dodson-Burk, B., & Hill, E. W. (1989). *Preschool orientation and mobility screening.* Alexandria, VA: Division 9 of the Association for Education and Rehabilitation of the Blind and Visually Impaired.

Hill, E. W. (1981). *The Hill Performance Test of Selected Positional Concepts.* Chicago: Stoelting.

Langley, M. B. (1980). *Functional Vision Inventory for the Multiply and Severely Handicapped.* Chicago: Stoelting.

Los Angeles Unified School District, Visually Handicapped Program—Division of Special Education. (1999). *Orientation and Mobility Assessment.* Los Angeles: Author.

Pogrund, R., Healy, G., Jones, K., Levack, N., Martin-Curry, S., Martinez, C., Marz, J., Robersen-Smith, B., & Vrba, A. (1995a). Assessment tool. In *Teaching age-appropriate purposeful skills (TAPS): An orientation and mobility curriculum for students with visual impairments.* Austin: Texas School for the Blind and Visually Impaired.

Pogrund, R., Healy, G., Jones, K., Levack, N., Martin-Curry, S., Martinez, C., Marz, J., Robersen-Smith, B., & Vrba, A. (1995b). Screening instrument. In *Teaching age-appropriate purposeful skills (TAPS): An orientation and mobility curriculum for students with visual impairments.* Austin: Texas School for the Blind and Visually Impaired.

Stetcher, S. (1996). *Orientation and mobility skills assessment for adults.* Marin, CA: Marin County Office of Education.

O&M Assessment Plan Form

Student's Name _____   Instructor _____   Date _____

Assessment Domain	Assessment Tool	Assessment Areas	Methods	Description of Assessment Activities
Personal				
Visual Functioning				
Mobility				
Orientation				
Conceptual				
Other				

Key: Assessment Tool—e.g., Los Angeles Unified School District, *Orientation and Mobility Assessment,* 1999
Assessment Areas—e.g., cane skills and residential street crossings
Methods—e.g., observation, interview, travel, game
Description of Assessment Activities—e.g., residential L-shaped route with 2 plus-shaped intersection crossings

2

Laying the Groundwork for Creative Instruction: O&M Plan Basics

CHAPTER PREVIEW

Goals and Objectives

Weekly Lesson Plans
   Goals and Objectives of the Lesson
   Location of the Lesson
   Instructional Materials
   Introduction to the Lesson
   Method
   Summary or Closing of the Lesson
   Daily Notes

Development of Instructional Units
   Traditional Curricular Units
   Alternative Instructional Units

Appendix
   2.A   Sample Lesson Plan Form
   2.B   Sample Instructional Unit: Learning the Address System

THE O&M specialist who knows the curriculum, is familiar with the training environments, and thoroughly assesses the abilities and interests of the student is well prepared to provide high-quality instruction. Maintaining a strong connection between assessment and instruction helps ensure the relevance of the instructional program. This chapter is intended to assist O&M specialists in developing appropriate goals and objectives, designing weekly lesson plans, and planning interesting learning units. When O&M specialists plan instruction and are well organized, they are more likely to create lessons that are clearly focused, appropriate to the student's needs, and logically ordered. They are also in the best position to produce and apply the creative strategies that will motivate their individual students.

O&M specialists, whether working in the educational or rehabilitation system, need to individualize the program plans for their visually impaired students. Long-term goals, short-term objectives or benchmarks, and weekly lesson plans are all part of their planning responsibilities. Although there are no set standards for these three planning activities and formats for recording goals, objectives, and lesson plans vary from region to region and program to program, there are some general guidelines that may be helpful to new O&M specialists.

GOALS AND OBJECTIVES

In public schools, an educational team establishes long-term goals for students with visual impairments as part of the IEP process. This team must include a program administrator, special education teacher or teacher of students with visual impairments, general educator, and family member. The visually impaired student, O&M specialist, and additional specialists and family members may be included as appropriate. The goals are developed with shared input from all the team members. Long-term goals are typically set for one year, but the duration can be shorter if the team members all agree. Although there is certainly no steadfast rule about the appropriate number of goals in each area (such as social skills, O&M, and activities of daily living), two to three goals per area are generally recognized as appropriate. The short-term objectives, or benchmarks, should be perceived as stepping-stones that lead to the achievement of the established goals. There are likely two to three objectives per goal. The objectives are commonly written in behavioral terms, for example, "The student will demonstrate appropriate scanning skills prior to crossing traffic light controlled intersections 100 percent of the time." Ways of formulating goals and objectives are discussed in more detail in Weekly Lesson Plans.

With adults, the planning process for the IWRP is similar to that used with children and youth. Long-term goals are set by the rehabilitation team (including the rehabilitation counselor-teacher, social worker, vocational specialist, O&M specialist, and student). The adult should assume an active role in planning. Staff meetings to review his or her progress are commonly used at rehabilitation centers and may occur weekly or monthly. Goals may vary in duration according to the student's needs, the frequency of instruction, and the typical length of the service period.

WEEKLY LESSON PLANS

Lesson plans are developed on the basis of the individual goals and objectives established for each student. It is recommended that lessons be tied to the goals and objectives and planned weekly, rather than daily. Weekly planning typically requires the O&M specialist to think sequentially when designing lessons and can help him or her avoid haphazard changes in the focus of lessons. Teaching on a daily whim shortchanges the student and limits the progress that can be made over time because the instructional program lacks focus, clarity, and meaning. When instructional programs are clearly linked to the results of the assessment and the student's and family's priorities, well-thought-out lesson sequencing is a logical result.

A wide variety of formats of lesson plans are used by O&M specialists. However, a few elements should be included in all quality lesson plans, including these:

- the goals and objectives of the lesson,
- location of the lesson,
- introduction to the lesson,
- method or instructional strategies,
- summary or closing of the lesson,
- instructional materials, and
- daily notes.

Each element is discussed in more detail in the sections that follow, and Figure 2.1 presents a sample completed lesson plan form. (A blank lesson plan form is provided in Appendix 2.A at the end of this chapter for the reader's use.) This sample is a simple format that can be easily used, but there are a variety of other options that may work just as well. Individuals may prefer to develop their own format, borrow formats from others, or modify this sample to best suit their lesson planning style.

Lesson Plan

Student: _Nick (adult who is blind)_

Instructor: _Sasha_

Date: _November 2, 2000_

Time: _11:15 am_

Lesson Location: _intersection of Haskell & Takeguchi Streets traveling east 3 blocks along Richmond and back to start_

Goal: _To cross safely at residential intersections_

Lesson Objectives:
1. Using the straight-line-of-travel method, the student will correctly align for residential street crossings four out of five times.
2. The student will identify "all quiet" at five residential crossings with 100 percent accuracy.

Instructional Materials: _long cane, portable tactile diagram of generic grassy strip along sidewalk_

Methodology/Instructional Strategies:

1. Begin lesson by asking Nick how he might make sure that he will be aligned correctly when he starts his first street crossing.
2. Acknowledge, but do not comment on, each of his ideas.
3. Tell Nick that today we will be learning an approach for aligning at residential crossings and we will see if it works as well as one of the methods he suggested earlier.
4. Introduce straight line of travel method to Nick at Haskell & Takeguchi Streets. Have him practice his approach until he is confident and consistently accurate.
5. Show him the tactile diagram of the sidewalk strip and how he is aligned. Allow him to use his cane to trace the line between the actual grassy strip and sidewalk to verify his alignment.
6. Tell Nick that he will be applying his new skill in a residential route, in which you will provide human sighted guide assistance for the street crossings.
7. At each approach, ask Nick to identify when the intersection is all-quiet. Give feedback as appropriate. Cross together when Nick correctly identifies "all quiet."
8. Give Nick feedback regarding his alignment at each corner. Use the tactile diagram of the sidewalk strip if needed.
9. Upon completion of the five block route, ask Nick to identify skills that he felt most confident in and what he would like more practice with during next lesson. Add instructor feedback and preview new skills that will be introduced next week.

Daily Notes:

Nick did a great job! He was very pleased that the straight-line-of-travel method was one that he thought of originally. The tactile diagram came in handy the one time that Nick veered on approach to the corner. Nick met all lesson objectives.

Figure 2.1

Sample Completed Lesson Plan Form

Keep in mind that the format of the lesson plan should have adequate space to include all important information in each of the specified areas.

Goals and Objectives of the Lesson

The goals provide the overall focus for the lesson or a sequence of lessons and may remain the same for the week or for a series of lessons. The objectives are more specific benchmarks that are geared to a specific lesson. Fulfilling individual objectives will eventually lead to the achievement of the goal. Goals for lessons are commonly written in general terms; for example, the goal in Figure 2.1 is "to cross safely at residential intersections." In contrast, objectives are typically stated in more specific behavioral terms; that is, they include a description of the behavior that the student is expected to achieve that can be observed and measured. Two behavioral objectives that correspond to the goal just stated are as follows:

1. Using the straight-line-of-travel method, the student will correctly align for residential street crossings four out of five times.

2. The student will verbally identify "all-quiet" at five residential crossings with 100 percent accuracy.

The objectives should include specified criteria for measuring success, such as, "with 100 percent accuracy" or "four out of five times." The method for measuring the success of an objective, which can be specified in the method section, can be as simple as observing the student's performance near the end of the lesson or presenting a specially designed culminating activity, game, task, or quiz to assess the student's level of skill or conceptual understanding.

Location of the Lesson

An important part of any O&M lesson plan is the selection of an appropriate location. Lesson locations are primarily selected based on the objective of the lesson and the student's abilities and interests. The availability of appropriate teaching environments within close proximity to the student's home, school, or work must also be considered. The location may be designated as

- a specific place in a building (like the cafeteria in a courthouse),

- an indoor route (such as the route from the hotel lobby to the conference rooms),

- a specific outdoor area (like the gas station at Habibi and Pouliot Streets), or

- an outdoor route (such as starting from the southwest corner of Oxley and Fair Oaks, traveling two blocks east and one block north, ending at the northwest corner of Bortondale Road and Levis Avenue).

The lesson location in Figure 2.1 was chosen because it was a quiet residential area in the student's neighborhood. In some instances, it may be simpler to sketch and label the route on the written lesson plan. For more detail on strategies for selecting appropriate training areas, see Chapter 6.

Instructional Materials

It is important to include a list of instructional materials in the written lesson plan for two reasons: First, the list serves as a reminder to bring all the materials needed for the lesson. Second, by leaving a space to include lesson materials, O&M specialists may be encouraged to think of how they may incorporate the use of props, maps, models, and manipulatives to improve learning. As an example, the O&M specialist in Figure 2.1 prepared and brought along a generic tactile diagram of a grassy strip along a sidewalk to help illustrate the alignment technique. It came in handy when the student veered on one approach to a corner and became slightly disoriented. For more information on the development and use of instructional materials in teaching O&M, see Chapter 7.

Introduction to the Lesson

Each lesson begins with an introduction. At the minimum, the introduction should provide the student with a preview of the lesson's objectives and learning activities to follow. Expectations for the student's behavior can be established at this time, and aspects of previous lessons that relate to the current objectives can be reviewed. The introduction also gives the O&M specialist the opportunity to pique the student's curiosity and to develop a sense of anticipation for the day's activities.

Introductions can be simply stated, as in, "Today we are going to practice your scanning technique at a variety of intersections." This approach can be informative and efficient, but over time, both the teacher and student may enjoy some variety in approach. A lesson can also be introduced with a question that focuses the lesson in an interesting manner, as in, "As we transition from residential travel to the light business area, what do you anticipate will be the differences in the travel environment?" The lesson introduction to the sample lesson in Figure 2.1 also used a question format that allowed the student to suggest ideas for strategies that might be effective in aligning for a street crossing. Interesting introductions can set the stage for meaningful learning activities.

Method

The method is the manner in which the lesson will be conducted. It should be selected for individual lessons according to the teaching and learning styles of the O&M specialist and the student and the specific curriculum that is being taught. In the written plan, the O&M specialist describes the teaching activities, including their sequence, and any specific instructional strategies that will be used.

Several approaches to sequencing activities in a lesson can be used. One approach is to concentrate on teaching just one skill or element of the O&M curriculum at a time. For example, an entire lesson could be devoted to remediating a particular cane skill (for instance, staying in step while using the touch-and-drag technique). The method for this lesson may include the following:

- Review the importance of developing the refined skill.

- Demonstrate the correct skill.

- Give the student physical prompts, as needed, to help him or her perform the skill correctly.

- Ask the student to demonstrate the technique along a stretch of familiar sidewalk, providing verbal prompts as needed.

- Continue to practice the skill as needed in a residential area.

- Close the lesson with a review of the student's progress in developing the skill.

The method in the sample lesson plan in Figure 2.1 is very similar and is effectively used for the introduction of an important street crossing skill.

Although there is nothing technically wrong with this "drill-and-practice" format, another approach is to embellish a lesson by integrating more than one skill or concept within it. Integrative curriculum approaches often help students to see the relevance and application of skills and concepts that may otherwise appear disconnected. In addition, combining two or more skills and/or concepts within a lesson may increase the student's interest and motivation for learning, as well as provide additional opportunities for reinforcement and practice. Lessons can be layered like a sandwich. For example, the first layer of a lesson may be a review of previously learned cane skills, followed by a layer of route travel in a residential area, and concluding with a layer of time to put a new entry into the student's O&M journal. Layering is one way that orientation skills and mobility skills can be combined in a single lesson, as depicted in Figure 2.2. Multiple components of a lesson can be integrated simultaneously (for instance, practicing cane skills while looking for landmarks) or separated into distinct parts (such as 20 minutes of residential travel, followed by 20 minutes of work on constructing a map). (For more ideas for creative instructional strategies, see Chapter 5.)

Summary or Closing of the Lesson

Each lesson should contain a summary or closing that encourages the student and O&M specialist to review the day's accomplishments. During this debriefing, the student may be asked to critique his or her mobility techniques, orientation skills, or social interactions during the lesson. The closing can also be an opportunity to share feelings and thoughts about recent travel experiences. The O&M specialist can assist the student in this process by asking open-ended questions and providing feedback as appropriate.

The closing is also an excellent time to set the stage for future lessons. Giving a brief preview can help to build a sense of anticipation for and connection to upcoming lessons.

Daily Notes

Daily notes form the basis for an ongoing record of O&M learning experiences for the student. For accountability purposes, both progress and setbacks are noted for each lesson as appropriate. Additional details on factors that contributed to the student's success and explanations for objectives that were not achieved can be included. Daily notes also provide a format for O&M specialists to reflect on and critique their own teaching.

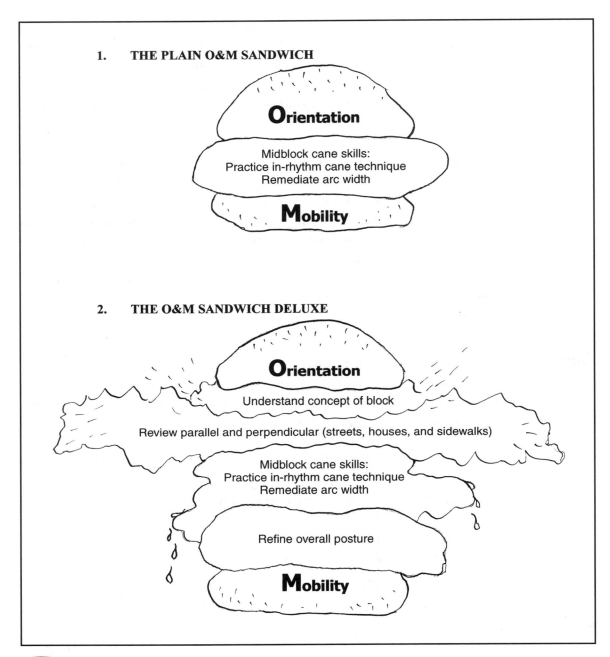

1. THE PLAIN O&M SANDWICH

Orientation

Midblock cane skills:
Practice in-rhythm cane technique
Remediate arc width

Mobility

2. THE O&M SANDWICH DELUXE

Orientation

Understand concept of block

Review parallel and perpendicular (streets, houses, and sidewalks)

Midblock cane skills:
Practice in-rhythm cane technique
Remediate arc width

Refine overall posture

Mobility

Figure 2.2

The O&M Sandwich: Layering Lessons

Two O&M lessons with the same general goal can be layered for a narrow or broadened focus. In the first illustration, the O&M lesson simply focuses on the development of specific mobility skills. In contrast, the second lesson incorporates instruction in and a review of concepts, as well as posture refinement, in the context of teaching the same mobility skill.

DEVELOPMENT OF INSTRUCTIONAL UNITS

As was already noted, weekly planning assists O&M specialists in sequencing lessons to achieve established O&M goals and objectives. Although goals, objectives, and weekly lesson plans are the basics of the O&M plan, the development of instructional units can help the O&M specialist to plan in a larger, more integrated fashion.

Planning instructional units provides the O&M specialist with a framework for sequencing lessons in a way that will be the most effective for individual students. An instructional unit is simply a logical grouping of elements that need to be taught in a curriculum to make instruction more meaningful, regardless of the content that is being taught. (A sample instructional unit, Learning the Address System, is presented in Appendix 2.B at the end of this chapter.) A well-planned unit incorporates a sequence of skill development in which skills are built upon or refined as lessons progress. In order to unify the lessons, the O&M specialist may develop a theme or project that will be worked on throughout. For example, in the sample unit on the address system found in Appendix 2.B, an address Bingo game is used across three lessons. A culminating activity in the sample unit, such as planning a lunch date, is commonly used to allow students the opportunity to put all the skills they have learned together in a meaningful and rewarding way. When appropriate, the well-planned instructional unit can lead to more in-depth teaching and learning. Skills and concepts can be effectively integrated within the context of the unit plan. For example, in a unit on "landmarks," mobility skills (such as shorelining), orientation skills (like searching on the right and left sides), and concepts (for example, classifying types of driveways) can be interwoven as the student learns how to select and locate useful landmarks in a residential area. Additional opportunities to apply landmarking skills in new or different travel environments can also be incorporated in the same unit.

The skills and techniques for independent travel can be grouped and presented in different ways. Unit planning should be more time efficient for the O&M specialist because the major work for the lesson plans can be done before the unit is started. Furthermore, with advance planning, the O&M specialist will have the opportunity to include a variety of instructional strategies and to develop instructional materials that can be effectively used for parts of the unit or the entire unit.

Moreover, the unit design helps the student to understand the purpose of the sequence of lessons. Thus, completion of the unit provides a sense of closure and a feeling of accomplishment for the knowledge and skills achieved.

The next section discusses traditional units in the O&M curriculum that may be used. The O&M specialist may want to devise alternative instructional units as well.

Traditional Curricular Units

Traditional units in the O&M curriculum are often grouped according to specific related skills to be taught or the environmental training area to be used. Some traditional units are basic travel skills, cane travel in indoor areas, travel in residential areas, travel in light business areas, travel in metropolitan-urban areas, and travel under special circumstances and in special areas. Some units, as logical sequences of lessons to teach a group of skills or concepts in depth, are really subunits of much larger traditional units. For example, the sample unit on Learning the Address System presented in Appendix 2.B is commonly taught *within* the traditional light business travel unit. This sample instructional unit incorporates a variety of learning activities that can be used with students of various ages. The O&M curriculum is commonly presented in either a traditional sequence, in which instruction starts with basic skills and builds up to more complex skills, or in a critical skills model, in which skills that an individual needs immediately are taught first.

Traditional Sequence

The traditional sequence, as typically presented in O&M curricula, starts with the simplest skills. These basic skills are often taught in familiar or quiet areas. The instructional sequence then builds on that foundation to develop increasingly complex skills that are applicable for a full range of travel environments. (For sample presentations of the O&M traditional sequence, please refer to Hill & Ponder, 1976, Jacobson, 1993, and La Grow & Weessies, 1994). The sequencing of the skills (for example, learning to cross on all quiet at a small residential intersection before learning how to cross with the parallel traffic surge at a traffic light-controlled intersection) ensures that "prerequisite" skills are taught first (Hill & Ponder, 1976).

Skills learned through a hierarchical sequence are typically considered to be well refined and of a higher quality than are skills that are developed out of sequence. For example, if individuals were to be given a sequence of ski lessons in which skills were fully developed in order from most basic to most advanced, they would have the potential to ski safely, gracefully, and skillfully on many slopes. An individual who was introduced to skiing at the top of an intermediate hill might also be able to get safely down the hill, but would certainly not demonstrate the same grace and skill as the individual who had been taught sequentially. This refinement occurs as new skills are introduced that expand on prior lessons and are based on the student's readiness and demonstrated competence. A thorough sequence allows for ample practice and application of skills before the student goes on to a more advanced level of skill.

The traditional sequence is commonly used in center-based rehabilitation facilities that serve adults who are adventitiously blind or visually impaired. It can also be used successfully with many school-age children who attend public or residential school programs. Some adults can learn this sequence in a manner of months, but the curricular sequence for school-age children may span many years and needs to be tailored to fit each child's developmental abilities and chronological age.

One advantage of the traditional sequence is that the skills and travel strategies that are learned are usually generalizable to new environments. For example, a blind veteran who learns the entire sequence of O&M skills and techniques at a residential rehabilitation center for people who are blind in one state should be able to apply the same general principles to independent travel in his home state. This ability to generalize travel skills from one environment to another is the ultimate goal of O&M training. However, the traditional sequence is not the only effective approach for designing or providing an appropriate O&M training program.

Critical Skills Model

Not all blind or visually impaired students need or benefit from receiving the entire O&M traditional sequence. A critical skills approach may be more appropriate for some students. Critical O&M skills are those that an individual needs immediately to travel safely. These skills may or may not be specific to a particular travel environment. For example, an O&M specialist may teach a specific alignment procedure to a student who needs to cross a skewed intersection. The alignment technique may incorporate the use of a landmark that is present only at this intersection and may be limited in its application to other skewed intersections.

In another case, an O&M specialist may teach a student to use public transportation before training in cane skills is completed because the student needs to take a bus to get to the facility for further training. In contrast to the first example of critical skills instruction, the bus skills taught in the second example should eventually be applicable to other travel areas. Sidebar 2.1 compares the elements of the traditional sequence and critical skills models of O&M instruction.

There are many variations in use of the critical skills model for O&M training. For example, if an older adult chooses to receive O&M training only in a familiar residential area, the skills critical to safe travel in that environment could be considered priorities, and the O&M specialist could still use the traditional sequence for that portion of the curriculum that represented the immediate need. Similarly, an adult with stable low vision may have little need for sighted (human) guide or protective techniques even though these techniques are commonly taught at the beginning of the O&M sequence. In this case, instruction may focus on the more immediate need to improve the person's lane-by-lane visual scanning at complex, traffic light-controlled intersections that the person needs for safe travel to and from work.

A child who is visually impaired and has severe cognitive disabilities may learn best when skills are taught as needed within the context of naturally occurring routines and environments. For example, the route to the cafeteria may be most appropriately taught at lunchtime—the natural time to travel there. At that time, presumably the child is hungry and is motivated to get to the cafeteria, along with other children lining up to go to lunch. Teaching within the context of naturally occurring routines is also commonly referred to as a functional approach because it addresses travel priorities and occurs within the natural environment with such a frequency that there is ample opportunity to practice and integrate skills (Fazzi, 1998).

In some instances, use of the critical skills model may lead to the development of *splinter skills,* which develop when an individual learns or understands only parts of a particular skill. Splinter skills, though often functional, are not always fully refined. For example, when attempting to teach stair travel to a person who cannot physically ascend stairs with alternating feet, the O&M specialist may be able to teach the person how to navigate the stairs using a long cane. The technique would probably be functional and get the person safely where he or she needed to go, but it would not be graceful. Thus, the O&M specialist

Sidebar 2.1 *Comparison of the Traditional Sequence and Critical Skills Models*

Traditional Sequence

- The assessment focuses on the student's skills and abilities for projected long-term travel needs.

- Skills are built from the simple to the complex.

- Skills are generalized across environments.

- The result is the refinement of skills.

Critical Skills Model

- The assessment focuses on travel demands for specific environments in combination with the student's ability level.

- Skills are taught to meet immediate needs.

- Instruction takes place in actual "natural" environments.

- The result is the development of splinter skills in some cases.

would have to spend additional time teaching alternating foot placement on stairs to refine the person's stair-travel skills. Similarly, if a child with a visual impairment is taught to use the constant-contact cane technique without a full awareness or understanding of the left and right sides of the body, the technique could probably be functional in providing body-width coverage, but might appear to be sloppy or uneven. When splinter skills develop, it may be necessary to take the time to break them down into their physical or conceptual components so that the entire skill can be learned. Improvement in skills may be evidenced by the student's increased ability to correct himself or herself when the technique is not performed correctly. However, there are other instances when the splinter skill is fully functional and the O&M specialist needs to concentrate on working on other areas.

The traditional sequence may be most effectively used when

- the student needs to learn a majority of the O&M curriculum, and

- the student is able to generalize skills from one environment to another.

The critical skills approach may be more effective when

- the student has an immediate need to learn a particular aspect of the curriculum out of sequence, and

- the student has difficulty generalizing skills across environments.

The traditional sequence and critical skills model need not be mutually exclusive. Critical skills may be introduced because of an immediate need (such as orientation to a new workplace), and then instruction within the traditional sequence may follow. When using a functional approach, the O&M specialist can determine which routes and travel tasks are priorities so the student can learn only the simplest skills needed to complete initial tasks and develop more complex skills in future routes.

Regardless of the approach or approaches that are ultimately used, it is important that the O&M specialist thoughtfully consider the options available. Haphazard approaches are often the result of day-to-day planning and inefficient time management and instruction. It is the professional's responsibility to plan the most appropriate O&M program for each student and to make necessary adjustments along the way.

Alternative Instructional Units

Although traditional curricular units in O&M serve a useful purpose for teaching many blind or visually impaired students and provide a framework that O&M specialists can easily follow, there are alternative curricular units that can be developed and successfully utilized. Alternative units may be used instead of or *in* addition to more traditional units. They give O&M specialists more latitude for grouping skills and/or concepts in ways that will be most meaningful and fun for individual students. Alternative units may be especially useful for addressing a set of skills that are not confined to a specific environmental training area or teaching specific concepts. They may be particularly helpful when working with congenitally blind or visually impaired students or those who have been exposed to the traditional model and need further work with or the remediation of particular developmental skills. Examples of topics for alternative units include scanning, analysis of intersections, landmarking, body imagery, self-advocacy, and mapmaking. O&M specialists may develop alternative instructional units that represent a temporary divergence from the traditional sequence or may develop a completely different framework for teaching units.

Unlike traditional curricular units, the presentation of alternative units may not fit into a traditional sequence or critical skills model. Depending on the nature of the alternative unit and the individual student, the O&M specialist can determine the appropriate sequence for presenting the particular content of the curriculum. Alternative units can take many forms; two examples—temporary tangent mini-units and feature units—are discussed next.

Temporary Tangent Mini-Unit

While working on a traditional O&M unit, either the student or O&M specialist may notice a need to address a particular skill or concept in more detail than was previously planned, or the student may express a strong interest in learning a skill or concept. In this case, the O&M specialist could develop a mini-unit that would be a brief tangent from the current unit. For example, if the O&M specialist observes, during a unit on traveling in a light business area, that the student is having difficulty with auditory alignment to traffic, he or she could present a temporary tangent mini-unit that addresses the specific auditory skills needed to ameliorate this problem.

Temporary tangent mini-units may also be developed around a strong interest expressed by the student. For instance, if a student with low vision shows a strong interest in the concept of fences during a residential travel unit, the O&M specialist may consider conducting a few lessons on this concept, continuing to reinforce appropriate O&M skills throughout the mini-unit. The O&M specialist could chose routes with interesting fences, so the student could locate and compare the fences. Once the student located a particular fence, some time could be spent discussing its shape, color, texture, size, and height, as well as the material it was built with, the types of gates and latches, and the part of the property that the fence encloses. This type of information is important when recognizing and describing the characteristics of landmarks in general and is essential for students to learn as part of their orientation skills. Depending on the student's level of interest, lessons could be expanded to include taking photographs of or drawing the fences that have been explored, making miniature model fences, or finding architectural and gardening books at a library or bookstore to learn more about fences. The temporary tangent mini-unit on fences would still include the practice of important mobility skills (such as street crossings, cane skills, or monocular skills), but it would be presented as a mini-unit on fences that would be particularly rich for conceptual development and interesting for the student. A similar tangent mini-unit could be developed on other environmental features (like windows, doors, roofs, or driveways) that are commonly found during lessons. For some students, this type of unit may be more highly motivating than a regimented unit in a residential area that focuses primarily on the development of travel skills.

Feature Unit

Featuring a concept or skill that is not linked to a specific training environment can be an effective alternative for teaching aspects of the O&M curriculum to some students. A feature unit provides in-depth instruction in an assessed area of weakness or strong interest or priority, as opposed to touching briefly on an area in one lesson and then addressing it again later when it seems relevant. The feature unit is an extended curricular unit, rather than a temporary unit, as is the tangent mini-unit.

As an example, an instructional feature unit on landmarks could easily be designed for a blind or visually impaired student. The concept of a landmark could be introduced within the context of learning a route in the home neighborhood and featured in a series of lessons over several weeks, with opportunities to explore different types of landmarks in a nearby residential area. Even though the student may not be ready for independent travel in a light business area, further lessons could involve traveling along the main street in town to recognize and describe landmarks (such as a church, park, library, or fire station) that are typically found in more advanced training areas. In one instance, a unit on landmarks was chosen for an older student who was adventitiously visually impaired who had been a homemaker for many years because she had difficulty selecting landmarks that were useful and often forgot the sequence of landmarks along a route. The O&M specialist had the student create a landmark recipe box—a box filled with index cards that described the many landmarks that were found along O&M travel routes. The student had to select landmarks that were permanent, unique, and easy to find and told the student where she was. Then the student labeled an index card for each landmark on which she described the landmark's shape, texture, size, or color and placed the card in the O&M recipe box. Once the box was complete, the student and O&M specialist used the cards to design routes or make maps of the areas in which the student traveled the most frequently.

Another feature unit could focus on scanning skills by featuring scanning at a variety of intersections, rather than addressing scanning skills on an as-needed basis during a unit on travel in light business areas. In other words, instead of learning about a particular intersection through scanning and other means, as in a more traditional unit, the student would learn to scan by going to a variety of intersections. Once the scanning unit was complete, the student would feel confident applying these skills while traveling in other light business areas. (Figure 2.3 contains a form that can be used to help students with low vision work on horizontal and vertical scanning. Examples of teaching materials that can be used in a unit on scanning appear in the Appendix to Chapter 7.)

The feature unit need not encompass the entire instructional time; rather, it can be presented as a portion or strand of each lesson (for example, as a 10-minute motor development warm-up unit at the beginning of each lesson). This format may work best when the unit features a skill, such as the use of monoculars, that may be considered tedious or fatiguing. Unit strands can also be used when two separate goals need to be worked on simultaneously. For example, a student may need to work on both mapmaking concepts and residential cane skills. A strand of each lesson could be devoted to mapmaking and another portion could be devoted to the refinement of cane skills. In one scenario, the map being constructed could be reviewed at the start of each lesson, followed by practice in cane skills in the area being mapped. Time could also be spent exploring a new landmark to add to the map at the end of the lesson. The unit strands allow for changes in activities during lessons. This approach can be especially useful when pairing a strand that develops a student's area of weakness with one that expands on a student's strength.

Alternative instructional units can make learning independent travel skills more interesting for both the O&M specialist and the student. The initial challenge may be to find sources of fun and meaningful ideas.

Generating Ideas for Alternative Units

Whereas content for traditional O&M units can readily be reviewed in available professional books, O&M specialists need to be creative in generating ideas for alternative units. In many cases, ideas are sparked by the student's and specialist's interest in particular areas. It is also beneficial to explore additional avenues to develop interesting or novel instructional units (see Generating Ideas for O&M Instructional Units). The extra time spent doing so should make teaching more interesting and learning more fun and meaningful for the student.

O&M specialists in schools may discover alternative units by finding out what is being taught in other academic and nonacademic

Study Sheet for a Unit on Visual Scanning

Directions: Travel environments have lines, edges, and surfaces that are parallel and perpendicular to one another. Find each of these items listed below, put a check next to the item, and practice your scanning technique to view the item completely. Scan with or without the monocular as appropriate.

1. Scanning "horizontal side to side" at ground level. Can be found perpendicular to viewer's line of sight and viewed from left to right, or vice versa.

    Inside:

    ❏ Edges of room (where floor and front/back walls meet)

    ❏ Design of flooring (panels or lines that run side to side from the viewer)

    Outside:

    ❏ Edges of sidewalk sections (expansion joints)

    ❏ Edges of nearside/farside curbs of perpendicular street

    ❏ Center line and lanes of perpendicular street

2. Scanning "horizontal near to far" at ground level. Can be found parallel to viewer's line of sight and viewed from front to back, and vice versa

    Inside:

    ❏ Edges of room (where floor and side walls meet)

    ❏ Design of flooring (panels or lines running near/far to the viewer)

    Outside:

    ❏ Edges of top and bottom of driveway

    ❏ Edges of parallel building line and curb

    ❏ White or yellow pedestrian crosswalk lines

3. Scanning "horizontal side to side" above ground level.

    Inside:

    ❏ Edges where ceiling and front/back walls meet

    ❏ Words written on a chalkboard or bulletin board

    ❏ Window blinds (horizontal slats)   *(continued)*

Figure 2.3

Study Sheet for a Unit on Visual Scanning

Outside:

❏ Edges of steps of stairways viewed from in front

❏ Words/numbers read on signs

❏ Tops of buildings viewed in front

4. Scanning "near to far" above ground level.

Inside:

❏ Side walls

❏ Edges where ceiling meets side walls

❏ Side edges of tables and chairs

Outside:

❏ Stairway railings as they ascend/descend

❏ Side edges of steps as they ascend/descend

5. Scanning "vertical up and down" from the ground up.

Inside:

❏ Flagpole

❏ Floor lamp

Outside:

❏ Goal posts

❏ Trees

❏ Traffic light poles

❏ Parking meters

❏ Parking signs

❏ Other street hardware

GENERATING IDEAS FOR O&M INSTRUCTIONAL UNITS

- Consider using traditional units (like those on indoor cane travel, residential street crossings, or bus travel) as presented in O&M curricular textbooks.

- Create O&M instructional units (such as on transitioning from school to work, using the rest room independently, or traveling in the home neighborhood) that relate directly to the student's or family's identified priorities for learning.

- Develop O&M instructional units around age-appropriate activities that similar-age peers are commonly engaged or interested in (for example, *preschool*—adventures of cartoon characters, *elementary*—collecting the toy trend of the year, *high school*—cruising the mall, or *adult*—transportation options for nondrivers).

- Adapt ideas from students' current academic curricular units that may relate to O&M (for instance, *geography*—O&M mapmaking unit, *reading*—an O&M sight-word vocabulary monocular unit, or *math*—O&M money survival-skills unit)

- Collaborate with other teachers and specialists to team teach a unit (such as a cooking unit with a *rehabilitation teacher* and O&M components; using a communication board with a *speech teacher* during an O&M lesson; a plants-and-flowers unit with a *general education teacher* and an O&M component of collecting or photographing various plants in the neighborhood).

disciplines. For example, a visually impaired student may be in a middle school social studies class that is studying ancient Egypt, and a map has been given in class for several specific assignments. Simultaneously, the O&M specialist could introduce an O&M mapmaking unit to teach the student about different kinds of landmarks and ways to locate and indicate them on a tactile map of a local training area. With input from the social studies teacher, the O&M specialist could devise a special O&M project for one or two lessons that would include making a tactile map of ancient Egypt that is based on the map given in class. Natural landmarks like rivers, mountains, and the desert could have different shapes and textures, and the main cities could be pinpointed with raised dots. Braille labels could be made, and the student could show the map in the social studies class, allowing the sighted classmates to learn a bit about braille letters and tactile maps. The alternative unit on mapmaking could then be extended to compare the map of ancient Egypt with the one of the student's travel area. Landmarks could be compared as to whether they were natural or manmade, large or small, or used daily by people in the area. A mapmaking unit like this gives a visually impaired student an opportunity not only to practice mapmaking skills, but also to share learning experiences with his or her classmates. It also helps the student participate more fully in class and reinforces valuable O&M skills like landmarking and mapmaking.

A complementary approach to developing alternative O&M units is collaboration with others. Whether in an educational or rehabilitation setting, O&M specialists can generate relevant topics or themes for units by sharing ideas with other professionals. Working in collaboration with a rehabilitation teacher, the O&M specialist may develop a grocery store unit to complement the cooking goals that will be addressed. While the rehabilitation teacher is teaching the student to organize the kitchen, prepare a shopping list, manage money, and cook and clean in the student's home, the O&M specialist could be teaching the student how to use a monocular, figure out cardinal directions, ask for assistance, apply cane techniques in congested areas, and use orientation strategies in a food market. Instruction can be coordinated so that the student travels to the market to purchase the food needed for the following cooking lesson. This form of collaboration makes learning O&M skills more relevant for the visually impaired student.

Regardless of the way lessons are grouped into units or the type of unit selected, O&M instruction can be further enhanced by the use of creative instructional strategies. The next chapter explores different ways of generating innovative ideas for making learning both meaningful and fun.

Sample Lesson Plan Form

Lesson Plan

Student: _____

Instructor: _____

Date: _____

Time: _____

Lesson
Location:

Goal:

Lesson
Objectives:

Instructional
Materials:

Daily Notes:

Methodology/Instructional Strategies:

Sample Instructional Unit:
Learning the Address System

This sample unit was prepared for two junior high school-age students who have low vision. When planning this unit, the teacher assumed that these two students had all the prerequisite knowledge of concepts and mobility skills to participate fully in the learning activities that would be provided. The teacher planned to teach the concepts of the address system in a seven-lesson unit.

The unit addresses the following concepts:

1. Grid pattern layout of a city

2. Block numbering systems

3. Central dividing streets

4. Location of even and odd addresses

5. Location of places within a block according to the last two digits of the address

6. Address numbering systems for corresponding parallel streets

The following games and activities (some of which are described more fully in other chapters) are used in the unit to teach these concepts:

- Use of a graphic aid of a grid pattern of a mock city (large-print diagram)

- Placing address cards on the graphic aid

- Doing homework to discover the address system used in the home neighborhood

- Verifying the address-system pattern in the training area

- Using an interactive model

- Locating a central dividing street

- Using mnemonics to remember the locations of odd and even addresses
- Estimating the locations of destinations using the last two digits of an address
- Completing the Address Bingo Card
- Planning a lunch date
- Singing the "Address Rap"

Lesson Plan

Students: _Sasha and James (low vision, junior high age)_

Instructor: _Tom_

Date: _____

Time: _____

Lesson Location: _____

_____

_____

Goal: _To develop an understanding of the address system_

Lesson Objectives:
1. _To recall the names of the two central dividing streets in the city_
2. _To identify the block-numbering system, from 100 to 500 with 100 percent accuracy_
3. _To identify four addresses and their pattern along a familiar I-shaped route_

Instructional Materials: _a graphic of the grid pattern of a mock city, address cards, tape, monocular, clipboard, felt-tip marker_

Daily Notes:

Methodology/Instructional Strategies:

1. Tell the students that the letter carrier mistakenly delivered a neighbor's letter to your house, but that you are not sure where along the street the house is. Ask them how you can figure it out so you can return the letter.

2. Introduce the concept of the address system if the students are unfamiliar with it. Tell them that if they help you figure it out, you will be able to return the letter in a couple of days.

3. Orient the students to a graphic aid of a grid system of parallel and perpendicular streets for a mock city. Tell them that the grid pattern is used to organize the houses and streets and is usually used for address numbering.

4. Show the students the largest dividing streets and let them know that these streets are where the numbers start and then increase in increments of 100. Tell the students the names of the two central dividing streets in the local community.

5. Starting at the central dividing street, ask the students to help you attach large-print address cards (100N, 200N, and so forth) to the blocks in the appropriate places. Review the progression of the numbering system.

6. Remove the numbers, and ask the students to replace them correctly.

7. Go outside to the local training area. Let the students know that it is their job to determine what the addresses are along a familiar street. They can decide who will use the monocular and who will record the information on the clipboard paper (or they can take turns). Assist them as needed.

8. After they have recorded the addresses, study together to determine the numbering pattern on this block.

9. If time is available, continue in the same direction and record the addresses on two additional blocks and review the pattern.

10. Ask the students if they now know where the neighbor's house is. Review the information they give. Thank them for their help.

Learning the Address System: Lesson 1

Lesson Plan

Students: _Sasha and James (low vision, junior high age)_

Instructor: _Tom_

Date: _____

Time: _____

Lesson Location: _____

_____

_____

Goal: _To develop an understanding of the address system_

Lesson Objectives:
1. _To locate the central dividing street for north–south addresses within 20 minutes_
2. _To locate the central dividing street for east–west addresses within 20 minutes_

Instructional Materials: _a graphic of the grid pattern of a mock city, monocular, clipboard, felt-tip marker_

Daily Notes:

Methodology/Instructional Strategies:

1. _Ask the students if they recall the names of the central dividing streets within the training area. Ask them how they would verify the names if they were unsure of them._
2. _Review the beginning address system concepts on the sample grid system. Show the students how the central dividing street changes the addresses (for example, from 100N to 100S)._
3. _Tell the students that for today's lesson, they will be doing two things. Using the address numbering system, they will need to verify the location of the central dividing streets for the north–south addresses and the east–west addresses. Tell the students that they will be working as a team and that they will have 20 minutes for each task. The only tools that they will be given are a monocular and clipboard and pen. Suggest that the students discuss/plan their strategy while they are riding in the car to the training area._
4. _At the training area, ask the students to share their plan for locating the central dividing streets. Give them feedback._
5. _Once the students have located the first central dividing street, check their work. Ask how they know it is the central dividing street and verify that they understand it is for the correct direction (north–south or east–west)._
6. _If the students had difficulty, review the necessary concepts and then start the search for the second central dividing street._
7. _After the assignment is completed, review their success and pinpoint areas to continue to work on in future lessons._
8. _Preview the next lesson—how addresses may be different on one side of the street from another._
9. _Assign homework: Ask the students to identify and write down their home address and two houses on both sides of it and then the three houses across the street._

Lesson Plan

Students: *Sasha and James (low-vision, junior high age)*

Instructor: *Tom*

Date: _____

Time: _____

Lesson Location: _____

_____

_____

Goal: *To develop an understanding of the address system*

Lesson Objectives:
1. *To identify which side of the street a given address should be located four out of five times*
2. *To locate the approximate location of a given three-digit address on a mock street, two out of three times*

Instructional Materials: *numbered foam squares large enough to stand on (found in a children's jigsaw floor puzzle), tape/string, address cards*

Daily Notes:

Methodology/Instructional Strategies:

1. Ask the students for their homework assignment from the previous lesson. See if they can figure out the pattern of addresses in their neighborhood. If necessary, explain that even- and odd-numbered addresses are typically on opposite sides of the street.

2. Tell them that there are mnemonics to help remember which side of the street odd- and even-numbered addresses are typically found: "NOW"—north and west sides are often odd and "SEE"—south and east sides are often even.

3. Introduce the interactive model of the address system that will be used today: jigsaw foam floor pieces (see photographs in Chapter 7). Ask the students to help you arrange the pieces on the floor.

4. As a warm-up, simply place the numbers in order, 0–9 (representing the 100, 200–900 blocks of a city). Review block numbering by taking turns with the students jumping from one block to another as a block number is called out. Ask which block is one, two, or three blocks south/north or east/west. Expand on this activity by placing a string or contrasting tape on the floor to designate a central dividing street.

5. Then ask the students to separate the odd and even numbers and place them across the imaginary street from one another.

6. Give the students a one-digit address card and ask them to find the right square on the floor and identify whether they are on the north or south or east or west side of the street according to the information on the card. Expand to two-digit addresses and then to three-digit addresses as the students develop mastery.

7. As the culminating activity, you and the students each secretly select a three-digit address. Play a game in which the other two try to guess the address by moving along the floor squares and asking simple yes/no questions (such as Is your house one block north from here?)

Learning the Address System: Lesson 3

Lesson Plan

Students: _Sasha and James (low vision, junior high age)_

Instructor: _Tom_

Date: _____

Time: _____

Lesson Location: _____

_____

_____

Goal: _To develop an understanding of the address system_

Lesson Objectives:
1. _To describe the numbering address system for parallel streets, using a graphic aid_
2. _To locate two addresses with the same three digits along two parallel streets_

Instructional Materials: _address system quiz, address cards and Address Bingo cards, felt-tip markers, monoculars_

Daily Notes:

Methodology/Instructional Strategies:

1. _Give the students the address system quiz worksheet (Figure 2.B.1) to complete together. Check their understanding._

2. _Until now, you have been concentrating on addresses on one street at a time. Introduce the concept of corresponding addresses for parallel streets._

3. _Given the central dividing street and its corresponding addresses, ask the students to place given addresses for various other streets within the grid._

4. _Once the students are consistently successful, ask them to give directions from one of the labeled locations to a new destination not labeled on the grid._

5. _Introduce the students to the Address Bingo cards (see Chapter 3 for a sample). Let them know how they are going to fill them in over the next few lessons and that when they have completed the address card together, they will be able to choose a destination for lunch for the following week._

6. _In the training area, ask the students to describe how they will locate two addresses with the same last two digits along two separate streets. Prompt as necessary to get them to talk about the numbering system and corresponding parallel streets._

7. _Start the students on the block where they will find the first address. Have them locate two addresses and circle those numbers on their Address Bingo cards. Remind them to include a brief description of the location (such as red house, shoe store, wooden fence)._

8. _Review the strategy that the students used to find the two addresses and provide feedback as needed._

9. _Preview the next lesson by telling them that they will be filling in four more numbers on their Address Bingo cards._

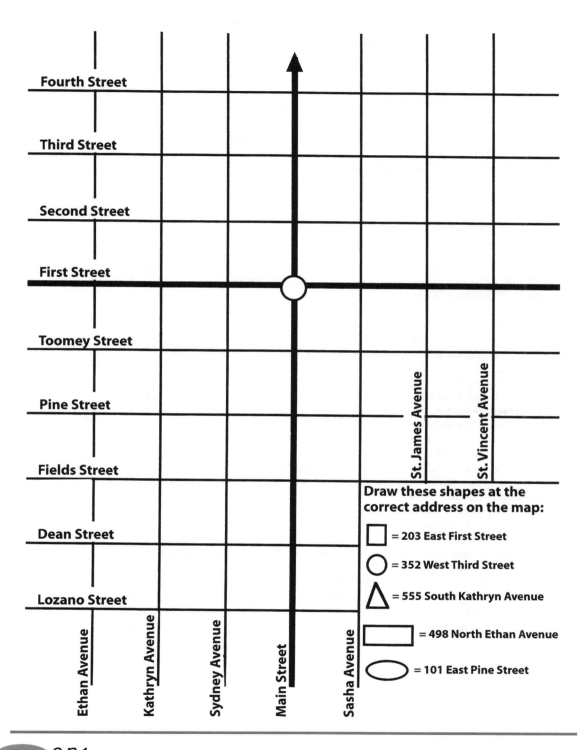

Draw these shapes at the correct address on the map:

☐ = 203 East First Street

○ = 352 West Third Street

△ = 555 South Kathryn Avenue

▭ = 498 North Ethan Avenue

⬭ = 101 East Pine Street

Figure 2.B.1

Address System Quiz

Lesson Plan

Students: _Sasha and James (low vision, junior high age)_

Instructor: _Tom_

Date: _____

Time: _____

Lesson Location: _____

_____

_____

Goal: _To develop an understanding of the address system_

Lesson Objectives:
1. _To estimate the within-block location of a place, given its address, with 80 percent accuracy_
2. _To locate four addresses, using address-system concepts, with 80 percent accuracy_

Instructional Materials: _a graphic of a grid pattern of a mock city, Address Bingo cards, felt-tip markers, monoculars_

Daily Notes:

Methodology/Instructional Strategies:

1. In the travel area, review address-system numbering concepts on the graphic aid of the mock city grid pattern. Include a review of the mnemonics "NOW" and "SEE."

2. Ask the students if they would check every address on this block to locate a place at 150 Chehalem Street? What about 192 or 108?

3. Explain that the last two digits can sometimes give you an idea of where a destination may be located in a block.

4. Give the students a few three-digit and four-digit addresses to estimate locations. Give feedback as necessary until they become at least 80 percent accurate.

5. Give the students their Address Bingo cards. Have them find an even and an odd number on this block to fill in on their card. Make sure they verify whether the last two digits indicate the location in the block accurately.

6. At the corner, ask the students to locate an even- and an odd-numbered address along the perpendicular street. Have them add these numbers to their Address Bingo cards (six should be marked).

7. When they have completed their cards, ask the students if they have any questions about the address system.

8. Ask the students to check how many numbers are left to be circled on their Address Bingo cards and where they would like to go on the following lesson to find the remaining addresses (at least get them to choose a street, neighborhood, or area to start at).

Lesson Plan

Students: _Sasha and James (low vision, junior high age)_

Instructor: _Tom_

Date: _____

Time: _____

Lesson
Location: _____

_____

_____

Goal: _To develop an understanding of the address system_

Lesson
Objectives:
1. _To maintain independent orientation using the address system_
2. _To locate four addresses, using address-system concepts, with 100 percent accuracy_

Instructional
Materials: _Address Bingo cards, felt-tip markers, monoculars_

Daily Notes:

Methodology/Instructional Strategies:

1. _Drive the students to a location near the area that they chose to search for their remaining four addresses to complete the Address Bingo card._
2. _Tell them that they will need to find not only the four addresses, but also the address where they are beginning the search because this is where you will meet them when they have finished. Once they have discovered the starting address, review the address-system concepts that they will use to maintain their orientation._
3. _Monitor the students from a distance (1/4 of a block) as they search for the remaining addresses for their Address Bingo cards. Intervene only if you are concerned for their safety or they appear to be lost._
4. _Discuss the lesson with the students at the ending point and check their Address Bingo cards to see that the cards are complete. Compare the variety of types of places that they found in completing their cards (such as houses, apartments, and stores)._
5. _On returning to school, have the students select the lunch spot for the following week._
6. _Back at school, have the students phone the information number to get the phone number of the restaurant and then call the restaurant to get the address/location and any major cross streets._
7. _Look at a map with the students using a closed-circuit television and plan your route for the lunch outing._

Lesson Plan

Students: *Sasha and James (low vision, junior high age)*

Instructor: *Tom*

Date: _____

Time: _____

Lesson
Location: _____

_____

_____

Goal: *To develop an understanding of the address system*

Lesson
Objectives: 1.   *To locate a given restaurant using the address system*
              2.   *To recite the words to the "Address Rap"*

Instructional   *words to an "address rap"*
Materials:

Daily Notes:

Methodology/Instructional Strategies:
1.   While driving the students to a location near the restaurant that they have chosen for lunch, teach them the words to the "Address Rap" (See Appendix 5.A for an example). Park the car and have the students lead the way to the restaurant.
2.   After lunch, practice singing the "Address Rap" on the way home in the car.

3

Making Learning Meaningful and Fun: Elements of Innovative Instruction

CHAPTER PREVIEW

Encouraging Students' Initiatives
  Teaching Requested Routes
  Capturing Learning Moments
  Using Discovery Learning
  Encouraging Students' Curiosity
  Sharing Decision Making
  Facilitating Students' Participation in Meetings and Lessons
  Encouraging Reluctant Students
  Use of Games and Activities
  Turn Taking
  Board and Computer Games
  Group Games
  Active Games

Use of Role-Play Scenarios

Use of Group Activities
  Group Games
  Interactive Models
  Creative Group Activities
  Off-Campus Travel
  Mini-Units
  Field Trips
  Group Discussions

Special Considerations for Students with Additional Disabilities
  Natural Routines
  Task Analysis

Reverse Chaining
Use of Prompts
Shaping

CREATING INTERESTING instructional strategies is beneficial for both O&M specialists and their students. Teaching a new concept or skill can be more effective, and students have a greater chance of understanding this information more thoroughly, when O&M specialists use a variety of techniques for explaining what a concept or skill is, how it is used, or why it is important. Units of instruction, whether they focus on beginning residential travel skills, street-crossing skills, or bus travel, for example, can all be presented using a number of interesting strategies to motivate students and enable them to learn more thoroughly.

Creative teaching strategies can help motivate students as they practice and refine their O&M skills. Students who are motivated to progress in their skills enjoy coming to their O&M lessons, and their positive attitude is a benefit to the O&M specialists who work with them. The creative give-and-take between student and instructor, which often occurs with motivated students, brings fresh ideas and approaches to learning and understanding concepts and skills. O&M specialists are less apt to suffer burnout when these kinds of exchanges take place. Motivated students also often progress at a faster pace when they enjoy learning.

O&M specialists can design lesson units that are based on the traditional sequence, yet incorporate nontraditional teaching strategies. For example, within a traditional sequence, an O&M instructor may collaborate with other teachers between lessons or team teach a lesson or series of lessons with another O&M instructor or teaching professional. Other types of lessons may include teaching several students at the same time, rather than just one student, or involving the student in an O&M presentation to his or her homeroom or general education class.

The suggestions presented in this chapter indicate how these nontraditional approaches, such as the use of students' initiatives, games and activities, role-play scenarios, and group lessons, may benefit some learners and make teaching more fun and relevant for them. Additional considerations for teaching approaches that may be useful when working with students who have multiple disabilities are also provided.

ENCOURAGING STUDENTS' INITIATIVES

Although some of the O&M curriculum must be teacher directed, students have opportunities to be more actively involved in choosing what they will learn and/or how they will learn during certain lessons. With these opportunities, students become active participants in the learning process, rather than passive learners. The following lesson formats or situations may provide opportunities for student initiatives in O&M:

- teaching requested routes,
- capturing learning moments,
- using discovery learning,
- encouraging students' curiosity,
- sharing decision making, and
- facilitating students' participation in meetings and lessons.

Teaching Requested Routes

Students sometimes need to learn a specific route or routes because of a change in the location of their classes, schools, jobs, housing, or other regularly visited places or because they want to learn how to get to a new area (see Environments by Demand in Chapter 6). As a departure from the planned O&M curriculum, teaching requested routes is similar to the critical skills model discussed in Chapter 2. Students should be made aware that it is appropriate for them to explain these needs to their O&M specialist. Even if a student tells the O&M specialist about such a need at the beginning of a lesson, the O&M specialist can postpone the planned lesson to accommodate the student. This approach is more effective than ignoring the student for the sake of a set curriculum or putting off the student's request until a later lesson. Having discussed the need, the student and O&M specialist can then work together to gather information about the most efficient way to travel to the new destination, given the starting point, method of travel, and time of day. (A form to help students gather information about a new neighborhood appears in the Appendix to Chapter 6.)

Capturing Learning Moments

There are other advantages to being flexible when teaching the O&M curriculum. There may be occasions during a lesson when learning opportunities occur spontaneously and O&M specialists can capture the "learning moment" for their students. If these opportunities are related to the student's IEP or other valuable learning experiences, it may be to the O&M specialist's advantage to digress from the particular objective of that lesson and take time out to explain or show the student what is happening at that moment.

For example, suppose a student has been learning about three-way traffic signals and is planning to cross one of these large intersections for the first time. On the way to the intersection, she or he crosses a smaller, familiar traffic light-controlled intersection and then hears a whistle. The student stops and asks the O&M specialist why there is a whistle sound. Rather than proceed with the student to the next intersection, the O&M specialist stops to answer the student's question, explaining that a police officer is blowing a whistle while directing traffic because the traffic lights are not working and describing how the police officer is directing the flow of traffic. She or he also explains that the traffic lights are being replaced by two city workers who are in a truck parked along the centerline of one of the streets and describes what the traffic light housing looks like while the lights are being replaced and how the workers are positioned above their special truck in the bucket of their cherry picker. From this diversion, the student learns firsthand two or more facts about how traffic light-controlled intersections work. Experiential learning like this is motivating to students and increases their understanding of the environment.

Using Discovery Learning

Discovery learning is another method to encourage students' curiosity and interest in the areas where students travel. While traveling in a new area, the O&M specialist can prompt the student to notice one or two particular elements of the environment (including the shapes of corners, the contours of the building line, the textural surfaces of the sidewalk, the length of the blocks, or the types of sounds heard). Rather than being told about everything on the lesson by the O&M specialist, students are free to explore the environment in their own way and to "discover" unusual features of elements typically found in these areas (such as square-shaped versus diagonal-shaped corners or the slopes in a sidewalk caused by big tree roots) or try to determine on their own the significance of certain unfamiliar sounds, like the unusual sounds of a factory or one-way street. Figure 3.1 presents a sample lesson plan that

Lesson Plan

Student: _Kathryn_

Instructor: _Diane_

Date: _February 24, 1999_

Time: _11:48 A.M._

Lesson
Location: _West side of Fair Oaks Avenue between_

California and Mission Streets

Goal: _To develop independent travel skills for light business areas_

**Lesson
Objectives:**
1. _Identify two pieces of street furniture (hardware) located along a given block_
2. _Use the touch-and-drag cane technique to locate 80 percent of business entrances along a given block_
3. _Describe four differences between residential and light business travel areas_

**Instructional
Materials:** _a long cane, tape recorder, blank tape_

Methodology/Instructional Strategies:

1. _Tell Kathryn that today we are transitioning from our familiar residential area to a new light business area._
2. _Ask her to share ideas on what may be different in the new area; if necessary, probe:_
   Traffic   _Grassy strips along sidewalks_
   Sidewalks   _Houses_
3. _Ask Kathryn to walk one block north, using her best cane skills, and note any differences or interesting features of the light business area into a handheld tape recorder (monitor safety closely)._
4. _At the completion of the block, listen to the tape recording of Kathryn's discoveries. Discuss the features and return with Kathryn to examine any areas of confusion._
5. _Guide Kathryn for street crossing._
6. _Briefly review the touch-and-drag technique and its purpose. Ask Kathryn to follow the building line to locate each business entrance and tape her description of the door and entry mat._
7. _Repeat step 4._
8. _Guide Kathryn for street crossing._
9. _On the third block, have Kathryn explore street furniture (hardware) located on the street side of the sidewalk. Ask her to tape her description of the items._
10. _Repeat step 4._
11. _Return to the starting point using the sighted (human) guide technique._
12. _To end the lesson, ask Kathryn to describe four differences between residential and light business travel areas._
13. _Play the entire tape in the car on the way back to school._
14. _Preview the next lesson._

Daily Notes:

Each of the three lesson objectives were met. Kathryn had some initial difficulty in sidewalk travel that was due to veering as she discovered there were no grass sidewalk strips. The tape recorder was highly motivating, but awkward (try to find a neck strap or smaller recorder for future) lessons). Kathryn found all but two of the doors in the second block. She has some difficulty staying in step with touch and drag. This was the first time she had seen a newspaper rack. In the next lesson, we can purchase a paper and scan an article into her computer to read.

Figure 3.1

Sample Lesson Plan: New Discoveries in Light Business Travel

shows how discovery learning can be incorporated into other types of instruction—in this case, a lesson on travel in a light business area. Discovery learning helps put students in charge of the lesson and of the learning for that lesson, which is an active and energizing role for them.

Encouraging Students' Curiosity

Students' initiative can be encouraged and included in lessons in other ways as well. For example, students can be asked questions during the lesson, as appropriate, to pique their curiosity. This approach is especially effective on lessons dealing with orientation. When encouraged to participate in a lesson by responding to questions about the environment or sharing relevant information about their own experiences, students often learn to participate more spontaneously and soon begin to ask questions on their own. Positive statements like the following encourage students' curiosity and help build their self-confidence: "You

 IDEAS FOR ENCOURAGING CURIOSITY
IN LEARNING O&M

- Praise the student for initiating thoughts and questions that demonstrate critical thinking during O&M lessons (for example, "I think it's terrific that you are considering other options for handling this detour" or "That's an excellent question about why they chose to put a four-way stop sign at this intersection.")

- Ask questions before beginning the travel route to pique the student's curiosity about a given environment (for instance, "Last week there was construction along this route. I wonder what type of machinery we may find this week?" or "Do you think the bus will be empty or full at this time of day?")

- Have the student identify an environmental feature of interest and count the number of those items found along a given block or route.

- Play "I Spy" with a young student with low vision to increase his or her environmental awareness and scanning skills.

- Design two alternate routes to a destination and ask the student to guess which is longer, faster, easier, and more populated and then travel the two routes for comparison.

were really curious today. That's great!" "The more you know about where you are, the safer you'll be." (See Ideas for Encouraging Curiosity in Learning O&M.)

Curiosity usually makes students more aware of what they are learning and of the environment in which they are learning. A greater awareness heightens students' desire to travel and increases students' safety. Students who are more alert and more knowledgeable are usually safer, since they are able to anticipate and respond to unexpected problems or hazards more quickly and effectively. The following sample questions to encourage curiosity can be asked of students of all ages and abilities:

- "Let's take a little break. Did you notice . . . ? Why is it here?"

- "I saw you hesitate back there. Were you curious about something?"

- "Have you ever seen [touched] one of these before? What about in your home area?"

- "Do you have these near your house [apartment]?

- "How many ——— do you think you can find along here on this block?"

- "Do you think there will be more or less ——— on the other side of the street?"

- "I'd like to point out something to you here. Is this typical or unusual for this area? What do you think it is? How did it get here?"

For young students, O&M specialists can use "curiosity" cards to encourage questioning skills. In this particular example, students are asked to select one or two "curiosity cards" (prepared in braille or large print as appropriate) as the focus of one of their orientation lessons, presented to them in a fan shape like a hand of playing cards. Each card contains a different word with the type of questions they will ask (a what, why, where, who, when, or how question). The student is instructed to find three objects during the lesson—such as a tree, gate, and fire hydrant—and use the words on the cards to formulate a question about each object. For example, if a student chooses a what and how card, he or she may ask "What is this?" and "How is it made?" or "How did it get here?" or "How do we use it?" The student is then challenged to answer the questions about the given item. The O&M specialist gives assistance as needed in answering the questions. When students are curious about their travel environments, O&M specialists can easily develop motivating lessons.

Sharing Decision Making

Asking students to make decisions during the lessons is yet another example of encouraging students' initiatives. Decision-making skills are important for students to learn because they help foster problem-solving strategies, independent thinking, and the ability to learn through consequences. Offering opportunities for decision making can be used in lessons for students of all ages and abilities. Examples range from a decision between two simple choices given to the student (for example, "Would you like to turn left or right at the end of the hall?") to more complex decisions that are recognized and identified by the students themselves (for instance, using maps and bus schedules to choose the best route among several to reach a desired location).

Students are often used to being told what to do in an O&M lesson and have little opportunity to give input during the lesson about what skill to use or route to follow. When O&M specialists make all the decisions for their students, the students do not have an opportunity to learn through experience, that is, to learn from the consequences of decisions that they have made.

For example, if a student is practicing walking in step along a residential block, the O&M specialist may ask him or her to choose a direction at the corner to continue to practice the cane skills and to learn about something new and different in the environment. The O&M specialist then describes what the student will find in each direction: The choices are (1) turn and continue walking around the block—the easiest choice, with an interesting mailbox to see midblock; (2) continue straight and cross the perpendicular street, where there is no grass between sidewalk and street, which would be interesting and different; or (3) turn and cross the parallel street, where there is a fun store to check out, but the street crossing is difficult.

Another example may be to give a student choices about how he or she would like to analyze an intersection if the unit being studied is on different types of intersections. The O&M specialist may ask the student if he or she would like to begin analyzing a particular intersection by writing answers on an intersection analysis form with the clipboard and pen (see Appendix 5.A) or by drawing the intersection, with its traffic patterns and traffic signal hardware, on a dry-erase board with marking pens (see Chapter 6 for a discussion of ways to analyze environments). The next few lessons would continue at that intersection, with the student completing either the analysis form or the drawing. Students may like to use both methods of learning about an intersection and, when given choices, may switch back and forth between these two approaches as they travel to new intersections and learn about them. Many students are resistant to this approach at first, finding it easier to say "I don't care," rather than to think about an answer. Eventually, however, most students recognize the value of thinking things through and acting on their own decisions. They have learned from experience that the consequences of decision making are positive and enable them to learn more about where they are traveling and what they may find while traveling.

Facilitating Students' Participation in Meetings and Lessons

O&M specialists can encourage students to participate in lessons and meetings that concern them. Students can keep a file or notebook of their work, an O&M student portfolio, which they can bring to their IEP or IWRP meetings to show the educational or rehabilitation team what they have been learning in O&M lessons. Student portfolios can be used by children of all ages and adults and may include the following:

- a copy of the student's medical eye report and emergency medical information,

- list and copy of all student identification cards,

- note cards describing important routes,

- journal entries of various travel experiences,

- tapes of telephone interactions with representatives of the local bus company,

- maps of areas traveled,

- drawings of O&M landmarks,

- O&M tests,

- information review sheets,

- names and schedules of bus routes completed independently,

- a list of intersections determined to be safe for crossing,
- business cards from shops visited, and
- other information collected during O&M lessons.

Encouraging Reluctant Students

If students are reluctant to show initiative during their lessons, they still can be encouraged to participate as actively as possible as a means of eventually fostering more independence. For example, students can be encouraged to use O&M materials actively in as many ways as possible and to help with materials during each lesson. School-age students can carry, open, and close the Chang Kit (a commercially available kit that uses Velcro shapes to create grid patterns or simple maps; see Chapter 4). They can assemble and put away the mapmaking materials, handle safety scissors and adhesive tape, and glue additions onto their maps on their own. They may choose to wear a waist pouch (sometimes known as a fanny pack) to carry needed O&M supplies, such as a handheld magnifier, measuring tape, bold felt-tip marker, index cards, and zipper-fastened plastic bags).Giving this pouch a name, such as "scout pouch," creates a sense of exploration and adventure about O&M lessons.

Students can also carry and operate their own note-taking equipment (a tape recorder, slate and stylus, clipboard, or Braille Lite) on lessons. Assuming responsibility for such items as one's umbrella when it is raining or baseball hat and special tints, filters, or sunglasses when there is glare is another important aspect of developing independence. Young children may enjoy using the O&M specialist's car key to unlock the car door or trunk. Adults can sometimes assist in navigating while the O&M specialist is driving or help to pump the gas if they wish to.

Encouraging students' participation in any small way can be the first step toward greater initiative that the student may demonstrate later on. It is important to realize that encouraging students' initiatives at any level will enhance the learning process.

USE OF GAMES AND ACTIVITIES

Games and activities are valuable tools to use while students are learning about a concept or skill. These kinds of teaching tools are used once students understand what the concept or skill is and its importance to them as visually impaired travelers. Practice and repetition in learning

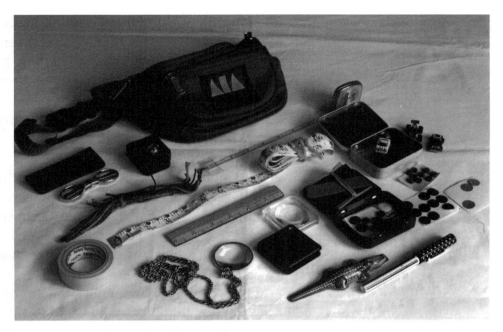

Photo 3.1

Suggesting that students wear a "scout pouch" to carry their supplies may help motivate reluctant students and add a sense of exploration to O&M lessons. Items in the pouch, moving clockwise from top right, include retractable measuring tape; measuring tape with tactile markings; miniature cars; assorted felt, foam, and plastic circle adhesives and storage box; pen; alligator clicker; hand-held pocket magnifier; hand-held magnifier on a chain; ruler with tactile markings; masking tape; Wikki Stix; retractable scissors and casse; and car compass.

a skill are usually more enjoyable and motivating if they are done in different ways and/or in different places. The games and activities described here are often used for one lesson or part of a lesson to help students practice skills in an enjoyable way. In addition to the information presented in this chapter, Appendix 5.A in Chapter 5 describes additional games and activities that may help students learn and practice specific O&M skills.

Turn Taking

Strategies involving turn taking with other students or with the O&M specialist are fun for students, even those who are in high school or older. With this approach, the O&M specialist and the student become more equal partners in the learning process. Obviously, the teacher still assumes responsibility for the lesson, and the student understands that the O&M specialist is in charge. The turn-taking strategy is used to encourage the learner to be more actively involved in the lesson. If they are working on a map or tactile graphic or using word cards to learn compass cardinal directions, the student and the O&M specialist can take turns asking questions and responding; they can also alternate giving the route to follow on the map. If they are traveling outside, they can take turns giving routes, so the student sometimes becomes the instructor. Traveling in a familiar area, cane travelers can take the O&M specialist, using the sighted guide technique, and point out landmarks and other interesting parts of the travel environment.

Other sharing games help students learn what is typical of a particular environment or about landmarks and what they are. Variations of I Spy are fun for some students. The student and O&M specialist take turns choosing something in the environment that they can touch, hear, or see and give clues about what it is and where it is until the other person guesses it. This game works well in such locations as grocery stores, hardware stores, or fabric stores. An adaptation of the game In My Suitcase is another enjoyable activity for students with low vision to practice their listening and memory skills. The O&M specialist may start by saying, "I'm going walking in the residential area and will take a monocular in my O&M scout pouch." The student then repeats what the specialist said and adds one more item to take in the scout pouch. The two continue to take turns adding to the scout pouch. The challenge is to remember the order in which the items were included. In another version, which uses visual scanning and monocular skills, as well as environmental concepts, the O&M specialist and student take turns finding new things they see at a particular location. The specialist can start the game by saying, "I'm standing at Western and Elm, and on this northwest corner is a Laundromat," and the student can respond: "I'm standing at Western and Elm, and on this northwest corner is a laundromat and a bakery." They can then take turns adding things that can be seen.

Board and Computer Games

Board games and other classroom activities can be adapted tactilely for students or purchased from companies that design products for people who are blind or visually impaired (see the Resources section at the end of this book). These games give students the chance to practice their interpersonal and communication skills, and many can be related to other O&M skills. Checkers, chess, and tic-tac-toe help reinforce spatial and route-planning skills (see Sidebar 3.1). Puzzles and manipulative toys

---

Sidebar 3.1 Board Games That Can Be Used to Teach O&M Skills

The games listed here are examples of commercially available board games that can be used to motivate students and to teach and reinforce spatial, number, and landmarking O&M concepts. The O&M specialist can create tactile adaptations for the games, and some games can be purchased in already adapted forms from specialty vendors. (See Resources section in this book.)

Game	Adapted/Purchased	Skills Practiced
Chess	Both	Spatial concepts; route planning
Checkers	Both	Spatial concepts; route planning
Tic-tac-toe	Both	Spatial concepts
Monopoly	Both	Spatial concepts
Dice/die	Both	Counting, even-odd concepts
Playing cards	Both	Visual and memory skills
Guess Who	Purchased	Visual identification and discrimination
Connect Four (vertical tic-tac-toe)	Purchased	Spatial concepts

---

like LEGO and similar variations help develop fine motor skills and are motivating for students to explore and understand spatial concepts like size, proportion, and dimensionality. Specific shapes that students hear about and will be exposed to while traveling (including tunnels, ditches, holes, and bridges) can be explained and demonstrated more easily using manipulatives, in addition to verbal explanations.

Computer programs that involve mapmaking and map reading (such as the Neighborhood Map Making Machine for Apple computers, or the Rand McNally StreetFinder program for personal computers and the street-finding program on the Rand McNally web site) can be used with students who have low vision. Dino Park Tycoon is an example of a computer game that asks students to design an amusement park and gives them a chance to practice their business skills.

Action games, such as Red Light, Green Light, tag, or relay races, can also be used as teaching strategies and are motivating for active students and those who learn better through movement experiences. They give students the opportunity to practice many of their orientation skills and to work on their physical skills, like their stamina, overall coordination, or balance. The O&M specialist can play these games with an individual student during a lesson or with several students together.

Group Games

Group games like treasure hunts or scavenger hunts are motivating for students of all ages and can be used with two or three students looking for the same landmarks or for something hidden by the O&M specialist either during the same lesson or during their individual lessons. If the students are searching on their own, they can ask questions or share information with the other O&M students who are playing the game via notes or audiotapes. Red Light, Green Light is a fun game to play with several students and helps them practice their listening skills and understanding of body references and/or compass cardinal directions. By replacing the labels in the hopscotch squares, hopscotch can be adapted in various ways to teach basic body references, compass cardinal directions, or the address system. Students can pick up body reference cards on various squares or call out address numbers as they hop from one and to another. Checkers can be adapted with rug squares that are placed in a formation like a giant checkerboard, and students (or one student) can move in various ways from square to square practicing specific route directions. To prevent possible slipping, carpet squares should have rubber nonslip backing and be placed on coarse surfaces, such as cement.

Address Bingo can be used to teach address concepts. In this game, the contents of the squares on the cards are the last two numbers of various addresses, and the column headings are the block on which the addresses in that column appear (for example, the 100–200 block), which tells the student the first number of the address (see Figure 3.2). To fill in the squares, a student must locate the indicated address, circle it on the card, and give a brief description of the location to prove that he or she has found it. Students can complete the cards in a group or compete against each other. (See Appendix 2.A for an example of lesson plans using Address Bingo.)

Active Games

Physical warm-ups for the legs and arms heighten overall body awareness and increase strength and flexibility. (See Appendix 5.A for an example of warm-ups for stair travel.) These warm-ups, which use movements and exercises adapted from physical education and dance classes,

0–100 block	100–200 block	200–300 block	300–400 block
16 location description:	92 location description:	85 location description:	57 location description:
49 location description:	12 location description:	34 location description:	27 location description:
76 location description:	53 location description:	19 location description:	24 location description:
61 location description:	39 location description:	65 location description:	44 location description:

Figure 3.2

Sample Address Bingo Card

can also reinforce correct gait, stair travel, placement of the cane, and correct movement of the cane. In a lesson, the O&M specialist can have a short human-guide race with an active student. Running with a guide or side by side, the O&M specialist and the student can race to the north or south, toward a particular building or landmark, or east and west between placed orange pylons as a way of practicing compass cardinal directions. The races may include skipping or turning to reinforce body image, laterality, and directionality. Variations may include exaggerated big and small steps or quick or slow steps to reinforce the student's spatial concepts and sense of timing. Interesting landmarks can be placed at the beginning and end of the racing route, so the student knows where to begin and end the race.

Other active challenges include asking the student to find as many doors in a hallway, walkways, driveways, or poles as possible in a given amount of time. Perhaps students could compare several objects in a given amount of time to see which is the biggest, smallest, shortest, tallest, or noisiest.

USE OF ROLE-PLAY SCENARIOS

Another creative strategy, role-playing, is enjoyable for students and can be used over a period of several lessons or longer. During role-play, students work on particular O&M skills in the overall context of a role they have chosen. The range of role-play activities that can be applied to community travel is seemingly endless, although different role-playing strategies may work better with students of different ages.

Role-playing activities and role reversals, in which the student becomes the teacher, can be used effectively with blind or visually impaired students of various ages. Students of all ages commonly enjoy assuming the role of teacher for the day. During these occasions, the O&M specialist can assess the students' understanding of specific skills or concepts, and the student has an opportunity to practice verbalizing certain information. In some situations, peer teaching may also be an effective teaching strategy. Elementary-age students may be able to teach one another specific routes around the school neighborhood. Older students may be able to teach some advanced travel skills, such as obtaining information on a bus route over the phone. These types of lessons should be planned carefully so they go as smoothly as possible and are successful in building confidence and developing skills.

During role-play activities, young students often like to pretend they are characters from books, popular television programs, or movies. Other children enjoy fantasy role-play that may take place in this world or some other imaginary environment. Pretending to be someone or something else can be appropriate as long as the students know they are using make-believe as a device to practice a skill (like maintaining a good cane arc or lining up at a corner) or to learn about orientation (such as locating landmarks or identifying left and right). For example, some students like to pretend that they are robots or that the O&M specialist is a robot. Walkie-talkies and robot-style speech make the robot role-play enjoyable, and students who do not like to practice their mobility skills are often more willing to practice carefully or for longer periods when the O&M specialist gives them suggestions or comments in a robot voice. As Master Controllers, students like to give route commands to the O&M specialist, especially when the specialist "robot" purposely makes mistakes to trick them. Some of the other roles that are fun for young students include being a pirate, a detective, a police officer, an alien from outer space, and an astronaut.

For high school- or college-age students, role-play is especially effective when it is related to careers that students may choose or jobs that their relatives or friends have. A student who role-plays being a real estate agent, for example, has an opportunity to notice a neighborhood in great detail and to practice a variety of O&M skills like landmarking, map reading, compass cardinal direction and body references, street crossings, bus travel, monocular skills, effective communication skills, and skills for organizing information. A student who role-plays being a newspaper or television reporter can practice these same skills while covering a beat or specific "assignment" (such as examining a new office building for compliance with the Americans with Disabilities Act). If the student is motivated, he or she can visit a local cable television or radio station or the office of a community newspaper to interview staff members and learn more about the kinds of jobs that are available in this line of work.

Self-advocacy skills are an important part of students' communication skills and can be practiced in role-playing, mock interview, or real interview situations like these. Other role-playing choices include being a newspaper or mail carrier, social worker, health care worker or visiting nurse, city or traffic engineer, lawyer, or computer consultant. All these jobs involve travel to locate various destinations on foot or using public transportation; students would find these types of destinations during their O&M lessons as part of the role-plays. Other lessons could focus on the typical travel experiences that these types of people have on weekends, from running household errands to participating in leisure-time activities. These types of destinations could be discussed, and students could learn how to plan the most efficient routes to complete various errands (such as the quickest way to go to the dry cleaner, the bank, and the grocery store). More role-play ideas for older students may include college student, store clerk, manager of a business, parent, teacher/professor, actor, physician, city planner, traveling salesperson, musician, or designer.

Adults can also benefit from role-play and other similar learning activities. Some adults may enjoy role-playing the interaction between a bus driver and a passenger. Others may like to take a turn at being the O&M specialist to demonstrate their competence in a particular skill. Hypothetical scenarios can be easily integrated into O&M lessons to make them more interesting for adults. For example, a hypothetical (or "dream") vacation can be researched. This activity would involve gathering information via a telephone or computer, bus travel to the travel agency, travel to and inquiries at the post office about obtaining a passport, and even a field trip to the airport to become familiar with the terminal. Although it is unlikely that adults would be interested in role-playing careers in the same manner as school-age students, some lessons can be based on previous or current work experiences to give adults a chance to share their expertise that is related to specific O&M skills.

USE OF GROUP ACTIVITIES

Students sometimes learn a concept better when they participate in a group learning activity, peer teaching experience, field trip, or group discussion. Members of such groups should be selected with care to ensure that all will benefit from the group lesson, and care should be taken to avoid making the members feel self-conscious about differences in skill levels in the group. The formation of groups may vary according to the given activity, but the use of these guiding principles may be helpful:

- Make sure that the learning activity is of interest to all the participants.

- Make sure that each participant has a level of skill or knowledge that will enable him or her to contribute to the activity.

● Make sure that the activity is appropriate to each participant's learning modality (for example, auditory information for participants who are totally blind or large-print materials for those who have low vision).

● Make sure that adequate supervision that is appropriate for the size of the group and the type of activity is provided.

Several types of group learning activities are effective for students who enjoy learning and sharing with other students or who can benefit from more interactions with their peers. Games and other activities, shared public transportation lessons, mini-units, field trips to a variety of destinations, and discussions or rap sessions are all examples of motivating ways to review concepts and skills from the O&M curriculum.

Group Games

As was mentioned earlier, board games or action games are motivating and help students learn various skills in groups. Games with two or three students together are generally effective for teaching or practicing such skills as body and spatial concepts, effective communication, auditory awareness and discrimination, and appropriate social interaction. For example, variations of hide-and-seek are challenging for two or three students who need to practice their auditory-awareness skills or give orientation references to one another like "in front of," "behind," "across from," or "to your side." In these games, students use sound or follow verbal directions as they try to find a hidden person or object. One such variation is Louder, Softer, in which an object is hidden and a student is chosen to find it. As the student moves closer to it, everyone else claps louder until the object is located. If the student moves farther away from the object, the clapping becomes softer. Games like these are even more fun when the students use walkie-talkies to communicate with one another. Telephone is another motivating game for a group of students to practice their listening and speaking skills. In an O&M variation of this children's game, the phrases or sentences that are whispered in turn to each person around a circle are O&M terms or descriptions of a route.

Interactive Models

Using interactive models is an effective way to have students learn concepts together. In an indoor or campus setting, a mock community can be set up so that a small group of students can use address-system concepts to find given destinations or assign appropriate addresses to make-believe buildings located on opposite sides of the street. Similarly, mock intersections can be constructed with high-contrast tape on the floor, so the students can assume the roles of various cars as they may move through the intersection. (For more information about interactive models, see Chapter 5.)

Creative Group Activities

Singing and drawing activities as part of an indoor group lesson are fun for students to review O&M concepts and skills. Making up lyrics and singing songs with an O&M theme (such as parts of the cane, cane technique, street-crossing skills, and the address system) are enjoyable activities for students who are working together on a lesson. The addition of percussion (hand clapping, foot or table tapping, or snapping the fingers) adds interest. If students have musical instruments that are portable, they can bring these instruments on another day when there is a group lesson and perhaps record the songs to share later with classmates. Another indoor activity may be to have several students who share a training area work on a map together. The students could discuss the kind of information needed for the map, like adding the compass cardinal direction north, street names, and landmarks. They could take turns adding symbols and words directly on the map or in a legend referring to the map. (For more information on mapmaking, see Chapter 7.)

Off-Campus Travel

Group lessons can involve travel off campus as well. Two students can travel on a bus route together or use another form of public transportation together during a lesson. If they are both at the same level in their training, the students can share their experiences with public transportation with each other at the end of the lesson. If one of them is completing bus travel while the other is just starting this unit, the student with more knowledge can act as a peer teacher and help to introduce bus travel by traveling on the bus with the less experienced student. Peer activities like these are typically most effective when they are done for one or two lessons.

Mini-Units

Other kinds of group lessons can be organized as a mini-unit with two or three students (provided there is ample supervision) who are at about the same level and who are training in the same general area. The group lesson (or lessons) would be the culmination of what the individual students have been learning for several weeks on their own. During their individual lessons, each student could "specialize" in knowing a certain section of the training area (such as certain intersections, landmarks along one side of a street, or businesses within a two-block radius). During the group lesson or lessons, the students could show each other the particular section they had studied and knew well. Each student would have a chance to teach the other students and share with them the materials used in the individual lessons, like maps, audiotapes, drawings, notes, purchased items, or analysis sheets. The culmination lesson or lessons would give the students a chance to practice both their listening and speaking skills.

Field Trips

Field trips are another way to present or reinforce skills and concepts from the O&M curriculum within a group context. These types of lessons are more fun with several O&M students and often involve an extended lesson and greater distance than is usual in an O&M lesson. Field trips are a convenient and efficient way for students to travel in unfamiliar yet significant environments that they may have heard or learned about but not visited. Examples of such destinations are the financial, cultural, or business center of a city; a subway station; a central bus station; an industrial park; an airport; a college campus; a nature preserve; an observatory; the pier or shore of a lake; a river; or an ocean beach. These kinds of trips usually take a half day or a full day and are often conducted during summer school or near the end of the school year when students have more free time. They typically involve a ratio of two or three O&M students per instructor. The instructors may be two O&M specialists, an O&M specialist and teacher of students with visual impairments, or an O&M specialist and classroom teacher if general education students are included in the field trip. Although preparing for the trip may take some time, the students can be part of the preparation process and help organize the details of the trip. Adult students enjoy going on O&M field trips as well and can help plan them. Adult O&M students gain as much as school-age students when they spend time together visiting a special place on a field trip.

Field trips are more effective if the O&M specialist discusses the field trip ahead of time—what the destination is, why it is important, what its function is, and where it is—and gives the students an opportunity to examine maps or other materials so they know where they are going. Students who are familiar with the route from their school to their destination (traveling by car on a highway, by bus along a main street, or by subway) may be more interested in following along.

Students can also be divided into groups and given study cards to take on the trip. These cards can have five or six simple questions for the students to ask and/or to answer, so they can practice their orientation skills throughout the trip and share this information with one another. For example, some students can be responsible for pointing out all the compass cardinal directional references of travel; others, for asking about the names of the streets on which they are walking; and still others, for asking about or describing significant landmarks they see or examine tactilely. Although field trips focus on reaching a destination and spending time there, students would also have an opportunity to practice many of their O&M skills while traveling throughout the day. In addition to the orientation skills mentioned earlier with the study cards, students would probably also be practicing many of the following: sighted (human) guide skills, street-crossing skills, cane skills, monocular skills, stair or escalator skills, elevator skills, purchasing skills, and skills for interacting with the public.

Group Discussions

Group discussions can be beneficial to people who are blind or visually impaired, especially those who are adventitiously blind or visually impaired and are adjusting to life with vision loss. People often feel better knowing that others experience similar difficulties learning or applying a particular skill (such as the address system, analyzing complex intersections, or the order in which to scan before crossing a street) or may want to share how they finally accomplished a particular skill. Some students appreciate time to share their thoughts and feelings (positive and negative) about their travel experiences, such as what happened to them on an O&M lesson or on a weekend when they traveled alone or with friends. This kind of sharing can take place when students meet in a group and use an O&M lesson as a rap session about various topics related to travel. Students can use this time to describe the frustrations they feel with bus drivers or clerks who are not helpful or buses that are late, as well as positive experiences, such as the first time they crossed an intersection near their home and walked to a familiar destination or were able to problem solve when they were disoriented. This advice may be particularly helpful to students who are just beginning to learn a skill. The rap sessions need not always be part of O&M lessons; students can meet during lunch or coffee breaks. Furthermore, these sessions do not have to be held on a regular basis, unless the students want to meet regularly.

SPECIAL CONSIDERATIONS FOR STUDENTS WITH ADDITIONAL DISABILITIES

Games, role-play activities, and group activities can also be used with blind and visually impaired students who have additional disabilities. However, there are a number of approaches to make these strategies more effective for such students. First, teaching O&M skills during natural routines may be the most effective. Second, a task analysis can be useful in determining the specific miniskills that will be needed to complete an activity with minimal or no assistance. Third, certain general teaching strategies may be particularly helpful when working with students who have additional learning challenges: presenting lesson sequences using reverse (backward) chaining, presenting information with effective verbal strategies, or using various prompting and shaping approaches.

It is especially important to be consistent when presenting information to students with cognitive-processing and recall difficulties. Teamwork with others who are involved in working with students who have multiple disabilities is an important factor in maintaining consistency and continuity to promote the learning and retention of O&M skills. O&M specialists need to work as a team with other professionals, staff, and family members who are involved in helping students practice a skill or travel along a specific route. Everyone involved needs to use the same terminology when interacting with the student and to make sure that the student is practicing skills or routes in the same way through proper repetition. Teaching aids (such as landmark cards, simple maps, or tactile cues) prepared by the O&M specialist can be shared by other people who are assisting the student as he or she travels on a specific route (see the Appendix for Chapter 7 for sample materials).

Natural Routines

For a student who has difficulty generalizing skills, the most effective time to schedule lessons is the actual time the student will be using the route, rather than at the convenience of the O&M specialist's schedule. For example, it is likely to be more motivating to practice a route to the music classroom immediately before the student has a music class. The successful completion of the route would then result in a positive natural consequence of having time to sing or play an instrument. Routes can be presented using the critical skills model (introducing skills that are specifically needed for completion of the route).

Task Analysis

In the task analysis process, skills are broken down into small, sequential steps that can be taught one at a time. In this way, O&M specialists can address each skill separately, if needed, to build the student's overall competence with skills. For example, the constant-contact cane technique involves a combination of skills that include grasping the cane, positioning the arm, positioning the cane, moving the cane from side to side, and coordinating the movement of the cane and placement of the foot. By completing this task analysis, the O&M specialist can determine which miniskills to teach in which order.

Reverse Chaining

The sequence or order of routes need not be presented in the traditional way (from the beginning point to the end point). It may be easier and more motivating for some students to start learning a route from the last segment, so they have the reinforcement of reaching the end point of the route each time they practice it.

In this teaching strategy, known as reverse or backward chaining, the O&M specialist first analyzes the route to be taught and determines where it can be broken up into smaller "teachable" sections (the process of task analysis). Having done so, the O&M specialist assists the student in completing all the sections of the route except the last section, which the specialist then teaches. Once the student has learned this last section, the student practices the route with the O&M specialist's assistance until the last section, which the student completes independently. The student then learns the next-to-last section and is assisted along the route until the last two sections, which he or she completes without assistance. This teaching strategy continues "in reverse" until the student has learned all the sections of the route (with the end of the route reached each time in this way).

Use of Prompts

While most O&M students are prompted verbally and physically at some point when they are learning skills, students with additional disabilities generally benefit from more frequent prompting so they can recall what they are learning and practice their skills correctly. The most direct form of prompting involves physical assistance of some kind so that the correct movements are modeled for the student through hand-on-hand or other forms of tactile cueing. For example, a physical prompt to support the shoulder or back can be used to remind a student to use correct posture, or a tap from the O&M specialist's cane to the student's cane can be used to prompt a wider arc movement. When the student understands the skills and performs them with more consistency, physical prompting can be reduced until only verbal prompting is used—a process known as fading. Verbal prompts are then gradually reduced, so the student becomes more independent in executing skills, recalling a route, or correcting a problem while traveling. The use of natural cues needs to be encouraged when possible. For example, a consistent veer to a grassline alongside a sidewalk could be a natural cue to remind a student to center his or her hand placement with the long cane versus a verbal prompt from the instructor. The reliance on natural cues helps to reduce the student's dependence on the O&M specialist's prompts.

Shaping

As an instructional strategy in O&M, shaping means reinforcing all the student's movements that resemble or approximate the desired movements of the final skill being taught. This approach encourages and motivates the student to continue to move and to make progress toward learning a particular skill. Verbal or other forms of reinforcement are given each time the student demonstrates a behavior that is close to the target behavior. For example, the student who refuses to use his cane when traveling to lunch is rewarded when he simply holds it in his hand and walks with a sighted guide. He is further reinforced when he holds the cane in the correct hand and keeps the tip on the ground and when he uses a better grip and moves the cane from side to side. The student's correct use of a modified two-point touch then is reinforced through successive approximations of the desired technique.

These teaching strategies and approaches can be used with a wide range of students. Their effectiveness with students who have multiple disabilities must be determined on an individual basis. For more specific information on creative ways to present lessons to students, including those with multiple disabilities, see Chapter 5.

This chapter has presented a variety of strategies that motivate students and O&M specialists alike in teaching both traditional and less traditional units from the O&M curriculum. Discovering new ways to explain or reinforce part of the curriculum helps to keep O&M specialists and students interested and challenged. Offering students several ways to learn a concept or practice a skill gives them opportunities to understand more thoroughly what is being presented to them. Encouraging students' initiative and role-playing and using games, action activities, and group lessons are all ways to bring creative strategies into each O&M lesson and challenge each student to learn the necessary skills.

4

Teaching Concepts Creatively: Theory and Best Practices

CHAPTER PREVIEW

Concept Development
  Concepts in O&M
  Formation of Concepts

Assessment for Teaching Concepts
  Assessing Conceptual Knowledge
  Assessment Approaches

Instruction in Concepts
  General Strategies
  Instructional Grouping
  Teaching Structures
  Special Considerations

Appendix
  4.A   Sample Instructional Unit on Residential Block Concepts

THERE ARE many techniques that can be used to assist individuals who are blind or visually impaired to achieve independent or semi-independent travel, but mobility methods and devices are rendered useless without the many concepts necessary for purposeful movement. To maintain independent orientation, blind and visually impaired travelers need not only the physical skills and abilities to move from one place to another, but also a conceptual understanding of body, environment, and physical space. There are an infinite number of concepts that are relevant when teaching O&M skills for independent travel. The O&M specialist needs to be prepared for the challenge of incorporating the development of appropriate concepts into the overall O&M plan for each student.

CONCEPT DEVELOPMENT

With concept development being an essential component of independent travel, O&M specialists need to be familiar with the types of concepts that are most commonly related to O&M. Understanding the theory behind the formation of concepts and how the presence of a visual impairment poses unique learning challenges will help them provide high-quality instruction in these concepts.

Concepts in O&M

Concepts are mental representations or understanding of people, places, things, physical properties, events, actions, and reactions. Conceptual understanding provides the purpose for movement and the basis for orientation within a variety of environments. There are virtually an infinite number of concepts that relate specifically to an individual's ability to get around independently. Standard basic concepts related to O&M can be grouped according to the following categories: body image; space; laterality and directionality; time, measurement, and distance; and environment.

Although it may seem obvious that O&M specialists should address these types of concepts with children who are congenitally blind, relevant elements must also be assessed and taught to children with low vision and adults who are adventitiously blind or visually impaired. Children with low vision may also have incomplete or inaccurate conceptual knowledge. Adults may need to learn new concepts related to traveling safely as pedestrians or find ways to apply conceptual knowledge to interacting with the environment in a more tactile manner. Increased conceptual knowledge can lead to more productive, efficient, and enjoyable travel experiences for all people who are blind or visually impaired.

Body Image

The development of concepts of body image (also commonly referred to as body awareness) related to O&M includes the ability to locate and label body parts, identify the functions of body parts, and understand the range of movements of body parts.

An understanding of body parts and body planes and how they work together is beneficial when a student is learning motor skills or basic skills and cane skills. For example, when teaching the upper hand-and-forearm protective technique, the O&M specialist may be able to describe the proper positioning using specific concept words to students with good body awareness, who can probably demonstrate the technique with only a few minor adjustments from the O&M specialist. In contrast, students with poor body concepts may struggle to figure out how to turn their hands so the palms are facing outward or may move their entire shoulders upward to lift their forearms to face or chest level. It is essential to help students move beyond the simple identification and location of body parts to learn the function, movement, and coordination of movements that individual and clusters of body parts can make.

Body concepts are also important to an individual's orientation while traveling. The body forms a frame of reference that the person will often rely on to establish his or her location in space (for example, placing one's back and heels against a wall to square off; facing north, or aligning one's foot parallel to a parkway.) Body movement experiences can contribute to the ability to understand spatial orientation.

Spatial Concepts

Spatial concepts help travelers understand the placement, arrangement, and spacing of persons or things in relation to one another. It is this knowledge, along with other skills, that enables visually impaired travelers to recognize the placement and sequence of landmarks along a familiar route or to use traffic sounds to establish parallel alignment for street crossings. Whereas body awareness—also known as *egocentric* form of reference—relates to orientation in relation to one's own body, *topocentric* forms of reference use positional concepts that include the use of prepositions to define location, such as "I am between my desk and the teacher's desk" (Long & Hill, 1997). (See Sidebar 4.1 for definitions of terms related to spatial concepts.) Positional concepts are also useful in executing mobility skills like keeping the hand centered at the midline for the two-point-touch cane technique, maintaining a consistent arc width that is 2 inches beyond each shoulder, or tracing a crosswalk line across the street (with a monocular) to find a pedestrian signal box.

Spatial understanding is closely linked to body awareness and

Sidebar 4.1 Forms of Spatial Reference

The terms defined here correspond to different forms of spatial reference. Orientation and directions can be given in each of these forms or in any combination. Each form of reference provides individuals with a different level of spatial conceptual understanding that can be used in independent orientation.

Term	Definition	Example
Egocentric	Relation of self to one's surroundings	*"The grocery store is on my right-hand side."*
Topocentric	Positional concepts that include the use of prepositions to define location in relation to oneself	*"The grocery store is in front of me."*
	The position of objects in the environment in relation to one another.	*"The grocery store is next to the post office."*
Cartographic	Organizational patterns, such as floor plans, grid patterns, and the address system	*"The grocery store is located at 123 East Middletown Road."*
Polarcentric	Relative positions in space or routes according to compass directions	*"The grocery store is on the east side of the street, one block north of the railroad tracks."*

Source: Adapted from R. G. Long & E. W. Hill, "Establishing and Maintaining Orientation for Mobility," in B. B. Blasch, W. R. Wiener, & R. L. Welsh, Eds., *Foundations of Orientation and Mobility,* 2nd ed. (New York, AFB Press, 1997), p. 40; based on B. B. Blasch, R. L. Welsh, & T. Davidson, "Auditory Maps: An Orientation Aid for Visually Handicapped Persons," *New Outlook for the Blind,* 67(4), 145–158.

supports the development of advanced environmental concepts. *Cartographic* forms of reference involve organized systems of spatial arrangements, including these:

- grid patterns (such as the arrangement of parallel and perpendicular streets in a residential area),

- floor plans (like the layout of aisles, reading areas, and checkout counter of a library), and

- address system (the numbering system used in a city or town— a home located at 4413 Dentith Place, for example).

Each of these varied aspects of spatial concepts contributes to the ability of blind or visually impaired individuals to understand their location in space and arrangement of their surroundings.

Laterality and Directionality

Laterality (understanding of left and right sidedness) and *directionality* (understanding of the points or lines toward which something faces or moves) can also be important to developing good mobility skills, but are even more important to visually impaired individuals' orientation while traveling. The ability to make accurate turns is incorporated into route travel, and directions given in left and right turns provide an egocentric form of reference for simple routes. Directions given in left and right turns can ultimately be limiting, however, because they are dependent on the direction a person is facing and route reversals may be confusing.

More advanced concepts can be applied for maintaining directionality during independent travel. Descriptions of the shapes of routes (such as I, L, U, and Z) can serve as organizers for keeping track of left and right turns, directional facing, and route reversals. The use of cardinal compass directions (*polarcentric* frame of reference) provides the traveler with orientation information that can be readily converted for use from multiple locations during route travel. Cardinal directions are clear because they have a constant reference point and remain the same, regardless of the direction in which an individual is facing. Concepts of cardinal directions are more difficult to develop but ultimately provide the traveler with a more reliable frame of reference for maintaining orientation. (See Chapter 6 for applications of these concepts to various environments.)

Time, Measurement, and Distance

Concepts related to time, measurement, and distance are integral components of independent travel. Time concepts are essential to route planning and the use of public transportation in real-life situations (for example, knowing what time to be at a bus stop and how long it should take to arrive at a destination). Concepts related to measurements can be helpful to such O&M tasks as discriminating landmarks (as in making comparisons in sizes), understanding environmental concepts (like knowing the difference in widths between a walkway and a driveway), maintaining orientation (for instance, locating a bus stop that is 12 feet from the corner), and effectively using a magnifier or monocular (such as understanding a 4-inch focal distance).

Practical knowledge of distances can help with route planning, depth perception (or perspective taking), visual efficiency, the appropriate use of monoculars, and accurate echo perception. Estimating when one has traveled to the middle of a block and then moving over to a building line to locate a landmark for a specific shop are less restricting and more efficient than is trailing an entire building line. The combination of time and distance awareness can increase the efficiency of travel for individuals with visual impairments.

Environmental Concepts

The range of concepts relevant to independent travel that describe one's surroundings or environment is nearly infinite. Environmental concepts include natural phenomena (such as the characteristics of sun, wind, and sound patterns) and man-made elements (like sidewalks, traffic controls, and buildings). The depth of understanding of one's surroundings (often based on experience) contributes to both mobility and orientation skills for travelers who are blind or visually impaired, as in the following examples:

- Recognizing the slope of a wheelchair ramp can confirm for the cane user that the constant-contact technique should be used to detect the lip of the curb.

- Understanding that many residential blocks are shaped like rectangles can help with orientation when a traveler determines that he or she is on the long side of a block.

- Identifying a unique fence in a residential area can help the traveler use the fence as a landmark for orientation purposes.

- Detecting the correct audible pedestrian signal can assist a traveler in making a safe street crossing.

Exposure to a variety of environmental concepts can also be motivating for O&M lessons. Learning about the world can be an exciting process, and such knowledge ultimately provides a greater sense of control for individuals who are blind or visually impaired as they move about with purpose in their daily lives.

Formation of Concepts

Typical Concept Development

To be able to teach the concepts that are important for orientation and travel, O&M specialists need to have a grasp of how people learn concepts. In general, people develop an understanding of specific concepts by classifying or grouping things that are similar. This process begins with

- an awareness that something (like a ball) exists,

- an opportunity and desire to interact with it (by touching, exploring, reading about, or playing with it) (Skellenger & Hill, 1997),

- other people supplying "labels" for it (such as "See the yellow ball?" "That's a soft ball." "Catch the bouncy ball."), and multiple experiences with different types of the object or thing in question, combined with

- the ability to classify objects of different shapes, sizes, and materials that fit the concept in question (for example, a basketball, golf ball, beach ball, and even the oddly shaped football).

For infants, the repetition of simple sensorimotor patterns (such as reaching, touching, kicking, and grasping) facilitates interactions with the environment. Touching a mother's face, kicking at the foot of the crib, or reaching for a musical mobile each provide an infant with contact with the surrounding environment. Each contact has the potential to result in initial ideas about things in the infant's immediate world. For example, kicking at the foot of the crib feels a certain way and makes a certain sound. Kicking while on the floor would feel and sound different to the infant and help to create initial ideas about concepts like hard and soft or rough and smooth.

The understanding of concepts and ability to more discriminate accurately between categories of concepts (like dog versus cat or chair versus table) develop and become refined with increased exposure (Recchia, 1997). Language provides the labels for concepts that are commonly used. Parents seem to provide those labels naturally to their sighted children when they do everyday things, such as look at picture books ("See the little girl!") or take a trip to the market ("Look at the pretty flowers!"). As children develop a generalized understanding of a concept, language is expanded so that labels are used to include all the appropriate exemplars of the concept.

An example of the development of concepts is the natural process that young children may go through to understand the concept of a rocking chair. The children would first learn the characteristics and properties of a rocking chair in their houses by being rocked in it, climbing on it, banging it with a toy, pushing it, rocking a doll on it, and so forth. Adults supply the label for it and may provide some guidelines on its proper use; for example, "If you stand on that chair, it will move and you may fall." To refine the concept further, the children begin to compare and group similar chairs that they see in books or movies or at friends' and families' houses: kitchen chairs, armchairs, desk chairs, recliners, and the like. A full understanding of the concept comes when the children can distinguish among different kinds of chairs and identify the properties that a chair must have to be classified as a *rocking chair*.

Individuals may attain varying levels of understanding for various concepts, depending on their interest, ability, and experience. Different types of conceptual understanding can be categorized as follows:

Concrete: the characterization of objects or events that are perceived through the senses as belonging to a particular group or classification of concepts. For example, when viewing a picture with a bus, motorcycle, and car, a child can accurately identify the car.

Functional: the identification of the natural or expected use of an object or end result of an activity or event, either verbally or by appropriate performance. For instance, at a traffic light with a left-turn arrow, a teenager can identify the sequence of the traffic cycles and cross at the correct time.

Abstract: the formation of a thought or idea apart from specific instances or material examples of the concept, as when designing a new travel route using cardinal directions.

Some concepts lend themselves more readily to one form of understanding than another. For example, the concept of tree can easily be understood at the concrete level because it can be perceived through the senses and many examples of trees can be found in the environment and in pictures. Tools are often described in terms of their functionality, so it may be easier to identify a compass by how it is used than by its general physical characteristics. In contrast, abstract notions, such as honesty or north, are usually understood at the abstract level because they cannot be perceived by the senses and are difficult to characterize by function.

Challenges to Conceptual Development for People Who Are Blind or Visually Impaired

The process of developing concepts does not always proceed along identical lines for people who are blind or visually impaired as it does for sighted people. Because vision plays a major role in the early formation of concepts for sighted children, children who are blind or visually impaired, especially those with congenital blindness or low vision, must find alternate or supplemental means of learning about the world. Adults who are adventitiously blind have the benefit of having visual referents for understanding O&M skills, but may have these similar challenges when learning new concepts. A number of aspects of the typical course of conceptual development pose particular challenges to blind or visually impaired individuals.

Visual Input

In general, young children use vision constantly to understand the world around them. "According to some researchers, vision is usually involved in 90% of the learning that takes place in early development" (Ferrell, 1996, p. 89). Children who are blind or visually impaired must rely more heavily on other forms of sensory input.

For example, a young sighted child sitting in a car seat can look around to see why Dad is stopping the car. The child may see a red light or a lot of other cars all stopped. This information will help the child learn concepts about traffic. In a similar situation, however, a child with a visual impairment would receive a lot less sensory information from which to draw conclusions about the car stopping. The child may hear only the engine idling and the car radio playing. This information will not be helpful in building concepts related to traffic.

Distance Sense

Vision is the most accurate and efficient distance sense that humans possess; that is, it can be used to perceive objects and other aspects of the environment that are not within arm's reach. Although hearing is also a distance sense, the information provided through auditory channels is more challenging to interpret without visual referents.

For example, as sighted adults walk through a residential neighborhood, they may notice a variety of interesting hedges and flowers ahead that they want to stop and look at. While auditory information obtained through the use of echolocation (reflected sounds) may let travelers who are blind know that there is something up ahead, the travelers need to explore the hedges and plants tactilely to confirm details about them. Flowers with a strong fragrance might also be noticed from a distance, but in order to accurately determine the location of the flowers, the individual would have to get much closer.

Sensory Integration

People who are sighted rely heavily on vision to integrate input from their other senses, but those who are blind or visually impaired must develop additional means for processing multiple pieces of sensory information. For example, although most people have the auditory ability to localize the sound of a fire truck siren accurately to determine its approach into an intersection, those who are sighted also commonly look for flashing lights to verify visually the direction from which the truck is approaching. Vision quickly and accurately confirms what is heard and enables people to make integrated, adaptive responses. In this example, a driver would respond by stopping the car or pulling over to the side of the road, depending on where the car was in relation to the fire truck. A person with a visual impairment might use remaining vision, hearing, or verbal descriptions from others to confirm the same information and make a good decision to initiate the street crossing later when the fire truck was gone.

Whole-to-Part Learning

Vision enables individuals to experience and learn about many new concepts by starting with the "whole picture" and then learning details about the parts that constitute an object or action. For example, young sighted children see a yellow school bus and then discover its many parts (including the wheels, the windows, and the seats). Learning about new concepts in this manner is effective and often occurs with little formal teaching. In contrast, congenitally blind children learn about most new concepts in a "part-to-whole" sequence, accumulating details that are eventually integrated into a complete concept. For example, the tactile, auditory, olfactory, and kinesthetic senses are all used to gather information about this large object, part by part, until these impressions are integrated fully into the concept of a school bus. Ideas about school buses may include the following:

- the smell of the exhaust,
- the smell of the vinyl seats,
- the sound of the engine,
- the sounds of children in the bus laughing and talking,
- the sound of the door opening and closing,
- the muscle memory of climbing the stairs,
- the feel of the rubber tires,
- the bumpy sensation of riding in the bus, and
- the notion of the size of the bus as estimated by walking around it on both the outside and inside.

The *wholeness* of the concept of school bus, then, is dependent on the children's ability to integrate many pieces of sensory information without the advantage of seeing the whole entity. Thus, for the children to gain an accurate and complete understanding of the concept, their teachers and family members need to provide them with numerous high-quality experiences with the school bus.

Incidental Learning

In contrast to sighted children, who develop many life concepts incidentally by unplanned observation of others and the world around them in the course of their everyday lives, congenitally visually impaired children often need well-thought-out interventions to achieve similar results. For example, sighted children learn many aspects of the concept of walking prior to taking their first steps by observing others as they move about the house or play yard. Children who are blind or visually impaired may need opportunities to feel the leg movements of others as they walk to understand the same concept fully.

Teaching concepts to blind or visually impaired children who face the additional learning challenges just described requires planning and creativity. Although a number of instructional strategies can be described, before the O&M specialist begins to teach, he or she needs to conduct an assessment of an individual student to determine what needs to be taught and the approaches that may be appropriate for the individual.

ASSESSMENT FOR TEACHING CONCEPTS

The starting point for planning high-quality learning experiences is to conduct a thorough assessment of the individual's conceptual development. The level of conceptual understanding that is necessary for the student to progress in his or her current O&M program must be considered when planning an assessment (see Chapter 1 for more detailed information on preparing for and conducting O&M assessments). For example, the O&M specialist may soon be presenting specific cane techniques that necessitate such body concepts as center of the body or midline, or environmental concepts like parking lots may be essential for maintaining orientation in a given training area. Since the spectrum of conceptual development is so broad, an understanding of concepts related to the portions of the O&M curriculum that will be taught in the near future, including body, spatial, and environmental concepts, should be targeted for assessment as appropriate.

Assessing Conceptual Knowledge

When assessing students' conceptual knowledge in a given area, O&M specialists must determine both the breadth and depth of understanding. To be thorough, they should determine whether an individual can *verbalize, demonstrate,* and *apply* the information in appropriate O&M situations. For example, in fully assessing conceptual understanding of the concept of parallel, the O&M specialist may ask a student to define or describe what is meant by the term *parallel* (verbalize), place two yardsticks so they are *parallel* to each other (demonstrate), and identify and cross with the surge of traffic on the *parallel* street (apply).

Less thorough assessments may yield misleading results, especially if the student's knowledge is assessed only on a verbal level. It cannot be assumed that an individual who is able to talk about or describe a particular concept understands it well enough to be able to apply the meaning in a variety of contexts. For example, a person may be able to describe or define the term "intersecting," but not apply that to form an understanding of how two streets intersect and then continue on through a town. Highly verbal children and adults may quickly convince others that they have a full understanding of given concepts as they converse, when they may not. Assessments need to provide the opportunity for students to demonstrate their understanding in ways that are relevant to independent travel, such as "Find two streets on this map that are parallel to one another" and "Tell me when cars are moving on your parallel street."

The presence of verbalisms can yield misleading results when assessments of concepts are conducted solely on a verbal level. *Verbalisms,* the use of words for which a person has limited or no sensory referent, have been commonly associated with individuals who are congenitally blind (Warren, 1984). This phenomenon may occur when the person's only experiences with a particular concept (like lanes of traffic) are verbal or written descriptions. Without opportunities for hands-on contact or exploration, the person may be able to talk about a concept (such as a coastline) without completely understanding the entity (that is, an actual coastline). The person might refer to the beautiful California coastline, but not understand that there is not a set line—rather an ever-changing place where ocean meets the land. Many environmental concepts are difficult to grasp fully at first because they are large or in an inaccessible location (such as 12-story buildings or traffic lights). The possibility of verbalisms makes it essential to conduct a thorough assessment of a student's conceptual understanding.

Assessment Approaches

Chapter 1 presented an overview of the general preparation for and approaches to assessments. The same general approaches apply to the assessment of concepts. The following are a few specific suggestions for assessing concepts related to O&M.

Body Concepts

Body concepts are most commonly assessed when teaching young children. One available assessment tool that can be used is the *Hill Performance Test of Selected Positional Concepts* (Hill, 1981), which can be used to assess both knowledge of body parts and positional concepts. This assessment tool provides the O&M specialist with a script and sequence to follow.

When conducting an assessment of body concepts with children, the O&M specialist can make use of games and activities to increase the child's motivation for participation. Simon Says can easily be used to assess a child's identification of body parts, movement, and related positional concepts. A high-contrast magic wand can be made by the student and/or O&M specialist to be used as a prop when identifying body parts during assessment or instruction. A version of Pin the Tail on the Donkey can be used with children with low vision by enlarging a picture or drawing of a person and having the children place stickers on the identified body parts. Body tracings can also be used with young students with low vision. By asking the children to color or decorate various body parts on an outline made by tracing their own body, the O&M specialist can determine their understanding of certain body concepts. Age-appropriate dolls and stuffed animals can also be used as props when assessing young children's body concepts. Similar activities can also be a fun part of an instructional program for concept development.

Spatial Concepts

With young children, positional concepts (such as in/out, front/back, side, and above/below) are commonly assessed. These concepts can be assessed in conjunction with body parts using the assessment tool just noted. The understanding of positional concepts can be assessed on multiple levels, including these:

- relation to self (for example, touch the *top* of your head with the *back* of your hand),

- relation of self-to-object (for instance, stand *next to* the sink), and

- relation of object to object (such as find the mailbox *behind* the fence).

Similar to assessing body concepts, simple games like Simon Says can be used to assess some spatial concepts in children. In addition, a tackle box with rows of drawers or a cardboard organizer for shoes or art supplies filled with interesting familiar or novel objects can be used to assess many positional concepts (like above, below, next to, beside). The O&M specialist can ask the student to locate certain objects using specific spatial terms (such as "Find the object that is next to the key chain and below the paper clip"). Alternatively, the student can place items in a compartment by following the O&M specialist's instructions or by describing where the item has been placed. A variety of computer games for young children work on positional concepts and can also be used for assessing students with low vision.

More advanced spatial concepts are frequently assessed with older children, adolescents, and adults. An assessment of a student's under-

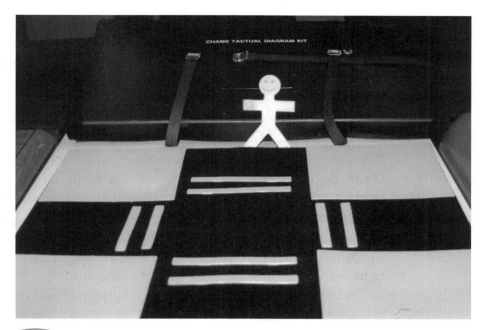

Photo 4.1

The Chang Kit contains bright yellow cardboard shapes with Velcro backings that can be attached to a black felt board to create grid patterns or simple maps to use for assessment.

standing and application of advanced spatial concepts may include cardinal directions, the address system, grid patterns, or physical layouts. O&M specialists may need to devise their own approaches to assessing these concepts because there is less available in the way of formalized assessment tools. Tactile or visual maps may be used to assess the understanding of cardinal directions, route planning, the address system, and general or specific floor plans (see Chapter 7 for more information on making and using maps). Tactile markers or pushpins with strings may be used to mark places for reference on a map and to create routes that can be later traced. The Chang Kit is an easy format that can be used to create grid patterns or simple maps for assessment. A commercially available kit, it contains a black felt board with bright yellow, heavy cardboard shapes with Velcro backings that can be temporarily attached to the board (see the Resources section for availability). Some students may like to use manipulatives (such as small cars or people) with the maps during the assessment.

In addition to assessing a student's verbalization and demonstration of conceptual understanding, it is also important to assess how a student applies these concepts to actual travel situations. These concepts can easily be embedded within route travel as problem-solving scenarios. Portable maps or dry-erase boards can be taken along as a supplement and used as needed to clarify questions or responses during the assessment.

Environmental Concepts

Because there are so many environmental concepts that are related to O&M, the challenge is how to narrow the focus for the assessment. The student's developmental level, chronological age, and previous travel experiences can provide a starting point for selecting appropriate environmental concepts to assess. In addition, the O&M specialist can select the concepts that will correspond to the mobility skills that he or she anticipates will soon need to be taught to the student.

Many environmental concepts can be assessed during the assessment route through the use of effective questioning (see Chapter 1 for details on effective questioning). Along the route, the O&M specialist may ask the student to

identify (for example, "Identify which form of *traffic control system* is used at this intersection),

label (for instance, "These *two lines* that are painted on the street, stretching from corner to corner are called what?"),

locate (for example, "Where should you be looking to find a *limit line?*"), and

describe functions and features (for instance, "Tell me what this *fire hydrant* is used for and how it works) of a variety of environmental concepts, such as sidewalk, curb, and crosswalk.

Young students with low vision may enjoy identifying certain objects or environmental features using enlarged photographs or diagrams and then matching them to actual objects found along the assessment route. A great deal can also be learned by asking students who are blind or have low vision to build or create an imaginary community with LEGO or other materials. While engaged in an interesting activity, the O&M specialist can note the features of the community that the students are familiar with, the vocabulary they use to describe things, and where they place things on the map.

More advanced environmental concepts need to be assessed with older children, adolescents, and adults. An assessment of an individual's understanding and application of environmental features relevant to given travel areas may include traffic control systems, intersection configurations, on-ramps, traffic islands and medians, and parking meters. Conceptual understanding related to the individual's travel needs is assessed initially through the formal assessment. However, the O&M specialist continues to assess concepts on an ongoing basis as part of the overall instructional process.

INSTRUCTION IN CONCEPTS

Through the assessment process, the O&M specialist may select a concept or series of concepts (such as arc width or body concepts) that need to be addressed with the student. Alternatively, the specialist may anticipate the need to introduce several concepts that are related to travel in a new area or a new area of skills. For example, the concepts of food court, department store, specialty shop, directory, and information kiosk would be taught for mall travel, and concepts related to time, money, and cardinal directions would be taught or reviewed for bus travel.

There are a number of ways to vary instruction in concepts for students who are blind or visually impaired. Some general approaches can be considered, and various groupings can be used to motivate students to learn about new things. Concept lessons can be structured in a variety of formats, depending on the needs of the students and the concepts being addressed. O&M specialists and teachers of students with visual impairments must be prepared to take a formalized approach to concept development for children and youths who are blind or visually impaired. A formalized approach would incorporate thoughtful planning of sequential teaching units so that children with visual impairments can be given meaningful learning opportunities that help them to integrate sensory experiences into fully developed concepts. Although good teaching practices can generally be applied to a wide range of learners, there are some special considerations for enhancing the learning of students who are blind or visually impaired and have additional disabilities.

O&M specialists must start early to address the conceptual needs of young children who are blind or visually impaired. By working together with family members and other professionals, they can greatly increase the effectiveness of early concept-development programs. Family involvement will help to ensure that concepts that sighted children learn incidentally are introduced to and experienced in a meaningful way by blind or visually impaired children. As the children get older, concepts can be expanded and increasingly complex concepts can be introduced. A thorough assessment of each child's conceptual development will assist O&M specialists in planning appropriate instructional units.

Adults who are adventitiously blind or visually impaired may not need the full complement of concept development required for congenitally blind children, but there are still some new concepts that should be addressed. For example, in a community where most people get around by car, an adventitiously visually impaired adult may need to learn some concepts related to pedestrian safety and intersection analysis. The advantage is that adult students are likely to have much basic knowledge about traffic and intersections from which they can build a more complex understanding. The challenge may be that they are now relying less on vision and more on tactile and auditory input to learn new things. The specialist should not overlook the conceptual needs of blind or visually impaired adults when planning individualized O&M programs. As long as planned activities are age appropriate, the principles of good instructional practices for concept development outlined next will be equally effective with adults as they are with children.

General Strategies

Instructional strategies for successful concept development should encompass a variety of integrated approaches that are based on the individual's age and ability level. Instructional practices like those outlined in Chapter 2 can readily be applied to concept development. Some general strategies that can be easily incorporated into a high-quality concept development program are presented in the sections that follow. They include encouraging young children to explore their surroundings, labeling and describing the surroundings and the children's own actions, collaborating with other members of the educational team, using appropriate conceptual terms, providing concrete experiences, using a variety of learning activities, and integrating instruction in skills and concepts. Additional suggestions for encouraging the development of basic concepts are listed in Instructional Strategies for Concept Development.

INSTRUCTIONAL STRATEGIES
FOR CONCEPT DEVELOPMENT

- Use real items (such as actual coins and bills) versus pretend items (like Monopoly money) to maximize hands-on experiences.

- Encourage parents to include their visually impaired children in typical family outings (to the post office, grocery store, bank, and other places).

- Use driving analogies, when appropriate, to help explain new or complex pedestrian concepts to adventitiously blind or visually impaired adults. For example, to explain the safety concerns for pedestrian crossings at T-shaped intersections, talk to the adults about driving patterns and behaviors at those intersections.

- Use clear, accurate, and consistent words when giving directions to persons who are blind or visually impaired (for instance, "The drinking fountain is on your left side, against the wall, beyond the first door," not "keep going on the left").

- Provide real items (such as spoons and bowls) for young blind and visually impaired children to play with, and model their functional uses (like stirring and mixing).

Early Interactions and Exploration

To develop a conceptual understanding of the world, children must be actively engaged with people and things in a wide variety of meaningful environments. Young sighted children interact with their surroundings primarily through play and exploration, and these forms of interactions are equally important for blind or visually impaired children. However, in some instances, families and/or teachers may be overly protective—fearful that the children may injure themselves if they are active and moving about. Parents of children with visual impairments can be reassured that sighted toddlers and preschoolers also get bumps and bruises as a part of active learning and that safe exploration should be encouraged as part of healthy development. Young blind and visually impaired children should be provided with accessible play environments that encourage safe and active exploration.

Family members and specialists can facilitate conceptual development by giving labels to objects, providing descriptions of their properties and functions, and including narration for the children's actions and their consequent reactions, as in the following example:

> Rachel, Mamma is opening the refrigerator. Feel the cold air? The refrigerator keeps our food, like milk and juice and eggs and butter, cold. Can you help Mamma put the milk in the refrigerator? That's right—it goes on the top shelf. OK, let's close the door of the refrigerator to keep the cold air inside it.

Early experiences at home and in school form the foundation for future learning and exploration.

Collaborative Approaches

O&M specialists assume an important role in facilitating conceptual development in students who are blind or visually impaired. Together with other professionals and family members, they can address body awareness, spatial concepts, and important environmental concepts in a consistent and collaborative approach. By sharing the results of assessments with teachers and family members, the O&M specialist can begin a dialogue with them regarding the student's areas of strength and need in concept development. Enlisting collaborative partners helps ensure that the student receives the necessary exposure to and reinforcement of important concepts. For example, if a young child who is blind needs help with body awareness concepts, the following collaborative activities can take place:

- Family members can work on the identification of body parts during bath time.
- The adaptive physical education specialist can provide a range of body-movement activities.
- The teacher of students with visual impairments can introduce the appropriate vocabulary of body parts in braille.
- The general education teacher can use songs and stories during circle time that emphasize a good body image.
- The O&M specialist can work on the function of body parts that are involved in basic skills and beginning cane usage.

Similar collaborative efforts can be used to address spatial and environmental concepts.

ENLISTING SUPPORT FROM OTHERS IN CONCEPT DEVELOPMENT

- Volunteer to teach a mini-mapmaking unit to the blind or visually impaired student's social studies class in an art-project format that incorporates the use of various interesting tactile materials.

- Give the general education teacher a brief list of concepts that are important to independent travel that may be related to the topic that is being taught to the class.

- Work with the adapted physical education specialist to adapt dances that may emphasize the rhythms or movements needed for using the long cane (such as in-step or wrist movements)

- Create an O&M bulletin board at the school to illustrate important O&M concepts. Model the appropriate use of color, contrast, print size, braille, and textures as appropriate.

Just by having the O&M specialist explain the importance of specific concepts to them, teachers and family members may be more likely to find ways to support concept development for children who are blind or visually impaired. Enlisting Support from Others in Concept Development presents additional suggestions for working with others in this area.

Using Appropriate Spatial and Environmental Terms

Effective instruction in spatial and environmental concepts involves using appropriate terms as the student moves through various settings applying appropriate O&M skills. Opportunities to reinforce these concepts by using the specific spatial terms are available during all kinds of routine daily activities, such as these:

- Family members can reinforce the concepts of right, left, and next to at the dinner table during meals by using the terms to describe the location of items on the table.

- General education teachers can reinforce the concepts of in front and behind by making a game of "who's in front and behind?" when children are lining up for lunch.

- Teachers of students with visual impairments can use the terms *top, middle,* and *bottom* when referring to the location of dots within a braille cell.

- O&M specialists can reinforce concepts of parallel and perpendicular when referring to traffic that is moving through an intersection.

O&M specialists can take advantage of the variety of environments in which they work with their students to provide concrete experiences with environmental concepts in natural settings. Concrete experiences with other concepts are also essential.

Concrete, Hands-on Experiences

When the input received from vision is either limited or nonexistent, concepts must be learned through alternate sensory channels (touch, hearing, and smell). Kindergarten and early elementary-age children often do some form of concept development at school with pictures for sorting, matching, and grouping tasks. As sighted children select all the pictures that have things that relate to baking a cake, for example, they are likely to have a visual image of the real object being depicted and occasions to see the objects being used to bake a cake. They may also have been given opportunities to help prepare the cake for baking. Functional and dramatic play commonly portray an understanding of cake baking and all the related concrete, functional, and abstract concepts. A blind child may be given access to the same picture-grouping task through adapted raised-line drawings. However, it is much more difficult to identify raised-line drawings accurately without a visual referent, and the child may not have a mental image of the real object being depicted.

How, then, does the blind child develop all the concepts related to baking a cake? Most important, the child needs concrete, hands-on, multisensory experiences, including touching, tasting, and smelling the ingredients; feeling the ingredients mixed in a bowl and poured into a cake pan; feeling the heat from the oven; listening to the ticking of the timer; and tasting the results. In addition, the blind child benefits from being shown how to explore his or her surroundings systematically. In the kitchen, for example, the child can be assisted in exploring the counter systematically to discover the arrangement of bowls, pans, and mixing spoons. If the child is given similar cooking implements to play with in a sandbox and provided with some creative modeling and expansion, he or she may begin to demonstrate some aspects of functional play that show an understanding of concepts related to cake baking.

It takes both time and creativity to provide children who are blind or visually impaired with the many meaningful experiences (such as accessible nature walks, participation in chores, exploration of household items, and so on), necessary to support the development of concrete, functional, and abstract concepts. When appropriate, hands-on experiences with multisensory components should be introduced, as was done in the cake-baking example.

High-quality experiences that are clear and thorough are most beneficial when they do not put the student in "sensory overload," with too much stimulation at one time. For example, talking to a student about his or her performance on a lesson while walking along a busy street or standing outside a store that is playing loud music while lots of pedestrians are talking and passing by is likely to place most students in sensory overload. Comments should be saved for a quieter area in which the student can process what is being said. Each person has his or her own tolerance for the level and variety of stimuli that can be processed. Children who are sighted frequently use vision to figure out the sources or context for the many sounds and sensations around them. Visually impaired children may "overload" more quickly if they have a limited context for the sounds they hear and the things they feel and may simply tune out (or not process) certain stimuli.

Learning Activities

A combination of clear verbal descriptions of concepts and meaningful hands-on learning activities help students who are blind or visually impaired to acquire concepts. Activities that are the most meaningful are those that provide concrete, hands-on experiences and promote positive interactions with the physical and social travel environment. Table 4.1 lists a variety of learning activities whose thoughtful use will promote the development of a variety of concepts.

Integrating Skills and Concepts

Each fully formed concept provides students with a foundation for future understanding and expanded possibilities for learning. While the focus of many O&M lessons may be to develop skills that can be used to travel independently, it is the conceptual component that enables individuals to apply these skills appropriately in a variety of environments.

Table 4.1 Learning Activities for Conceptual Development

Activity	Purpose	Example
Route travel	To apply conceptual knowledge to relevant O&M contexts	Using cardinal directions for route instructions
Functional tasks	To use conceptual knowledge in daily routines	Learning body concepts while bathing
Games	To practice concepts in a social context	Playing a game of Red Light, Green Light for positional concepts
Play	To explore the physical properties of toys and objects	Stacking blocks to learn about height and balance
Pretend	To exercise imagination in exploring conceptual applications	Becoming a superhero while exploring landmarks along a route
Role-playing	To exchange ideas through situational role-playing	Practicing bus-route concepts by assuming the role of the bus driver and passenger
Models	To illustrate things that are too large or inaccessible to explore tactilely	Examining a model of an elevator
Manipulatives	To provide hands-on materials for learning concepts	Using a wallet and real bills and coins for money concepts
Mapmaking	To create realistic or fantasy maps that incorporate the use of concepts	Placing landmarks on a map of a college campus
Projects	To make interesting products that showcase conceptual understanding	Creating a classroom bulletin board of the types of businesses found in a community
Field trips	To experience a concept firsthand	Taking a trip to the traffic control center for a city

Therefore, it is important to integrate skill and concept development in lessons whenever possible. Table 4.2 illustrates how teaching common O&M skills related to crossing streets independently can also be used to teach related concepts in all the O&M concept categories.

Table 4.2 Integrating Skills and Concepts in Teaching Independent Street Crossing

Concept Category	Skill	Concept
Body imagery	*Stepping* off the curb	with *proper foot placement*
Laterality	*Localizing* traffic sounds	heard on your *left side*
Directionality	*Labeling* the four corners of the intersection	according to *cardinal directions (NW, NE, SW, SE)*
Environmental	*Identifying* the type of	*traffic control* at a given intersection
Spatial/positional	*Aligning* with	the *parallel traffic*
Time	*Comparing*	the *timing of traffic cycles* at two different intersections
Measurement	*Estimating*	the approximate *width of a crosswalk* to position correctly for a street crossing
Distance	*Anticipating* the "up-curb"	on completing three quarters of the distance of a residential street crossing

Note: Words in italics represent the skills being taught and the concept that can be integrated into instruction in those skills.

Instructional Grouping

In addition to the use of different strategies, the O&M specialist may choose to teach students one at a time or in small groups. Either plan of instruction can be used effectively to teach concepts, but there are several considerations that may make one or the other plan more effective in particular circumstances.

One-to-One Instruction

Most O&M specialists are familiar with using a one-to-one teaching approach with individual students to work on concepts. In any case, the plan of instruction should consider both the developmental level of the student and the age appropriateness of the activity being used. When working with one student at a time, O&M specialists have the advantage of being able to individualize instruction and meet the learning style of that student (see Chapter 5 for an in-depth look at individual learning and teaching styles in O&M). Occasionally, however, the one-to-one format limits the type of activities that are beneficial and enjoyable, such as games and role-play activities.

Group Lessons

Some learning activities, especially games, movement activities, and projects that can be worked on with more than one student, are simply more motivating when done in a small group. O&M specialists do not need to limit learning possibilities because of the traditional one-to-one instructional format. With a bit of creativity and flexible scheduling, they may use small-group instruction occasionally or on a regular basis.

Group lessons may include other students with visual impairments or a combination of visually impaired and sighted students. For example, adapted versions of common commercially available games can be played by both children who are visually impaired and sighted—reinforcing spatial concepts and social skills simultaneously. (See Chapter 3 for a list of such games.) Similarly, blind and sighted students can be grouped together on treasure hunts in which the instructions are brailled and cardinal directions are used frequently to demonstrate the blind child's conceptual knowledge. Road car rallies have also been held with sighted drivers and blind navigators using braille maps and instructions. In any case, the plan of instruction should consider both the developmental level of the student and the age appropriateness of the activity being used. Small- and large-group learning opportunities can also be facilitated by collaborating with other teachers and specialists. For example, with some thoughtful planning, map concepts that are useful for orientation in the travel environment can be incorporated into a general education geography unit or a specialized lesson for using raised-line drawings. (See Lessons 6 and 7 of the Residential Block Concepts Unit in Appendix 4.A for more specific ideas of how this can be done.) This type of collaboration has the added advantage of integrating O&M concepts within the classroom and may provide the blind or visually impaired child with an opportunity to showcase specialized knowledge and skills (for more ideas on O&M group instruction, see Chapters 3 and 5).

Adults may also enjoy certain group O&M lessons. Map-skill concepts, monocular terminology, and address system concepts can be taught and practiced in a small-group, classroom format. This approach does not preclude the instruction that must take place in the actual travel environments where the concepts can be fully integrated with corresponding O&M skills.

Teaching Structures

Whether working with one student at a time or a group, O&M specialists can and should use a variety of structures for teaching concepts that are important for independent travel. A particular format may be selected because of the specific types of concepts being taught, the learning style of the student, or the actual timing of the concept unit in the individualized O&M program.

Within the Context of Mobility Lessons

There are two distinct approaches to teaching concepts within the context of O&M lessons. One approach is to address concepts on the spur of the moment in lessons, and the other is to plan the instruction of concepts.

Some O&M specialists prefer to teach concepts as the need arises within the context of O&M lessons. For example, concept development in the mechanics of elevators may be addressed during elevator travel if the student poses a few questions that warrant further exploration. There are certain advantages and disadvantages to providing concept instruction in this manner. The advantage of occasionally teaching specific concepts to a visually impaired student as the need seems to arise is that the O&M specialist can make the most of a "learning moment." While the student's curiosity is piqued, time can be spent teaching the important concept. This approach can quickly become a disadvantage if the O&M specialist relies mainly on it for concept development for the following reasons:

- The selection and order of concepts addressed becomes haphazard and dependent on the student's expressed interest or the time that is available.

- Students who are typically passive or less likely to express an interest openly may receive less concept instruction than may those who consistently ask questions about their travel environment.

- In addition, dealing with the "learning moment" precludes high-quality preparation for teaching complex concepts.

In the second approach, concept instruction is planned to take place within the context of the O&M lesson. The advantage of this approach is that skills and concepts can be thoughtfully integrated so that the relevance of each is made clear. By planning lessons in this manner, O&M specialists can prepare instructional materials and arrange for appropriate learning activities that will make learning both fun and meaningful.

Concept Class

Although O&M is traditionally taught on a one-to-one basis, the opportunity to teach concepts in a small class can be an exciting alternative. This format may be especially effective with preschool through upper elementary-age students who may really enjoy or benefit from learning through play, exploration, and creative projects in small groups of peers. *Body concepts* can be integrated into a movement class for preschoolers with visual impairments. For example, Figure 4.1 presents a sample lesson plan for teaching the concepts of left and right to a small group of preschool girls. This type of class can be taught collaboratively by O&M specialists with teachers, adapted physical education specialists, or physical or occupational therapists.

Pedestrian safety-skill concepts can be effectively taught to older children, adolescents, or adults in a class, similar to a driver's education class.

Intersection analysis concepts regarding the use of adaptive pedestrian signals and community advocacy skills can be introduced in a group with the use of appropriate guest speakers (such as traffic engineers), models, enlarged diagrams, and pertinent manipulatives. Application lessons—applying new concepts at actual intersections involving independent street crossings—should be done on an individual basis to ensure a student's safety.

Concepts related to bus travel and the use of public transportation can be taught in a class, with one-on-one instruction used for the actual bus travel lessons.

Concept-class groupings can be based on the availability of students (visually impaired and/or sighted) at one school site or facility, students' interests, or age and ability level. After locating a suitable space or area for instruction, the O&M specialist can develop concept units that are appropriate for each group of students.

Unit Teaching

Concepts can be learned most effectively when they are presented in a well-planned teaching unit (see Chapter 2 for more details on unit teach-

Lesson Plan

Students: _Veronica, Ceci, Paige, Carey,_

and Ayana (pre-K-age)

Instructor: _Mary_   **Assistant:** _Zulma_

Date: _October 6, 1999_

Lesson Location: _preschool classroom_

Goal: _To increase understanding of left and right sidedness_

Lesson Objectives:
1. _To identify left and right sides of their bodies with 80 percent consistency_
2. _To identify left and right sides of a given stuffed animal with 50 percent consistency_

Instructional Materials: _assortment of 20 toy bracelets or wristbands, jingle bell anklets and watches, 5 teddy bears, 5 carpet squares_

Methodology/Instructional Strategies:

1. _Before the lesson starts, make sure the teaching assistant knows what we are doing today and let her know that she should give individual support to Ceci and translate my instructions in Spanish._

2. _Set up the carpet squares in a semicircle and have each child stand on a carpet square in the semicircle. Do the usual warm-up song with stretching movements._

3. _Tell the children that they are going to practice finding their left and right arms and legs today. Start by allowing each child to select a bracelet or wristband. Tell the children to put the bracelets or wristbands on their right arms (ask the assistant to help those who need help)._

4. _Play Simon Says using only right-arm commands until the children are getting it right most of the time._

5. _Repeat steps 3 and 4 but with toy watches for the left arms._

6. _Tell each child to select a jingle bell anklet and place it on her right leg. Do the Hokey Pokey, so the children can shake their jingle bells (give assistance as needed)._

7. _Hand every child a teddy bear. Ask the child to find a matching bracelet for the bear and place it on her right arm. Ask the child to find the bear's right arm and then left arm._

8. _Do the Hokey Pokey again with the children holding onto their teddy bears._

9. _Pass around a sack for the children to put their bracelets, watches, and anklets in._

10. _Close the lesson by giving each child a smelly sticker to place on her right hand and a sticker for her bear's right paw._

Daily Notes:

Four of the children were able to identify their left and right arms 80 percent. They enjoyed the movement and music of the Hokey Pokey, but it was hard to get them settled afterward. Only one child was able to identify her teddy bear's left and right side 50 percent. Stick to children's body parts longer. Maybe do separate lesson with teddy bears once the children are more sure of themselves. Carpet squares worked well to keep places.

Figure 4.1

Sample Lesson Plan: Left and Right

ing in O&M). Adopting a unit structure enables the O&M specialist to combine related concepts in a meaningful sequence of instruction that addresses concrete, functional, and abstract levels of understanding. Planning ensures that important concepts are not left out and that the students are able to integrate sensory information, verbal descriptions, activities, and meaningful concrete experiences for a greater understanding of concepts that are important to daily life and future learning. These experiences should help the student integrate parts of information into a "whole" understanding.

For example, an O&M specialist could use a less effective approach and simply plan to teach residential street-crossing skills and address-related concepts as the need arises during the lesson. In this scenario, it is likely that the O&M specialist will rely primarily on verbal descriptions to teach important concepts and that the student will not develop a fully integrated understanding of intersection-related concepts. In contrast, an O&M specialist may plan a concept unit on the topic of residential street crossings. Intersection concepts (such as streets and crosswalks) could easily be combined with concepts of traffic control and pedestrian safety (like stop sign and all-quiet) within a unit framework. Verbal descriptions, models, games, projects, and field trips would all be used to assist the student in developing a full understanding of the concepts essential to residential street crossings. This conceptual understanding could be generalized to many residential intersections and would serve as a strong foundation for the development of street-crossing skills.

Appendix 4.A presents a sample instructional unit for developing concepts associated with residential block travel for an elementary-age student. In the sequence of lessons, the student begins to explore the residential block along the sidewalk in front of his school, which is most familiar to him, and expands beyond that in future lessons. The map-making activity helps the student integrate each sidewalk segment into a whole understanding of the block. Actual clippings from bushes and the like are used to create the map, as well as other materials to represent landmarks found along the way. The student demonstrates a more abstract understanding of block as he creates edible blocks from a Jell-O mold. The student is able to share what he learns in a culminating activity in which he helps his sighted classmates create tactile "fantasy" maps in class.

Integration into Daily Routines

Some concepts may be most effectively taught by integrating their functional use within the student's daily routine. For example, while a 5-year-old student is learning the concept of in, he or she could be given the responsibility of collecting the students' lunch slips and placing them "in" the special envelope to deliver to the office each morning. The concept that is being learned becomes much more meaningful because it is applied within a daily routine. Even with older students, it is important to find ways to integrate newly learned concepts into the daily routine when possible. After learning the concepts associated with a monocular training sequence, most students will follow through with greater consistency if there is a need to "trace," "scan," and "track" with their monocular to view the classroom chalkboard, read street signs during O&M lessons, or check the scoreboard at the Little League baseball game. Skills and concepts that are integrated within an individual's routine are more likely to become a permanent part of daily functioning.

O&M specialists can use a variety of instructional formats to teach concepts to their students. It may be appropriate to introduce a novel concept on the spur of the moment because a student's curiosity is piqued or because an unusual environmental feature is present. When it is anticipated that a student will need to be introduced to a new concept or to review previously learned concepts, it is generally a good idea to plan the instruction, rather than wait for a naturally occurring opportunity. Concept classes can be considered when it is feasible and there is an appropriate group of peers (children or adults) to form a class. Concept classes can be effective for children when they involve games and movement activities. When concepts are grouped to form a teaching unit, students benefit from the sequential instruction and connection between concepts. Integrating the application of new concepts within daily routines will support the generalization of conceptual understanding.

Special Considerations

Consistency is essential when addressing concept development in students with severe multiple disabilities. Effective instructional approaches cannot be established without collaboration, communication, and team planning. Family members are an integral part of the educational team and can be helpful in setting priorities for critical skills and concepts that will be the most functional and easily integrated within

SUGGESTIONS FOR TEACHING CONCEPTS TO STUDENTS WITH MULTIPLE DISABILITIES

- To address concepts that are priorities and those that are the most functional when working with students who have severe multiple disabilities, ask families and teachers to identify the two most important concepts that would increase the individual's independence (like survival money skills or orientation concepts).

- To teach concrete and functional aspects of important concepts, use common household objects, rather than plastic toys, when providing meaningful multisensory experiences for students with dual sensory impairments (for example, exploring fruits and vegetables in the produce department, rather than playing with plastic fruits or miniature wooden foods).

- Explore creative uses of the long cane as a probe for blind or visually impaired students who are semi-independent wheelchair users to increase exploration and interactions with the environment (for instance, a cane grip with just a tip on the end to facilitate trailing the wall and recognizing doorways and intersecting hallways).

the daily routine. When possible, instruction should take place in natural environments and during actual routines or times of day. This planning helps to assure that students receive sufficient repetition and meaningful opportunities for applying concepts to purposeful movement. (See Suggestions for Teaching Concepts to Students with Multiple Disabilities.)

Maximizing the use of residual vision and hearing when teaching concepts is especially important to students who are deaf-blind. O&M specialists and teachers must develop multisensory approaches to introducing and guiding learning experiences with environmental concepts. Concrete experiences in natural environments (such as helping to prepare lunch in the kitchen, assisting with gardening in the yard, or mailing a letter at the post office during an O&M lesson) help a student who is deaf-blind attach meaning to sensory information.

As with all blind or visually impaired students, concept development for those with multiple disabilities should maximize opportunities for concrete experiences and hands-on exploration. When blind or visually impaired students have additional physical disabilities that limit contact with the environment, the O&M specialist must find creative ways to increase their interactions with their surroundings. For example, although some students who use assistants to mobilize their wheelchairs may never be fully independent travelers, O&M specialists may be able to increase their participation in travel by working on concepts that may be relevant in the travel environment (like left and right turns or doors opening toward or away). Some students may be issued canes simply to serve as an extended probe into the environment and as a means for learning about concepts (such as a cane grip with just a tip to trail the wall and locate doorways and intersecting hallways). Students who have multiple disabilities can also benefit from mapmaking activities to promote concept development. Group concept classes can also be beneficial and provide opportunities for socialization as well.

A conceptual understanding of body, space, and environment provides the purpose for physical movement and helps foster the development of safe and efficient O&M travel skills. Although there are challenges to the development of concepts for individuals who are blind or visually impaired, thoughtful instructional approaches can provide meaningful learning experiences that promote understanding and interest in learning more about one's surroundings.

An individualized approach to concept development can be further enhanced by examining the different learning styles of the O&M specialist and students, as described in the next chapter, and incorporating them into O&M instruction. Paying attention to learning styles can generate creative approaches to instruction and many different activities, and Chapter 5 offers many examples.

Sample Instructional Unit on Residential Block Concepts

The sample unit presented in this appendix was prepared to teach concepts pertaining to residential blocks to an elementary school-age student who is functionally blind. When planning this unit, the O&M specialist assumed that the student knew all the prerequisite concepts and had the mobility skills to participate fully in the learning activities provided. (More details on the maps and mapmaking activities used in this unit are found in Chapter 7).

The unit specifically addresses the following concepts:

1. landmark
2. streets
3. sidewalk
4. residential blocks

The following games and activities are used in the unit to teach these concepts:

- mapmaking
- residential block travel and exploration
- making and eating an edible Jell-O map
- class presentation
- assisting classmates in making tactile maps
- preparing a classroom bulletin board

Lesson Plan

Student: _Vince (functionally blind, elementary age)_

Instructor: _Gina_

Date: _____

Time: _____

Lesson Location: _a residential block surrounding the school bordered by 22nd Street, Palm Street, Chehalem Road, and Vista Place;   L-shaped route (22nd Street)_

Goal: _To develop an understanding of residential block concepts_

Lesson Objectives:
1. _To identify two landmarks on a given side of a residential block_
2. _To place two landmark symbols on one side of a blank tactile map_
3. _To recall a given street name and two corresponding landmarks found along the route_

Instructional Materials: _one 8x10-inch foam board and one 8x10-inch sample map with LEGO pieces representing the school and houses, mapmaking materials, waist pouch ("scout pouch")_

Daily Notes:

Methodology/Instructional Strategies:

1. Tell Vince that in the next couple of weeks, we will be exploring the neighborhood around the school and making a map of it to share with the class.
2. Introduce Vince to a sample of the 8x10 map that he will be making and give him time to explore some of the materials that he may use.
3. Look at the sample block together and show him how it is shaped like a rectangle (two long sides and two short sides).
4. Ask Vince to trace the sidewalk on each of the four sides of the block. Tell him that you will be starting to explore the block on the sidewalk in front of the school.
5. Pack the mapmaking materials inside the waist pouch and tell Vince that this will be his "scout pouch" to use while he is exploring the block.
6. Walk along 22nd Street, examining any possible landmarks to include on Vince's map. Give student three rules for landmarks: (1) permanent, (2) unique, and (3) helps you know where you are. Vince can use scissors from the pouch to cut small samples (like leaves or bark) to attach to the map with tape. Wikki Stix can be used to represent walls or fences. Small spongy circles can be used to represent poles or fire hydrants. Get additional samples as needed.
7. Return to the school and examine the things that Vince has attached to his map. Ask Vince to identify two of the landmarks selected. Also ask Vince to recall the name of the street that was explored today.
8. Preview the next lesson. Tell Vince that we will return to 22nd Street to visit the landmarks that he chose and will go to the next side of the block.

Residential Block Concepts: Lesson 1

Lesson Plan

Student: _Vince (functionally blind, elementary age)_

Instructor: _Gina_

Date: _____

Time: _____

Lesson Location: _a residential block surrounding the school bordered by 22nd Street, Palm Street, Chehalem Road, and Vista Place; L-shaped route (22nd Street and Palm Street)_

Goal: _To develop an understanding of residential block concepts_

Lesson Objectives:
1. _To identify two landmarks on a given side of a residential block_
2. _To place two landmark symbols on one side of a blank tactile map_
3. _To recall a given street name and two corresponding landmarks found along the route_

Instructional Materials: _one 8x10-inch foam board student-made map, mapmaking materials, waist pouch ("scout pouch")_

Daily Notes:

Methodology/Instructional Strategies:

1. Review the map that Vince has started to make. Ask if he remembers the two landmarks and the street name of the first side of the block.

2. Begin the L-shaped route with a quick review of 22nd Street, checking that the landmarks selected are indeed permanent.

3. Spend most of the lesson on the second side of the block (Palm).

4. Walk along Palm Street, examining any possible landmarks to include on Vince's map. Vince can use scissors from the pouch to cut small samples (like leaves or bark) to attach to the map with tape. Wikki Stix can be used to represent walls or fences. Small spongy circles can be used to represent poles or fire hydrants. Get additional samples as needed.

5. Return to the school and examine the things that Vince has attached to his map. Ask Vince to identify two of the landmarks selected. Also ask Vince to recall the name of the street that was explored today.

6. Preview the next lesson. Tell Vince that we will return to Palm Street to visit the landmarks that he chose and will go to the third side of the block.

Lesson Plan

Student: *Vince (functionally blind, elementary age)*

Instructor: *Gina*

Date: _____

Time: _____

Lesson Location: *a residential block surrounding the school bordered by 22nd Street, Palm Street, Chehalem Road, and Vista Place; U-shaped route (22nd Street, Palm Street, and Chehalem Road)*

Goal: *To develop an understanding of residential block concepts*

Lesson Objectives:
1. *To identify two landmarks on a given side of a residential block*
2. *To place two landmark symbols on one side of a blank tactile map*
3. *To recall a given street name and two corresponding landmarks found along the route*

Instructional Materials: *one 8x10-inch foam board student-made map, mapmaking materials, waist pouch ("scout pouch")*

Daily Notes:

Methodology/Instructional Strategies:

1. Review the map that Vince has started to make. Ask if he remembers the two landmarks and the street name of the first and second sides of the block.

2. Begin the U-shaped route with a quick review of 22nd Street and Palm Street, checking that landmarks selected are indeed permanent.

3. Spend most of the lesson on the third side of the block (Chehalem).

4. Walk along Chehalem Road, examining any possible landmarks to include on Vince's map. Vince can use scissors from the pouch to cut small samples (like leaves or bark) to attach to the map with tape. Wikki Stix can be used to represent walls or fences. Small spongy circles can be used to represent poles or fire hydrants. Get additional samples as needed.

5. Return to the school and examine the things that Vince has attached to his map. Ask Vince to identify two of the landmarks selected. Ask Vince to recall the name of the street that was explored today.

6. Preview the next lesson. Tell Vince that we will return to Chehalem Road to visit the landmarks that he chose and will go to the fourth (and final) side of the block.

Residential Block Concepts: Lesson 3

Lesson Plan

Student: _Vince (functionally blind, elementary age)_

Instructor: _Gina_

Date: _____

Time: _____

Lesson Location: _a residential block surrounding the school bordered by 22nd Street, Palm Street, Chehalem Road, and Vista Place_

Goal: _To develop an understanding of residential block concepts_

Lesson Objectives:
1. _To identify two landmarks on a given side of a residential block_
2. _To place two landmark symbols on one side of a blank tactile map_
3. _To recall a given street name and two corresponding landmarks found along the route_

Instructional Materials: _one 8x10-inch foam board student-made map; mapmaking materials, waist pouch ("scout pouch")_

Daily Notes:

Methodology/Instructional Strategies:

1. Review the map that Vince has started to make. Ask if he remembers the two landmarks and the street name of the first, second, and third sides of the block.

2. Begin block travel with a quick review of 22nd Street, Palm Street, and Chehalem Road, checking that the landmarks selected are indeed permanent.

3. Spend most of lesson on the fourth side of block (Vista).

4. Walk along Vista Place, examining any possible landmarks to include on Vince's map. Vince can use scissors from the pouch to the cut small samples (like leaves and grass) to attach to the map with tape. Wikki Stix can be used to represent walls or fences. Small spongy circles can be used to represent poles or fire hydrants. Get additional samples as needed.

5. Return to the school and examine the things that Vince has attached to his map. Ask Vince to identify two of the landmarks selected. Ask Vince to recall the name of the street that was explored today.

6. Preview the next lesson. Tell Vince that next week, we will be making a map that we can eat. Ask Vince what his favorite flavor of Jell-O is.

Lesson Plan

Student: _Vince (functionally blind, elementary age)_

Instructor: _Gina_

Date: _____

Time: _____

Lesson
Location: _a classroom at the school_

_____

_____

Goal: _To develop an understanding of residential block concepts_

Lesson
Objectives:
1. _To count the number of blocks formed on an edible map with 100 percent accuracy_
2. _To trace parallel and perpendicular streets created on an edible map with 100 percent accuracy_

Instructional
Materials:
Vince's student-made map; Jell-O (sugar free if the student is diabetic), shallow pan, butter knife, spatula

Daily Notes:

Methodology/Instructional Strategies:

1. Get Vince from the bus in the morning to help make Jell-O before school starts. (See Chapter 7 for details of making an edible map.)

2. Review Vince's student-made map. Ask if he remembers each of the street names and the corresponding landmarks.

3. Tell Vince that we will be making a different kind of map today—one that we can eat after we are done.

4. Have Vince wash his hands and then examine the sheet of Jell-O. Help Vince use a butter knife to make a cut through the center of the pan of Jell-O, making a north–south street. Separate the two parts so Vince can run his finger between them as if it was a car traveling on the street.

5. Continue by cutting two more north–south streets and two east–west streets. Encourage Vince to examine all the blocks and streets surrounding them. Also ask Vince to count how many blocks there are.

6. Add toothpicks with flags to represent houses.

7. Allow Vince to eat one or two blocks; then discard the remaining Jell-O.

8. Wash the dishes together and preview the next lesson.

Residential Block Concepts: Lesson 5

Lesson Plan

Student: _Vince (functionally blind, elementary age)_

Instructor: _Gina_

Date: _____

Time: _____

Lesson
Location: _a classroom at the school_

_____

_____

Goal: _To develop an understanding of residential block concepts_

Lesson
Objectives:
1. _To prepare a class presentation for "our school block" with the O&M specialist's assistance_
2. _To describe Vince's student-made map by identifying street names and landmarks_
3. _To locate "his block" on a larger map by reading brailled street names_

Instructional
Materials: _Vince's student-made map, larger background map, samples of mapmaking materials, brailler, note cards_

Daily Notes:

Methodology/Instructional Strategies:

1. Remind Vince that he will be doing his class presentation on "our school block" next week. Let him know that today you will help him prepare and practice his presentation.

2. Ask Vince to practice describing what he has on his map. If needed, prompt him to touch the section of the map that he is talking about.

3. Show Vince the larger background map of the school community. Let him examine the street names to locate the block that he has explored. Show him how he can place his map on that block. Have Vince drive miniature cars around the block to practice the street names.

4. Plan the order of the presentation. Have Vince braille key words on individual note cards to use during the presentation. (Either number the cards or put them on a ring so Vince will not get confused if he drops the cards.)

5. Ask Vince to select the mapmaking materials that he would like to share with the class during his presentation.

6. Have Vince practice the entire presentation.

Residential Block Concepts: Lesson 6

Lesson Plan

Student: *Vince (functionally blind, elementary age)*

Instructor: *Gina*

Date: _____

Time: _____

Lesson Location: *a classroom at the school*

_____

_____

Goal: *To develop an understanding of residential block concepts*

Lesson Objectives:
1. *To conduct a class presentation for "our school block" with the O&M specialist's assistance*
2. *To describe his student-made map by identifying street names and landmarks*
3. *To assist other students in making "fantasy tactile maps" with the O&M specialist's assistance*

Instructional Materials: *student-made map, larger background map, samples of mapmaking materials, brailled note cards, 8x10-inch cards*

Daily Notes:

Methodology/Instructional Strategies:

1. *Introduce the presentation to the class and provide background on what Vince has been learning.*
2. *Have Vince present his map as practiced in the previous lesson, using brailled note cards as needed.*
3. *Give each student in the class an 8x10-inch card and mapmaking materials to make his or her own tactile map of a block. Allow the students to do maps of their home neighborhood, school neighborhood, or a "fantasy" block. Encourage them to put at least four items on their block.*
4. *Encourage Vince to assist the other students in coming up with ideas as appropriate.*
5. *When the students have finished their maps, have them exchange with a partner and examine each other's maps with their eyes closed to see if they can figure out some of the landmarks and objects on the block.*
6. *Place all the completed maps on a cork bulletin board for display, along with Vince's map.*

Residential Block Concepts: Lesson 7

5

Integrating Individual Teaching and Learning Styles: Motivating O&M Instruction

CHAPTER PREVIEW

Multiple Intelligences Theory
Linguistic Intelligence
Musical Intelligence
Logical-Mathematical Intelligence
Spatial Intelligence
Bodily-Kinesthetic Intelligence
Interpersonal Intelligence
Intrapersonal Intelligence
Naturalist Intelligence

Applying Multiple Intelligences Theory to Teaching O&M
Personal Assessment
Assessment of Students
Teaching Styles
Thinking about the O&M Curriculum

Matching Teaching and Learning Styles
Strong-Strong Match
Strong-Weak Mismatch
Weak-Strong Mismatch
Weak-Weak Match

Additional Considerations
Gender
Culture
Age
Additional Disabilities

Appendixes

5.A   Descriptions of O&M Activities, Sample Forms, and Materials
       Categorized According to the Eight Intelligences
5.B   Multiple Intelligences Inventory

O&M SKILLS and concepts are usually taught to people who are blind or visually impaired one on one. There are many advantages in designing lessons for students on an individual basis. First, the O&M specialist can concentrate on the specific mobility skills a student needs to learn at a given time and in a given setting. Second, it is more effective to teach such hands-on lessons, incorporating demonstration, practice, and correction, at a pace that is best suited for the student. Third, individual teaching allows the O&M specialist to enhance the student's understanding of the environment and application of orientation knowledge to various travel situations. In short, the ability to individualize lessons means that teaching can be tailored to meet each student's needs and goals.

With these advantages comes the added responsibility of designing a variety of instructional programs and lessons that optimize individual students' capacity for learning skills, techniques, and concepts necessary for independent and semi-independent travel. It is important to understand how each student learns best, which areas of the curriculum the student will enjoy most, and which areas may be particularly challenging so that teaching strategies that will maximize learning can be used. In the one-on-one learning situation, the need to teach and communicate effectively with one student is magnified and success is readily apparent. When an O&M specialist is unsuccessful in communicating the objectives of a lesson to a student or helping the student to learn a new skill or concept, it may be awkward and discouraging for both the student and the specialist. Challenges arise when the O&M specialist's style of teaching does not appeal to or match the student's style of learning. Such a mismatch of teaching and learning styles may occur, for example, with an O&M specialist who excels in explaining routes and various orientation concepts verbally and a student who responds only with shrugs, nods, and an occasional yes or no. This student enjoys computers and would prefer to work with a computer tactile graphics program to develop orientation skills for travel in light business areas. If the O&M specialist is unfamiliar with computers and uncomfortable using technology for instruction, his or her teaching would be more effective with this particular student if he or she took a computer class or collaborated with another teacher to develop computer-based O&M lessons that would be motivating for the student. In other words, teaching to the student's strength could help to increase the student's understanding of the material presented and ultimately improve the student's ability to communicate verbally with the O&M specialist.

While assessing visually impaired students' levels of skill and conceptual development in O&M, O&M specialists also need to assess the students' *individual learning styles* (the ways in which the students learn best) to increase the effectiveness of instruction. In addition, experienced O&M specialists need to examine their own teaching styles to recognize their own strengths, expand the variety of teaching strategies they use, and look for ways to improve upon their weaker areas. By doing so, they can select teaching approaches that are tailored for individual students in their caseloads, improve their present teaching performance, and possibly renew their interest in and commitment to teaching. For O&M specialists who are just beginning their careers, identifying areas of strength from which to draw on can be helpful in formulating creative and successful teaching strategies. Both experienced and inexperienced teachers can use Gardner's (1993) multiple intelligences theory, with its emphasis on individualized teaching strategies and outcomes, as a guide for formulating instructional programs in O&M for a range of students.

Multiple intelligences theory can be used to design a variety of individualized O&M programs. It provides a framework for effectively linking assessment, instructional practice, and learning. The dynamic processes involved in attaining the skills and concepts necessary for independent travel lend themselves to consideration of multiple entry points for teaching and learning. O&M teaching strategies, learning styles, and curricular components may involve the use of a combination of intelligences: linguistic, logical-mathematical, musical, spatial, bodily-kinesthetic, interpersonal, intrapersonal, and naturalist. Expanded teaching approaches can give individuals who are blind or visually impaired learning opportunities that lead to a fuller understanding of the environment and a greater ability to apply that knowledge to problem solving and performance in a wide range of travel experiences.

This chapter presents an overview of multiple intelligences theory and applies that framework to O&M instruction. Methods of assessing individual teaching and learning styles are highlighted, as are an array of teaching approaches that can be used to appeal to students who exhibit different learning preferences. Strategies for matching teaching and learning styles are given to maximize the effectiveness of instruction. Additional considerations for students of different cultures, ages, and genders and those who have multiple disabilities are also discussed.

MULTIPLE INTELLIGENCES THEORY

Although there are many different theories of learning and brain function, multiple intelligences theory readily lends itself to O&M instruction and individualized programming. The practical application of individual learning styles is well suited to meet the learning needs of students who are blind or visually impaired. Finding multiple approaches for teaching concepts and skills that are necessary for independent travel and interacting with the environment from a variety of perspectives provides the student with a means for learning about the world without the advantage of incidental observations.

Howard Gardner, a professor of education at Harvard University, reconceptualized intelligence from a multidimensional perspective. In his theory, he challenged traditional notions of intelligence as the accumulation of information and explored individuals' abilities to solve problems by applying understanding to new situations. Indeed, the ability to solve problems is the basis for negotiating environments with impaired or no vision.

According to Gardner (1993, p. 15), cognitive competence is "a set of abilities, talents, or mental skills, which we can call *intelligences*." The functions of intelligences are to enable individuals to solve problems (for example, in O&M, to find an efficient detour around a construction site to reach a desired destination safely) and to create end products (for instance, in O&M, to develop a tactile graphic of the layout of a school campus) that are relevant to particular cultural settings or communities. In addition, Gardner (1983, 1993) identified eight distinct intelligences:

- *linguistic* intelligence,
- *musical* intelligence,
- *logical-mathematical* intelligence,
- *spatial* intelligence,

- *bodily-kinesthetic* intelligence,

- *interpersonal* intelligence,

- *intrapersonal* intelligence, and

- *naturalist* intelligence.

Although individuals may be stronger in certain intelligences than in others, each child and adult with intact brain functioning is believed to have the capacity to learn using each intelligence and to develop a level of skill from each. The ability to take advantage of one's "stronger" intelligences may depend on how they are recognized, valued, and encouraged by teachers, families, and the community (Gardner, 1993). While the eight intelligences can be viewed as separate entities, they are used together to develop the abilities and skills necessary for everyday life.

Multiple intelligences theory is an interesting theory from which to examine individual teaching and learning styles that may enable students who are blind or visually impaired to be more successful in developing skills and knowledge for independent travel. Effective teachers often tap into many of these intelligences when they present lessons. The theory also provides a guide for assessing the most effective channels that individual students may use to understand a variety of types of information. Examining students' learning styles can spark ideas about activities and strategies that will be most effective in motivating the students. O&M specialists can also use this theory to analyze their own learning and communication styles. Descriptions and examples of each of the eight intelligences are presented in the following sections, along with teaching ideas that play to students' strengths and help them develop their weaker areas.

Linguistic Intelligence

Linguistic intelligence involves the use of written and spoken language. Some of the uses of language include the ability to

- understand the meaning and order of words,

- remember information (lists, rules, directions, instructions, or procedures),

- explain ideas or skills (in oral or written form), and

- persuade others to adopt a plan of action (Gardner, 1993).

People who are particularly talented in this area may be those who are skilled in writing (novelists, journalists, poets, playwrights, lyricists, or scholarly authors like historians) or in speaking (politicians, television interviewers, lawyers, or comic performers who improvise). They may enjoy reading, writing, telling jokes and stories, and doing crossword puzzles. They may have good memories for names and places, be naturally good spellers, and have well-developed auditory memories. For people who are deaf and hard of hearing, linguistic intelligence includes the ability to communicate using sign language.

For O&M specialists, linguistic intelligence is essential, since it enables them to communicate with their students. As part of the O&M specialist's job, language may be used to become acquainted with students, explain a concept or correct a skill, praise students for their work, question students to check their understanding of a skill or concept, and communicate with other professionals or family members orally or in writing. Students must also rely on linguistic intelligence as part of their O&M learning. Linguistic skills are important for students when they

- learn specific O&M vocabulary,

- become familiar with a concept prior to experiencing it through touch or sound,

- question and understand why something occurs or what something is,

- talk about how or why they are traveling in a particular way in a given environment, and

- recall verbal route directions or remember new information they gather when questioning others about a place.

In each lesson, words are used before, during, and after the particular activity that is planned as the focus of the lesson. The exchange of words between the student and the O&M specialist is important for the O&M specialist not only to monitor what is being learned, but also to determine at what pace the learning is taking place. Words, whether they are spoken, tape-recorded, brailled, or written in large print, can also be used as part of a teaching strategy. Students who have strong linguistic skills may find that playing with words while learning O&M is interesting and motivating. These students may enjoy poems that help them learn about safe travel, such as the following O&M poem:

CROSSING AT THE "T"

When I stand at the "top" of the T
It looks midblock to me.
I use my sight
To search for the light
To cross both day and night.

I look "in front" and "to the left"
To find the car I need
So I can get to school on time
To learn, study, and read.

This parallel farside left-turning car
Comes so <u>close</u> to Lynn
Good Heavens to Betsy, we don't want a scar
Not any scrape of skin!

"T", "T" be good to me
As I prepare to cross
I cannot be confused, you see,
Not totally at a loss!

When it says "WALK"
There's no time to talk
But scan from front to left
To see what car is out there
And cross with skills so deft.

Presenting a route as a limerick, a poem with a missing last line or word, or as directions with clues from an O&M crossword puzzle may be a challenge to students who have strengths in linguistic intelligence. These students may also enjoy learning the address system or how a bus system works by inventing "fantasy" maps. These maps would have street names and destinations they invented for fun before they looked at the real location where they would be traveling. (For additional suggestions and descriptions of sample activities for teaching students with strong linguistic skills, see Linguistic Teaching Strategies and Appendix 5.A at the end of this chapter.)

Teaching to students' strengths is reinforcing, but teaching to weaknesses is also a necessary part of O&M. Developing good communication skills is essential. If students need to improve their speaking skills,

LINGUISTIC TEACHING STRATEGIES

- Reinforce cane skills or route travel using verbal prompts, such as "good even arc" or "remember right turn at the ramp."

- Create crossword puzzles for students to review O&M vocabulary words or the names of destinations.

- Practice monocular skills by having students do a word search at the mall or grocery store (for example, find 10 words that start with the letter "A").

- Help a student or group of students to write a short story or skit about an imaginary character's mobility travels. Challenge the students to include three different cane techniques, two different street crossings, and four different landmarks in the story.

- Hold an O&M spelling bee for an individual or group of students that includes terms such as *parallel, perpendicular,* and *landmark.*

it is necessary to give them opportunities to use words effectively. Some students may need verbal prompts or written cues initially to assist them in asking appropriate questions or interacting with the O&M specialist or others in the community. Incorporating enjoyable experiences in O&M lessons (such as going to a music store for a shy student who plays an instrument) offers students a chance to begin talking more easily. Students may be more willing to talk about their interests and then, with some coaxing, what they accomplished in a given lesson.

Linguistic intelligence is a necessary ingredient in the content of the O&M curriculum and in the manner in which skills and concepts are taught. Content and strategy can be focused toward complementing students' strengths and improving students' weaknesses when designing O&M lessons for individual students.

Musical Intelligence

Musical intelligence involves a sensitivity to pitch, rhythm, and timbre. Like linguistic intelligence, it is perceived primarily through the auditory channel, but it uses musical notes as its notation system. Some of the uses of musical intelligence include the ability to recognize variations in pitch, rhythm, and timbre; compose or perform music; and appreciate musical expressions.

Individuals who are highly musical are often performers, singers, conductors, or composers. They may also enjoy going to concerts, listening to music when they study or read, collect tapes and CDs, play an instrument, keep time rhythmically, sing songs to themselves, and notice background sounds. Depending on the culture, music may be essential to a person's education and a society's religious or patriotic expression (Gardner, 1993).

Musical intelligence is important in the auditory training component of the O&M curriculum. Recognition of sounds and rhythms is vital to understanding a nonvisual environment. Music can also be a powerful motivator or area of interest for students who are blind or visually impaired as they practice a skill or learn a new concept.

Recognizing variations in pitch may help a student to determine the gender of a person from whom he or she is seeking assistance. Rhythm involves sensing a pattern of sound or movement, such as the movement of the long cane in step with one's gait. Timbre refers to the ability to identify different qualities of sound, like the difference between an idling Volkswagen and a Porsche. Musical intelligence enables a visually impaired individual to put these three elements together to interpret sounds that help him or her conceptualize the travel environment. For example, students who are blind or visually impaired may use their musical intelligence to help them use auditory cues to analyze the complexity of traffic light-controlled intersections, such as

- changes in *pitch* to identify the surge of accelerating cars,
- changes in *rhythm* to perceive the pattern of traffic at signal lights, and
- changes in *timbre* to recognize the sounds of different vehicles.

Students who enjoy listening to music; go to concerts, musical theater, or the opera; or perform in their school or community bands, orchestras, or choirs are likely to have well-developed aspects of musical intelligence. In addition to reacting positively to music and interesting sounds, they may also be more sensitive than other people to certain kinds of noises or react negatively to certain sounds that are too loud or too soft. They may be naturally alert to auditory cues and enjoy identifying environmental sounds, often volunteering information while walking on a lesson, like "That was a Karmann Ghia that just went by, wasn't it?" They are able to understand and progress in their auditory street-crossing skills, since they can identify accurately parallel versus perpendicular traffic and traffic surges. Students with high musical intelligence may learn auditory skills quickly because they are already able to listen carefully and attend to what they hear.

Young children who are musical may enjoy songs with familiar tunes with "O&M" lyrics or rhythmic chants to sing about their canes or body parts as they walk during their lessons. Teenagers and adults may be motivated by designing routes to a music store or video store or telephoning to find out what concerts are playing in their community. Students with multiple disabilities who respond to music may enjoy a "sound challenge," in which they tape each other's voices, listen to the tape, and identify who was speaking. (For additional ideas for teaching students who are strong in muscial intelligence, see Musical Teaching Strategies. For more teaching activities, see Appendix 5.A at the end of this chapter.)

It is important to recognize the importance of auditory awareness for safety in independent travel, even for students who are weak in the area of musical intelligence. To increase opportunities for success for such students, O&M specialists could start auditory training activities indoors where there may be fewer distractions and then apply auditory

 MUSICAL TEACHING STRATEGIES

- Practice sound localization with castanets, tambourines, jingle bells, and other percussive instruments.

- Teach the use of appropriate optical devices by having the student read sheet music.

- Design routes to practice cane techniques in environments that have interesting echoes.

- Preview a travel route by listening to music from different cultures found in that area.

- Challenge the student to recognize auditory cues (such as of a train, freeway, elevator, audible pedestrian signal) along a route and tape-record them.

skills to outdoor environments and intersections with distinct traffic patterns. Students who have both visual and hearing impairments may need alternative strategies for crossing streets safely, such as soliciting assistance.

Even with ample time for practice, some students with a poor sense of rhythm may not always be able to walk "in rhythm" or "in step" and may need to compensate with a longer cane or slightly wider arc width. Teaching cane-skill activities that require rhythm may be supplemented with fun poems or limericks or the use of physical prompts as needed.

Logical-Mathematical Intelligence

Logical-mathematical intelligence is based on the ability to manipulate physical objects, beginning with sensorimotor exploration and extending to the development of abstract theories in the fields of science, mathematics, and logic. Logical-mathematical intelligence includes the ability to

- understand the use of numbers, words, and symbols as they represent objects and functions (Gardner, 1993);

- work with and solve mathematical problems;

- analyze a sequence of events;

- use intuition to solve scientific problems; and

- handle long chains of logical reasoning.

People with this gift are often professional mathematicians or professors of logic, engineers, physicists, researchers in the biological or physical sciences, or physicians with different kinds of specialties. They enjoy abstract forms of logical thinking, compute arithmetic problems quickly in their heads, like to play chess and other strategy games, and solve problems using reason. Logical-mathematical intelligence is an important part of the O&M curriculum because it fosters curiosity and problem-solving skills; enables students to sequence events, places, or things in a logical way for orientation; and assists students in understanding the patterns of maps and the consistency of cardinal compass directions. Young students who are gifted in logical-mathematical intelligences are motivated by teaching strategies that enable them to explore, discover, examine, compare, analyze, measure, or research (find out about) objects and events in their environment.

LOGICAL-MATHEMATICAL
TEACHING STRATEGIES

- Challenge the student or a group of students to estimate and compare traffic speeds along several different streets or at several different intersections.

- Allow the student to look up bus schedules on the Internet at bus company web sites and select the most efficient transfer point for a given destination.

- Use a task analysis to present a lesson on negotiating doors with a guide in a logical step-by-step sequence.

- Design a drop-off lesson that will enable students to use their analytical skills to solve problems.

- Give the student a list of items to purchase at a grocery store within a limited budget. Give the student a calculator to keep a tally while shopping.

Having a student who is blind compare the textures of different walking surfaces or having a student with low vision examine the features of a variety of signs may encourage his or her logical-mathematical intelligence. O&M specialists need to set aside time for these students to ask their favorite "why" and "how" questions and present a choice of ways they can begin to "solve O&M problems." For older students, some lessons can be centered on learning about traffic signals: how they operate, how they are repaired, or when their timing is changed. Sitting at a table with a tactile or visual map, adults may enjoy debating the best way to find a destination and comparing in a logical way the distance and degree of difficulty of three different routes. (For additional ideas for motivating students who are strong in this area, see Logical-Mathematical Teaching Strategies. For more teaching activities, see Appendix 5.A.)

Students who have difficulty in the logical-mathematical area may need assistance in dealing with a long sequence of reasoning necessary for reorientation in complex travel environments. They may need to ask for assistance on some occasions to locate a familiar landmark or destination and may learn routes best when the routes are presented in smaller segments. Applying the principles of the address system to real travel situations may also be a challenge initially for these students. To ameliorate this problem, O&M specialists can teach elements of the address system one at a time. Mnemonics may be helpful for some students in remembering details of the system. For example, N-**O**-W reminds them that *odd*-numbered addresses are commonly found on the *north* and *west* sides of streets and S-**E**-E indicates that *even*-numbered addresses are commonly found along the *south* and *east* sides. Some students may benefit from O&M specialists providing a written system or checklist for logical intersection analysis. When teaching map-reading skills, O&M specialists can start with simple map concepts and route applications and gradually introduce more complex ones. Using the students' other strengths, they can help the students make maps that the students can most easily understand (such as verbal maps, written route-instruction cards, or tactile or visual maps).

Understanding how things work, where they are, and why they are there in a specific travel environment increases the safety of students who are blind or visually impaired. Teaching strategies that encourage curiosity and problem solving (see the section on Encouraging Student Curiosity in Chapter 3 for a review of these teaching strategies) motivate students who are naturally logical-mathematical and strengthen these abilities in students who have trouble in this area. As these students become better informed, they are able to make logical choices and decisions about where to travel, when, and why.

Spatial Intelligence

Spatial intelligence involves visual-spatial competence, whether it is reproducing a specific form or designing one that is original. People who are gifted in this intelligence are able to

- visualize in their minds various shapes or designs (Gardner, 1993),

- select materials necessary to help re-create forms in two- or three-dimensional expressions,

- understand spatial relationships, and

- maintain orientation to a variety of environments.

Painters, sculptors, architects, photographers, engineers, and navigators are able to use their innate understanding of spatial forms and relationships, along with their vision and sense of touch. They usually think in images and pictures, spend free time in art activities, easily read maps and charts, draw accurate representations of people and things, like movies and photography, and enjoy jigsaw puzzles and mazes.

They are able to recognize both the fine details of texture and color in a small corner of a building (the part) and the overall unifying shape of that same building (the whole).

Spatial awareness is fundamental to understanding one's environment and traveling within that environment in a purposeful way. For O&M students, seeking landmarks, understanding the shape of a route or compass cardinal directions, and responding to the environment to remain oriented are all part of spatial intelligence. For O&M students who are adventitiously blind, visual memory plays a key role in learning to recognize by sound or touch what they previously recognized by sight. It helps them understand the sounds of a traffic pattern or the proportional relationships of things, especially from a distance. Visual memory also enables students to know objects that are too big to comprehend all at once by touch or too far away to reach, like a mountain range. Students who have a gift for spatial understanding do not necessarily need to have had sight, however. Students who are visually impaired and strong in spatial intelligence are able to use their sense of hearing, touch, and time distance (the ability to perceive or estimate relative distance by the amount of time it takes to travel to a given location) to

- perceive and recall the shapes, sizes, and directional and proportional relationships of objects, places, and map routes they have traveled;

- explore new travel areas;

- make tactile maps and design routes on them to desired locations; and

- remember the sequence of turns they must follow on a route after they have traced the lines on a map.

Teaching strategies that these students enjoy include not only using a teacher-made map, but also finding or creating two- and three-dimensional forms with Play-Doh or Wikki Stix (nontoxic strands of wax-coated yarn that are bendable like pipe cleaners and temporarily stick to some mapmaking and other surfaces). Making shapes, such as an oval, sphere, rectangle, cube, or parallel lines, is a fun classroom activity and can be used to illustrate larger environmental concepts (like the parallel lines of railroad tracks). For additional teaching ideas for students who

SPATIAL TEACHING STRATEGIES

- Use road-sign cutouts (such as a stop sign, yield sign, or one-way sign) for coloring, matching shapes, and identifying traffic symbols.

- Incorporate a choice of compasses (braille, talking, globe, or pocket-watch style) to use on orientation lessons.

- Have the student select a variety of materials (such as a sponge, popsicle sticks, Play-Doh, and so on) to use in creating a student-designed map.

- Position Wikki-Stix on a piece of cardboard to illustrate route shapes, such as I, L, or U, or ask the students to place the given materials on the cardboard.

- Challenge the student to complete route reversals and route alternatives for traveling in a variety of environments.

are strong in spatial intelligence, see Spatial Teaching Strategies and Appendix 5.A.

O&M students who have a weak spatial understanding of their environment may have difficulty recalling the size, shape, or arrangements of objects in a room. For these students, rearranging the furniture can cause considerable hardship. Students who have poor spatial abilities may find it difficult to reverse a route from a place where they have traveled. It is easy for them to become disoriented and harder for them to solve problems using spatial cues in the environment. Since they may be able to use only simple tactile or visual maps that contain basic information, the first step may be to build a map with just one shape or line and to add details when the students become more comfortable using maps. Auditory or written route directions may be helpful for some travelers.

Bodily-Kinesthetic Intelligence

Bodily-kinesthetic intelligence enables a person to

- control bodily movements,

- manipulate objects with skill, and

- recognize bodily positions and the specific movements as they are made (Gardner, 1993).

For a person to accomplish a given physical task, the brain sends messages to instruct specific sets of muscles to contract. These muscles then send back messages to the brain indicating that they have done their job and give additional feedback. For example, in ascending the stairs, new information, such as the depth of the steps, is added, and the brain recognizes that physical adjustments need to be made. The brain sends appropriate neurological messages to the same sets of muscles to avoid overstepping. This neurological "conversation" takes place constantly and allows people to move with coordination, efficiency, and grace. People who are sensitive to this inner sense of position and movement are often athletes or artists. They may move their entire bodies through space in a breathtaking sequence of motion, like acrobats and dancers, or hold a part of their bodies still with smaller movements of the hands, like violinists, marksman, or surgeons. Gardner (1993) noted that people with a highly developed bodily-kinesthetic sense are often inventors, engineers, or "tinkerers" who enjoy using their hands to take things apart, rearrange them, or reconstruct them in a new way. They often move, tap, or fidget when sitting; engage in physical activities and sports; like to touch people when they talk to them; enjoy handicrafts (such as woodworking, pottery, or sewing); can mimic others' gestures and mannerisms; and learn best through movement and hands-on activities.

The ability to perceive and control one's movements is essential to O&M because it helps students learn about their environment through movement and touch. Bodily-kinesthetic intelligence helps students learn correct cane techniques and other safe travel skills (like how to step off curbs and consistently walk in a straight line to the other side of the street). It informs individuals who are blind or visually impaired about what is in the world through touch. It is especially important to develop this intelligence with young children who are blind or visually impaired while they are still formulating their movement patterns and beginning mobility skills. Young children who are blind or visually impaired who have been given high-quality movement experiences (rocking, swaying, bouncing, and so on) early on are able to find or regain their balance more quickly in a variety of physical activities. They can also perceive objects directly through their hands or other parts of the bodies or indirectly through tactile feedback from the long cane. O&M students who are naturally inclined in bodily-kinesthetic intelligence are usually able to

- maintain good posture and a smooth gait,

- learn cane skills with ease,

- recognize the slant of a driveway or slope of a wheelchair ramp, and

- make automatic body adjustments in response to the environment as they travel.

The need to explain or examine aspects of the environment through movement and touch is a fundamental way of presenting and learning the O&M curriculum. For example, Figure 5.1 presents a sample lesson plan illustrating how basic cane skills and campus orientation can be taught using strategies that take advantage of a student's bodily-kinesthetic intelligence. The need to move with the correct speed and range of motion and to avoid unnecessary or socially inappropriate movements are fundamental skills for all O&M students. The refinement of movement skills leads to increased safety and better orientation.

Teaching strategies for students who have particularly good bodily-kinesthetic intelligence may include rewarding them with time on a slide or climbing apparatus or shooting hoops with a basketball. Active games with running, hopping, and jumping can be incorporated into the instruction of concepts. When introducing a new route, O&M specialists may ask students with strong bodily-kinesthetic intelligence to travel the route before they examine a map of the area. Students who enjoy movement activities will enjoy interactive maps in which they play the role of cars moving through intersections or pedestrians walking around the block. (For sample descriptions of interactive maps, as well as other teaching activities, see Appendix 5.A at the end of this chapter. For additional teaching ideas that incorporate bodily-kinesthetic intelligence, see Bodily-Kinesthetic Teaching Strategies.)

For students who are weak in this area, approaches are needed to provide practice through the repetition of movements. The O&M specialist needs to assess exactly what a student's movement problems are and determine the best ways to correct them. One approach may be to begin with physical correction and monitoring the accuracy of movements while physically and verbally prompting the student through repetition. Students who have low vision may be able to watch the O&M specialist or another student do a physical activity to mirror the movements. Motivators could include incorporating music during physical

Lesson Plan

Student: _Elijah (age 4, no light perception)_

Instructor: _Cheryl_

Date: _May 12_

Time: _1:30 p.m._

Lesson Location: _the school campus_

Goal: _To develop basic cane skills and campus orientation_

Lesson Objectives:
1. _To use his hand to trail wall along the route from the classroom to the bathroom, 80 percent of the time_
2. _To keep the cane tip on the floor 100 percent of the time_
3. _To extend the cane across the front of his body 50 percent of the time_

Instructional Materials: _feather duster with plastic handle, piece of foam_

Methodology/Instructional Strategies:

1. Begin the lesson with a physical warm-up outside in the attached play yard. Ask Elijah to recall what trailing is. Probe to get something like "We trail something so we won't get lost. When we trail, we keep our hand on it all the way."

2. The physical warm-up today will be using the feather duster to trail the playground apparatus. Tell Elijah about his special warm-up "duster trailer" and ask him to dust (follow) all the bars along the playground. Have him try it in both hands. Reward him with a brief climb on the apparatus before practicing the route.

3. Start from the classroom door and review the route to the boys' bathroom. Ask Elijah about the foam landmark placed along the wall and show him the small version so he remembers it. Remind him to keep his hand on the wall and show him the correct cane position.

4. Provide physical and verbal prompts as needed to ensure success.

5. Take time to have Elijah wash his hands in the bathroom. Return to class using the sighted (human) guide technique.

6. At the end of the lesson, ask Elijah which body part he used to follow the wall. Praise him and say "good trailing." Ask him if he was able to keep the cane tip on the floor. Praise Elijah for locating the landmark (if he did).

Daily Notes:

Really able to see Elijah's coordination and balance today during the warm-up. His parents have encouraged his exploration at home, and he was very good at dusting the playground equipment and loved the climbing. He seemed to be more attentive after the physical warm-up. Will try to do one each lesson. He is still having difficulty keeping his hand on the wall; veers away and misses his landmark. Spatial tasks are hard for him. Next time, walk the route using the sighted guide technique first and then have him do so independently.

Figure 5.1

Using Bodily-Kinesthetic Strategies to Promote Basic Cane Skills and Campus Orientation

---

BODILY-KINESTHETIC
TEACHING STRATEGIES

- Teach dance steps (such as ballet positions or country line-dance routines) to explore a range of body-part movements.

- Use isometrics to develop the student's muscle memory of the correct positions for protective techniques.

- Travel to a sporting goods store to examine hand weights and other exercise equipment.

- Prescribe an adapted mobility device to enable the students to run safely on the playground and play games of tag.

- Create an imaginary intersection with ropes or tape and have a small group of students move through the intersection the way cars and pedestrians do.

---

practice or engaging in role-play activities, such as pretending to be a robot or, for older students, a computer consultant walking to a bus stop.

Interpersonal Intelligence

Interpersonal intelligence enables a person to become aware of other people and their needs, wants, and intentions. Individuals who are gifted in interpersonal intelligence are able to

- understand the intent and meaning of another person's words,

- perceive another person's emotions by observing the person's body language,

- listen skillfully to learn more about others, and

- communicate effectively and influence others (Gardner, 1993).

Teachers, religious and political leaders, those in the helping professions, businesspeople, and salespersons are examples of people with well-developed interpersonal skills. They are social, show empathy for others, are good at organizing people, enjoy group games and clubs, and learn best by relating to and cooperating with others in group activities.

O&M students who enjoy being with others, who have many friends, and who listen well have developed this intelligence. They are comfortable with group learning activities and may prefer to brainstorm with other people than to solve a problem by themselves. Teaching strategies they may enjoy include peer teaching (such as practicing compass cardinal directions), class presentations or show-and-tell, group activities (like field trips to the local fire station or community center), lessons traveling to a mall with another student, or sharing in the design of a tactile map with other students. For additional teaching ideas and activities that incorporate interpersonal intelligence, see Interpersonal Teaching Strategies and Appendix 5.A at the end of this chapter.

Students who have weak "people" skills are at a disadvantage because it may be difficult for them to ask for and get the help they need, including readers and persons to assist them with certain daily living activities. Poorly developed social skills may also make it more challenging to obtain and keep jobs. Improving these students' awareness of how other people think and feel is an important part of the O&M curriculum. For example, students should try to recognize variations in the tone of others' voices and be aware of how people may feel when asked for a favor, such as a ride to work on a regular basis. Teaching strategies to assist them may include role-playing scenarios in which they listen to

INTERPERSONAL TEACHING STRATEGIES

- Play Telephone or Whisper Down the Lane with a group of students using O&M topics. For example, start with "I was using the constant-contact technique when safely crossing counterclockwise at Confetti Avenue" and see how the phrase changes as students whisper it to the person sitting next to them.

- Encourage a small group of students to plan an O&M field trip together to a local mall, movie theater, or arboretum.

- Have the student plan and practice a bus route to a friend's house.

- Explore transportation options (such as a taxi, carpool, public bus, hired driver, and so on) for taking a date or friend to a dance or social event.

- Allow the students to design routes for one another, using maps or verbal directions.

and interpret accurately the intentions of other persons. For instance, was it the intention of the security guard who offered assistance to give brief directions or to accompany the student throughout the shopping mall? Role-playing afterward using different tones of voice and gestures may help students recognize subtle differences in intent.

Since O&M instruction involves teaching someone else, O&M specialists need to develop this interpersonal intelligence fully. Continued attention to the way students move, to their posture and gestural habits, is crucial in perceiving more accurately how students feel. For example, a change in posture may alert the O&M specialist to the fact that a student is feeling frustrated while trying to time a safe street crossing. The timing of when to present information and when to wait is also important in communicating with students. Part of being sensitive to others' dispositions is knowing when to talk, when to listen, and when to change the subject.

Intrapersonal Intelligence

Human beings are social creatures and, as such, are motivated to improve both their own well-being and their relationships within the community (Gardner, 1993). Therefore, as a complement to interpersonal intelligence, which enables a person to look outward to understand and empathize with others, Gardner (1993) described intrapersonal intelligence as the ability to recognize and develop a "sense of self," an awareness of one's inner needs and potential. Intrapersonal intelligence enables one to

- identify one's emotions,

- assess individual strengths and weaknesses,

- monitor and guide one's actions and words,

- recognize what motivates one and what makes one afraid or angry, and

- learn about oneself, who one is that makes one different from everyone else.

Those who have strong intrapersonal intelligence include writers who describe their innermost feelings in words; artists, composers, and choreographers who illustrate their feelings through visual, auditory, or movement expression; and therapists, who through their ability to listen and understand others, demonstrate that they understand themselves and are in touch with their own feelings. People who are gifted in this intelligence have accurate self-knowledge, make clear career and lifestyle choices, like to be alone to pursue a hobby, do well in independent projects, and are often intuitive.

O&M students who have well-developed intrapersonal skills may

- recognize and verbalize how they feel about what they accomplished or did not accomplish in a lesson,

- appear to be somewhat impatient during lessons, exclaiming, "I know . . . " or "Let me do it!" or

- feel positive or negative about having to ask for assistance or using their cane.

Students with strong intrapersonal intelligence are familiar with their own strengths and weaknesses and are able to accept compliments and listen to constructive criticism. For example, they may be able to acknowledge that they did not ask for assistance clearly and need to work on that skill, but also recognize and enjoy the fact that their cane skills have greatly improved. They may also have ideas about what career paths to pursue. The lesson plan in Figure 5.2 illustrates teaching strategies that can be used with an adult who is strong in intrapersonal intelligence. The student who is doing bus travel is allowed to make and evaluate independent choices for bus routes. The student is also encouraged to keep a reflective journal and asked to complete a homework assignment by herself.

Teaching strategies to motivate students who are strong in intrapersonal intelligence may include encouraging them to interview people in careers they find interesting or shadowing these people on their jobs for a day. For additional teaching ideas and activities that incorporate intrapersonal intelligence, see Intrapersonal Teaching Strategies and Appendix 5.A at the end of this chapter.

Students who are weak in intrapersonal intelligence are less able to verbalize their feelings about issues that are of concern to them, including what or how they are being taught. They may not recognize a talent they have, like public speaking, writing, or physical stamina or coordination. In addition, they may not recognize the anxiety they feel when they approach a particular intersection or may be more resistant to suggestions or constructive criticisms during a lesson. Students who are

Lesson Plan

Student: _Brenda (mid-30s, restricted field from retinitis pigmentosa)_

Instructor: _Earl_

Date: _September 5_

Time: _12:00 noon_

Lesson Location: _advanced residential and light business areas_

Goal: _To increase options for traveling to and from work_

Lesson Objectives:
1. _To obtain accurate bus transfer information via telephone prior to the lesson_
2. _To select and travel the complete route from home to work independently_
3. _To interact appropriately with the bus driver_

Instructional Materials: _bus schedules, student notes, area map with acetate overlay, grease pencil, student's O&M journal_

Methodology/Instructional Strategies:

1. Begin the lesson at Brenda's home and ask her to share the information she obtained regarding the bus transfer route. Have Brenda compare information with that printed on the bus schedule.
2. Ask Brenda to record the full information in her O&M journal filed under "bus routes."
3. Talk briefly about Brenda's new job and her work schedule. Review her route choices using the map of the area. Use a grease pencil to trace the route selected by the student.
4. Remind Brenda to ask for assistance from the second bus driver as the drop-off point will be unfamiliar. Review what a few good questions might be.
5. Monitor Brenda's bus travel from appropriate distances, depending on the activity.
6. After Brenda completes the entire route, ask her to evaluate the following:
   a. convenience of bus route and transfer
   b. safety of crossing at intersections
   c. the way she used her cane
   d. route to workplace from the second bus
   e. advantages and disadvantages of the route selection
7. End the lesson by asking Brenda to consider other options for getting to work (e.g., carpool). For homework, ask her to find out if there is a ride-share program at work and obtain the necessary information. She can write the information in her O&M journal. She should also write down her thoughts about the lesson (e.g., what she did well, where she needs to improve, things to continue working on, and how she felt traveling the new route) in the diary section of her journal.

Daily Notes:
Brenda is highly motivated and executed the route independently. She enjoys the homework assignments because she likes to work on things independently (she is high in the intrapersonal intelligence area). She is still trying to avoid talking with the bus drivers. The idea about a ride-share program went over like a lead balloon. Keep encouraging her to interact with others, as this is an area of weakness.

Figure 5.2

Increasing Options for Traveling to and from Work for the Intrapersonal Student

INTRAPERSONAL TEACHING STRATEGIES

- Incorporate career role-playing (such as of a news reporter, social worker, real estate agent, or newspaper delivery person) into purposeful travel in a residential or light business travel environment, giving the student a functional task to complete that would be appropriate for the given profession.

- Encourage the students to set personal goals for O&M training by examining their accomplishments in independent travel.

- Have the students maintain O&M diaries or journals in which they describe how they feel using a cane or asking for assistance.

- Give the student opportunities to explore new environments semi-independently (with the O&M specialist's supervision) at the beginning of a teaching unit.

- Assign O&M homework to allow the students time to work on independent projects (like developing a student portfolio, designing a map or model, or planning a bus route).

weak in intrapersonal intelligence may be reluctant to complete travel routes, projects, or assignments independently and may rely more on the teacher's prompts and assistance. For students who have not imagined themselves in a meaningful career, the O&M specialist can incorporate role-playing activities from a career-planning book into relevant O&M lessons. Other teaching strategies for improving intrapersonal intelligence may include the use of self-analysis inventories or tests, in which students rate their performance on a variety of skills or tasks; discovery learning, in which students are encouraged to learn about a new area or skill with a great deal of independence and self-initiative; student portfolios, in which students collect materials that document their various O&M accomplishments; and research on careers, in which students plan routes and go to local libraries or community colleges to obtain further information on such aspects of careers as job descriptions, required training, and typical salaries.

O&M specialists, too, need to develop intrapersonal awareness. It is important for them to examine their feelings about why they have chosen a "helping" profession and how this choice influences their teaching. Recognizing both their positive and negative feelings during and after a lesson enables effective O&M specialists to continue to use a teaching approach or choose a better one. They may want to ask themselves such questions as these:

- How do I feel about letting students experiment and learn through their "mistakes"?
- How do I react when a student takes a long time to learn a particular skill?
- Am I frustrated or angry because this student takes "too long"?

Whereas logical-mathematical intelligence helps O&M specialists analyze and organize lessons, intrapersonal intelligence brings them directly and immediately in touch with their feelings about a particular lesson. These feelings can serve as a guide for future lessons.

Both interpersonal intelligence and intrapersonal intelligence are important to the O&M curriculum. Students are encouraged to look inward to gain a better understanding of themselves and to focus outward to participate more actively in the community. Capabilities in these two intelligences enable O&M specialists to communicate and teach effectively.

Naturalist Intelligence

Naturalist intelligence involves the ability to observe, understand, and organize patterns recognized in the natural environment (Campbell, 1997). People who are gifted in this area and who study the natural world include botanists, oceanographers, and astronomers, and those who enjoy studying the habits of people and/or animals include biologists, sociologists, or archeologists. They often have keen sensory skills, like to be outside, like animals or plants, are concerned about the environment, and create scrapbooks or journals or have collections of natural objects or animal species. Naturalist intelligence is important to the content of the O&M curriculum because students who are blind or visually impaired are asked to observe, identify, and organize environmental information for independent travel. Students use this intelligence to

- collect information about travel locations,
- describe characteristics typically found in travel areas,

- organize information about different kinds of environments (such as intersections), and

- recall information to analyze new travel environments.

For example, learning the traffic-control characteristics of residential travel environments helps students to anticipate the sound of cars stopping at stop sign-controlled intersections.

Students who are gifted in naturalist intelligence may enjoy keeping notebooks or tape-recording descriptions of what they have seen or touched. They are curious about the environment and like to collect and label objects they have found or learned about. For example, after collecting and identifying leaves gathered while walking in a residential area, these students may choose to sort the leaves by shape, size, or texture and label them in a notebook. An O&M specialist could ask a student with low vision to use a monocular or magnifier to identify and categorize different objects found along a route. If the student noticed an interesting church steeple, he or she may enjoy categorizing different religious buildings by location, denomination, or characteristic shape or building material. Students may use any of this information in creating detailed

NATURALIST TEACHING STRATEGIES

- Have the student start a collection of logos or business cards from businesses encountered along travels in light business areas.

- Examine a variety of metal utility covers found along sidewalks, identifying size, shape, color, and texture.

- Incorporate a lesson about flowers found during residential travel. Take photos of the flowers that are found. Conduct a follow-up lesson at a bookstore or library to look up the name of each flower. Label the photos with the names of the flowers and paste them in a scrapbook.

- Plan a field trip to a local park, garden, or zoo and plan an activity that will require the student to categorize animals or plants found on the trip.

- Design a route and ask the student to identify man-made and natural landmarks along the way.

maps of travel areas. For additional teaching ideas and learning activities that incorporate naturalist intelligence, see Naturalist Teaching Strategies and Appendix 5.A at the end of this chapter.

Students who do not express an interest in collecting, organizing, or classifying information still need some of these skills for learning advanced environmental concepts and executing complex travel skills. It is more efficient to recall information if it has been categorized (for instance, knowing that odd-numbered addresses are often found on the north and west sides of streets). Teaching strategies may focus on students' stronger areas to help complete classification tasks. For example, highly linguistic students may be motivated to write down information on bus routes and organize it in various ways in a hanging file folder or on note cards in a recipe box for later use. Highly spatial students may enjoy making drawings of interesting landmarks and organizing them in a file by category.

Naturalist intelligence involves interests in the world of nature and in the world of man-made objects. O&M specialists can use this intelligence to help students identify and retrieve information needed for safe travel.

APPLYING MULTIPLE INTELLIGENCES THEORY TO TEACHING O&M

Sometimes it is a challenge to find creative strategies for teaching certain orientation concepts or reinforcing specific mobility skills. At other times, a strategy that works well with one student is not effective with another. In both instances, O&M specialists can use their knowledge about the eight intelligences to help generate teaching solutions.

Just three intelligences—linguistic intelligence, logical-mathematical intelligence, and intrapersonal intelligence—are generally emphasized in educational systems in the United States (Gardner, 1993) and thus are the ones with which teachers are the most familiar. Since the personal educational experiences of many O&M specialists may be based primarily on these three intelligences, the O&M specialists' lesson plans and creative strategies may, in turn, be based on these same three intelligences. The reliance on only a few intelligences for creating ideas, however, limits O&M specialists' teaching options. Since some O&M specialists may be equally strong or stronger in one or more of the other intelligences—musical, spatial, bodily-kinesthetic, interpersonal, or naturalist—tapping into these areas may be helpful in finding more kinds of creative strategies for teaching the O&M curriculum. Gardner's theory of multiple intelligences can help expand useful methods for presenting materials and information. A good starting point for O&M specialists may be to assess their own areas of strength in each of the eight intelligences.

Personal Assessment

Most teachers rely on teaching styles that reflect how they prefer to learn because these are the approaches they enjoy and that come naturally to them. However, not all students have the same preferences; thus, O&M specialists may need to examine their teaching styles so as to determine which ones meet the needs of their students. A fun way for O&M specialists to become more familiar with the eight intelligences and the ways in which this knowledge can be used in creative lesson planning is to start with a self-assessment of strengths and aptitudes. The process is simple and involves three steps:

1. reflecting on educational experiences in high school and college by recalling subjects that were enjoyable, those that were excelled in, and learning styles that were preferred;

2. identifying past and/or present hobbies, interests, and extracurricular activities; and

3. completing an informal aptitude assessment.

Reflecting on Educational Experiences

One of the quickest ways to tap into an inventory of abilities is to recall the particular subjects and activities that one enjoyed during and after school. Identify general areas of confidence and enthusiasm. For example, an individual may be talented in one or more of the following: language arts, mathematics, fine arts, or athletics. A general learning style or styles can be determined by thinking about how one best learns a particular skill or subject. For example, some people like to begin learning a new skill or concept through a detailed explanation (*linguistic*), a hands-on approach (*bodily-kinesthetic*), deductive processes and trial and error (*logical-mathematical*), working with other people to complete a project (*interpersonal*), or working on their own (*intrapersonal*). The descriptions of the eight intelligences may provide clues about the way a certain subject is usually taught—that is, the learning style that often accompanies it. O&M specialists who did well in a certain subject in school probably have strengths in the learning style associated with that subject and typically use this style to present O&M lessons to their students. Those who enjoyed science and did well in that subject probably learned by understanding a logical progression of information that helped them solve problems of increasing complexity. While studying science, individuals are typically encouraged to experiment, ask questions, design problems, and find solutions. To present the O&M curriculum to students, these O&M specialists may naturally use the same style of logical progression, moving from the simple to the more complex. Creative strategies would evolve from the "scientific" learning style so that information would be presented in a logical sequence and students would be encouraged to ask questions about their travel environment and how it functions.

Identifying Hobbies or Interests

Individual strengths can be recognized by identifying preferred past and current leisure-time activities and hobbies. These activities are related to the eight intelligences as well. Some activities that O&M specialists may remember enjoying while they were in high school and college may include writing articles for the school newspaper or yearbook (*linguistic*), taking and developing photos for the photography club (*spatial*), working in the computer lab (*logical-mathematical*), creating an insect collection (*naturalist*), playing on the soccer team (*bodily-kinesthetic*), singing in the choir (*musical*), and membership on a social committee for a school dance (*interpersonal*). Consider jobs and volunteer experiences as well (like working at a veterinary clinic, volunteering at a hospital, or working in a shop at a local mall) or hobbies (such as collecting records or CDs, comic books, or stamps). These early experiences and choices provide initial clues for determining one's aptitudes or talents.

Current interests and hobbies also provide insights. Some individuals enjoy being active and spend a great deal of time outdoors hiking, gardening, or sailing (*bodily-kinesthetic*). Others may belong to a church or community choir, orchestra, or band (*musical*). Still others may enjoy writing and keep a daily journal or submit articles to local newspapers (*linguistic*). Each of these activities relates to at least one of the eight intelligences and shows areas of preference.

Completing an Aptitude Test

The last step in the self-assessment of aptitudes is to use a more formal inventory. Such tools are often provided in workshops on multiple intelligences. A simple tool—the Multiple Intelligences Inventory—is included in Appendix 5.B at the end of this chapter. By taking a few minutes to complete the assessment, the O&M specialist will be able to clarify further and quantify his or her strengths in the eight intelligences. One can simply circle the statements that describe one *most* of the time and then total the number of circled statements for each section. After reading the small paragraph description, one can circle the number that corresponds to how accurately it describes one and then add the two scores together to obtain a numerical score for that particular intelligence. Higher numbers indicate a stronger aptitude in a given area.

Once the assessment is completed, O&M specialists should have a clearer idea of the areas in which they are most confident and can look in these areas for ideas on how to present the O&M curriculum. They can also identify teaching approaches that they have not previously explored but that may be helpful to try with specific students.

Assessment of Students

To plan lessons more effectively, O&M specialists will also want to identify students' strengths (and weaknesses) in relation to the eight intelligences. Learning styles and aptitudes can be assessed informally through observation, interviews, and reviews of students' files. For a more formal assessment, the same Multiple Intelligences Inventory in Appendix 5.B at the end of this chapter can be used to assess students' aptitudes.

With preschool-aged children, O&M specialists can try the following strategies to obtain an idea of each child's areas of strength:

- observe each child at home to see how the child plays,

- observe each child at home to see how the child responds to learning situations, activities, and praise from various family members, and

- talk with family members to learn about the child's needs, likes, and dislikes.

Formulating an impression of the child's learning style and aptitudes can be based on what the family members say and on how the child demonstrates the skills he or she has learned. A correspondence between the child's preferences, skills, and learning styles and the eight intelligences should be apparent.

To assess older students, O&M specialists can use several strategies.

1. Read students' files to obtain general information about students' success in particular subjects, citizenship grades, and social skills. This information may give O&M specialists a picture of students' aptitudes, especially if the students receive consistently high grades in particular subjects like English, foreign languages, history, science, or mathematics. It is also possible, however, that students may have strengths in certain intelligences but have low grades in the subjects because of absenteeism, lack of motivation, or other factors. For example, a student may have poor grades in an art class in school, but have a talent for detailing and painting cars as a hobby or part-time job.

2. Learn about students' hobbies and after-school activities to gain additional insights into students' strengths. Some students may have a talent for science and belong to a young inventors' club, while others may have strong leadership qualities as class presidents or as the organizing forces behind a community activity.

3. When possible, prior to meeting students, talk with family members, teachers, and other school personnel (such as coaches and counselors) who may know the students well. Information gleaned from such interviews may offer important clues to students' learning styles and aptitudes.

4. With adults, read the students' files and talk with the rehabilitation counselor to become familiar with the adults' interests before a home visit or assessment is conducted. During home visits, follow up on areas of particular interest with the adults. Approaches similar to those used with school-age students can be used to explore the interests and aptitudes of adults.

Further research on the nature of a particular visual diagnosis will also indicate how a person with that condition may respond in certain situations. Knowledge of each individual's eye condition and general associated characteristics help O&M specialists

- make curricular choices (like the traditional two-point-touch technique for a functionally blind student versus verification cane techniques for a student who primarily uses vision to navigate the environment),

- select appropriate instructional materials (such as limiting the use of color in map designs for adults with macular degeneration), and

- determine which instructional strategies will be most successful (for instance, moving a familiar target to encourage visual attention from a young child who is cortically visually impaired).

O&M specialists are likely to spend the first one or two lessons talking with and listening to their students. They can ask the students what they think their strengths are, what they like to do in school or on the job, and what leisure-time activities they enjoy. Some students may even tell them how they learn best (for example, "I like to try doing something right away to see how it feels") or what makes it difficult for them to learn (for instance, "I don't like it when it's noisy because it's distracting and I can't concentrate very well").

Having completed all the activities discussed, O&M specialists will have some knowledge of their students' strengths and weaknesses and how these strengths and weaknesses correspond to the eight intelligences. To gain more specific information on each student, they can use the Multiple Intelligences Inventory assessment in Appendix 5.B at the end of this chapter to help determine areas of competence with regard to the eight intelligences. O&M specialists can either complete the inventory based on their observations of a student or include the student in the assessment as a lesson activity.

Teaching Styles

Once the personal and student inventories have been completed, O&M specialists should have a clearer idea of their strongest areas for teaching and the areas in which their students are the most confident. They can also become familiar with strategies that they may have used less frequently, but may be beneficial to try with a particular student or group of students. That information is helpful when considering the range of teaching styles that can be used. For example, an O&M specialist who is weak in musical intelligence could still consider singing to a preschool child to help teach body concepts. Although a wide range of teaching strategies emerge from aptitudes in specific areas of intelligence, a few strategies that may correspond to each of the eight intelligences are highlighted next. Table 5.1 suggests learning activities for each type of intelligence that can be used in teaching various O&M skills

Table 5.1 O&M and the Eight Intelligences

	Cane Skills	Address System	Soliciting Assistance
Linguistic	Recite rhymes or poems while practicing the constant-contact or two-point-touch cane technique	Tell or write the story of how your "travel community" developed	Keep a diary on computer of information learned through telephoning
Musical	Practice wrist movements with the "grip cane" (grip with marshmallow tip on end) on a table to music or metronome	Compose and perform a rap song about address system	Visit a music store and talk with a salesperson about music/musical instruments
Logical-Mathematical	Keep chart for the number of times specific cane skills were used correctly	Alphabetize an address book with information on all the destinations visited in the training area	Complete "How to Find a Specific Destination" sheet for the address book
Spatial	Use arc to compare the width of objects or distance between objects	Use plastic colored acetate over a large-print map to identify even and odd sides of the street	Role-play correct and incorrect positioning when speaking with others; repeat only correct positioning
Bodily-Kinesthetic	Perform feet and leg warm-ups before stair travel	Learn center dividing streets by holding onto and moving along string (interactive model)	Practice appropriate gestures to confirm information when asking for directions

Intersection Analysis	Body Awareness	Visual Efficiency Skills	Maps and Mapmaking	Auditory Training
Select the correct order of cards describing individual procedures for crossing traffic light-controlled intersections	Match body-word cards with body parts by taping card onto body (like Pin the Tail on the Donkey)	Spot on letter targets of different sizes, colors, or fonts	Give an oral report to the class about a map you have made of a certain travel area	Listen to environmental sounds; write what each sound is on a card; use the cards to make sentences
Identify by sound: trucks, cars, buses, and motorcycles	Move the way different music feels: quick/slow, strong/light (or soft); sustained/percussive	Use a monocular to view an orchestra, choir, or band	Write lyrics to recall a route; sing them while traveling	Use a tape recorder to identify, compare, and contrast sounds heard during a lesson
Use a stopwatch to compare the timing of traffic light-controlled intersections	Select hands, arms, or feet to measure different body parts; record the measurements	Assemble a large visual puzzle (of the world, states, continents, and so on)	Use a ruler to make a grid pattern for a map	Count the number of cars passing through streets at a stop sign-controlled intersection
Photograph/draw shapes of different types of traffic light housings and their signals (housings with 3, 4, 5, or 6 lights in them)	Cut out cardboard tracings of the right and left hand and the right and left foot	Visually trace or scan lines or shapes on a target with a monocular	Assemble LEGO pieces to make a map of a real or imaginary place	Identify pictures/shapes of different utility vehicles heard (garbage truck, street cleaner, and so forth)
Play Red Light, Green Light with a group on parallel and perpendicular hallways/pathways	Climb a playground apparatus to strengthen and coordinate arm and leg movements	Learn correct hand/eye/head coordination to use a monocular effectively	Act out a neighborhood block on a rug with props (interactive model)	Practice keeping the feet still while turning the head to hear a traffic surge

(continued)

Table 5.1 *Continued*

	Cane Skills	Address System	Soliciting Assistance
Interpersonal	Walk with another cane traveler—compare what the two canes find along the way	Ask for help to find the correct address	Role-play in a group about how to talk to a bus driver
Intrapersonal	Assess own skill level of specific cane techniques	Find the addresses of places where you may want to work	Determine and use the most effective way for you to get assistance
Naturalist	Notice changes in texture of the environment using a cane	Classify addresses by geographic location or cultural similarities	Collect business cards from various shop owners

and concepts, some of which are described in Appendix 5.A. (See the Index of Activities for additional activities described in this book.)

If O&M specialists have a particular aptitude in *linguistic* intelligence, they can use words effectively to reinforce a student's skill along a route with a walkie-talkie or with O&M words brailled on cards. O&M specialists who are strong in this area may be particularly skilled at crafting clear explanations for a variety of unfamiliar concepts.

O&M specialists with *musical* aptitudes or those who are sensitive to sounds may have students select music they enjoy and play it on a tape recorder while instructing "in-step" and "in-rhythm" cane skills. Those who are strong in this area may enjoy singing to younger students while they practice basic travel skills or develop body-concept awareness. They may also effectively teach their students to use echolocation to assist in negotiating travel environments.

A strong aptitude in *logical-mathematical* intelligence may lead an O&M specialist to make simple models of an escalator to demonstrate

Intersection Analysis	Body Awareness	Visual Efficiency Skills	Maps and Mapmaking	Auditory Training
Play Orientation 20 Questions—a group game about street crossings/ intersections	Play Twister	Play the commercial board game Guess Who?; recognize and choose the same faces	Have a group discussion about route choices in specific travel areas	Play the Marco Polo game
Assess and categorize how other travelers cross intersections: Who are you like?	Look at magazine photos and guess people's emotions	Take a monocular test	Determine which type of map is best for personal use, such as verbal, tactile, or print	Role-play and interpret people's moods by their voice tones
Categorize types of intersection islands by shapes, hardware, and landscaping	Compare/contrast who has the longest, shortest, widest legs, arms, fingers, feet, and so forth	Use a monocular or magnifier to examine objects in the environment	Learn the names of physical features on maps of travel areas (like mountains, rivers, lakes, and oceans)	Visit a zoo and identify animals by their sounds

how the stairs move and then "fold" and where the machinery is that causes the movement. Students could travel on escalators and compare them to traveling on stairways or in elevators. O&M specialists who are strong in this area may be particularly good at finding meaningful ways to teach the use of the address system or how to figure out the timing of bus schedules.

O&M specialists with strengths in *spatial* intelligence may be motivated to design a variety of maps and models for use with their students and to encourage the students to create their own maps with them as the students learn a new campus or travel area. O&M specialists who are strong in this area may also be good at selecting a variety of interesting materials to use when making maps, models, or other teaching props.

O&M specialists who are strong in *bodily-kinesthetic* intelligence recognize the value of presenting much of the O&M curriculum through movement experiences, especially with young children. Inventing movement games, for example, along with rhythms and songs, would be a fun way to help young students learn about the parts of their bodies and the different ways their bodies move. O&M specialists who are strong in this area are likely to have the coordination necessary to demonstrate many of the more intricate cane skills to their students for modeling, whereas those who are not may find it easier to explain a particular motor skill.

O&M specialists who are strong in *interpersonal* intelligence may use peer teaching with their students. One student could leave notes (or a tape) for another student describing how to find a certain destination. Group lessons for students who have similar interests may include traveling together to a certain location or examining something of mutual interest (such as different kinds of fabric at a fabric store or drums sets in a music store).

Intrapersonal intelligence can be promoted by using students' self-evaluations of travel skills or by having students maintain O&M diaries. Career awareness or exploration can easily be incorporated into many O&M lessons. O&M specialists who are strong in this area should find it easy to evaluate the success of their teaching strategies and adapt them as necessary to meet the needs of individual students.

Using *naturalist* intelligence, O&M specialists may assist students in examining natural phenomena (such as a variety of textures of hedges or bushes in a residential area) along travel routes. They may also suggest the development of O&M notebooks to collect interesting items found outdoors or business cards gathered in a shopping mall. O&M specialists may also have collections of objects that can be incorporated as teaching materials for some O&M lessons. Those who are strong in this area may be interested in taking students on hiking or climbing field trips or to tide pools to examine some forms of sea life.

Taking the time to examine personal aptitudes and interests can be a valuable experience for any O&M specialist. Thinking about why one teaches in a certain way and how individual students respond to one's instruction may lead to opportunities to improve one's overall teaching effectiveness. Multiple intelligences theory provides a useful framework for expanding instructional strategies to meet the individual needs of a range of students who are blind or visually impaired. Varied teaching approaches that address multiple intelligences may also help O&M specialists reach students whose learning styles are different from their own.

Thinking about the O&M Curriculum

The eight intelligences provide an alternate or expanded way of looking at the O&M curriculum. O&M specialists can identify skill areas that students with particular aptitudes may excel in or enjoy. They can also anticipate areas that may be challenging for specific students and plan to use instructional styles that support learning and growth in areas of need. To begin with, O&M specialists can look at the O&M curriculum and identify where they are already using one or more of the eight intelligences. For example, using verbal, written, brailled, or recorded words (linguistic skills) enable students to understand and recall specific terms that are important to O&M concepts, such as *block, landmark, shorelining*, or *north.*

Sidebar 5.1 lists the eight intelligences and samples of corresponding O&M skills and competencies for students who are blind or have low vision, taken from the O&M curriculum. These lists can provide O&M specialists with a starting point for examining the O&M curriculum to see how multiple intelligences are incorporated into O&M instruction. O&M specialists can use these examples to help them consider how particular skills and aspects of O&M training depend on each of the intelligences. When they are teaching or remediating a particular skill, they can think over how that skill fits into the multiple intelligences classifications and whether they are taking full advantage of strategies that might correspond with that skill. It is important to keep in mind, however, that many aspects of the O&M curriculum rely on not just one, but several intelligences.

In examining the content of the O&M curriculum from a different perspective, O&M specialists may expand the types of educational experiences they provide to their students. There are endless possible strategies that may fit into the context of the learning environment that will be motivating for both students and specialists.

MATCHING TEACHING AND LEARNING STYLES

As was already indicated, the Multiple Intelligences Inventory in Appendix 5.B provides O&M specialists with important information about designing the content and teaching methods of lessons for students who are blind or visually impaired. Not all O&M specialists have the same strengths and interests as their students. Not all students learn the same way, nor do all O&M specialists teach students with the same strategies.

Sidebar 5.1 O&M Skills and Competencies in the Eight Intelligences

The following list shows examples of O&M skills or competencies for students who are blind or visually impaired that fall into each of Gardner's eight intelligences.

Linguistic

- using specific words to identify body parts (e.g., nose, heel, hip, forearm, and ears)

- demonstrating understanding of directional and positional terms (e.g., "in front of you," "behind the chair," "under the tree")

- learning environmental terms (e.g., "table," "curb," "door," "elevator")

- reviewing O&M vocabulary (e.g., "squaring off," "walk in step," "walk in rhythm")

Musical

- pinpointing the location of a specific car or traffic surge for street crossing alignment

- identifying an auditory cue along a familiar route

- using reflected sounds to negotiate obstacles

- perceiving a change in pitch of a car motor as it accelerates through an intersection

Logical-Mathematical

- sequencing landmarks along a rote route

- finding locations using the address system

- understanding the cause and effect of the intelligent disobedience of a dog guide

- interpreting the output provided by an electronic travel device

- completing an independent drop-off lesson

Spatial

- perceiving the size, shape, and relative proportions of objects in the environment

- recognizing the similarities and differences between two- and three-dimensional maps

- applying information gleaned from visual and tactile maps to follow or design a travel route

- learning simple and complex route shapes (e.g., I, L, U, and Z)

(continued)

Bodily-Kinesthetic

- maintaining efficient posture and gait

- positioning, stabilizing, and focusing a monocular

- coordinating the movement of the cane with one's footsteps to remain "in step"

- estimating the distance walked along a familiar block

Interpersonal

- using appropriate social skills to greet people

- telephoning to gather information about a specific business

- interacting with the bus driver during a route

- soliciting assistance to locate a desired destination

Intrapersonal

- selecting an appropriate "personal" (individual) mobility system (i.e., a long cane, dog guide, monocular, sighted (human) guide, or electronic travel device

- identifying realistic career options to explore in greater detail

- discussing with the instructor when and where the student would feel comfortable using the Hine's break or other methods of refusing assistance

- establishing goals for an Individualized Educational Program (IEP), Individualized Transition Plan (ITP), or Individualized Written Rehabilitation Program (IWRP) in collaboration with the instructor

Naturalist

- sorting items collected along a route in a rural area

- planning a trip to a local park

- finding and classifying types of fences found along a route

- taping birdcalls and identifying types of birds typically heard in a residential area

Assessing teaching and learning styles helps O&M specialists make the best match between the teacher's and student's strengths and weaknesses and between possible teaching approaches and the student's learning style as they adjust and design O&M programs for individual students. In general, lessons that address areas in which both the specialist and student are strong are usually effective and enjoyable for both the student and the specialist. When there is less of an optimal match between their areas of strength, there are a number of ways to address the more difficult material and compensate for areas of weakness in the specialist or the student.

Strong-Strong Match

When the O&M specialist and student have similar strengths in areas of intelligence, the specialist's usual approach to teaching is most likely to be effective and enjoyable for the students. The teaching and learning processes should go "relatively" smoothly because the specialist's natural teaching strategies complement the student's learning styles, communication has a seamless flow, the specialist and student may share similar hobbies or interests, and the specialist's problem-solving solutions are well suited to the student's strengths. For example, if both the O&M specialist and student are strong in linguistic intelligence, they will both respond well to role-playing that involves dialogue, such as role-playing a passenger and a bus driver. If both the student and specialist are strong in logical-mathematical intelligence, then introducing traffic-flow patterns using a logical number sequence will be easy for the specialist to explain and easy for the student to understand. When the specialist and student share similar interests and hobbies, it is easier to build rapport. Problem-solving disorientation scenarios are always a challenge, but when the specialist and student are strong in the same intelligence areas, the solutions just seem to make sense. For example, if both the specialist and student are strong in spatial intelligence, a variety of maps or visual-tactile teaching aids may be effective in regaining orientation.

Strong-Weak Mismatch

If the O&M specialist is strong in certain intelligences but the student is weak, there are several different ways the specialist can approach instruction.

The O&M specialist can initially start instruction in other areas of the O&M curriculum to teach to the student's strengths. When the student shows increased skill and confidence, the O&M specialist can transition to those areas of the curriculum that are more challenging for the student. For example, a student who is weak in logical-mathematical intelligence may not respond well to an introduction to the use of the address system at the beginning of a unit on travel in a light business area. He or she may feel overwhelmed or be easily frustrated with the concepts and consequently not enjoy the new training area. If the student is strong in interpersonal intelligence, he or she could talk to shop and business owners to determine addresses along a certain block and fill in the addresses on a teacher-made map. Later, when the student feels more comfortable in the new area, the O&M specialist could use the map for which the student obtained the addresses to begin to introduce the address numbering system.

The O&M specialist can also make compensations for areas of weakness by using instructional methods or approaches that match a student's learning strengths. For example, if a student has difficulty with spatial skills and tactile map reading but has a strong naturalist intelligence, he or she could concentrate on the use of landmarks (such as unique types of trees) in the residential area. These landmarks could be presented in sequential order as words, pictures on a card, or parts of real objects found along the route and presented in calendar-box form. (A calendar box incorporates the arrangement of real objects that represent activities into a sequence that helps students anticipate daily schedules. For example, a swatch of carpet, representing carpet squares for "circle time," would be the first thing in the box because it would be the first activity of the morning.)

The O&M specialist can provide a rationale for working on areas of weakness. The student and O&M specialist may decide that an area of weakness, such as interpersonal skills, needs to be addressed as part of the curriculum because it is a necessary skill for independent travel. After the student understands why a particular skill is important, even if it is difficult for him or her, the skill can be incorporated into a small part of a lesson, experienced in a simple way, or done with the help of another person (the O&M specialist, a friend, or a family member). For example, a shy student may not be asked initially to interact with the public on lessons, but may first practice asking for information from the O&M specialist. After demonstrating increased verbal skills and self-confidence, the student would then be asked to speak with the public in a nonthreatening situation.

Weak-Strong Mismatch

Knowing that there are areas in which the O&M specialist is weak and the student is strong alerts the O&M specialist that he or she cannot rely on typical teaching strategies. Finding more effective ways to teach students who are stronger than the O&M specialist in a certain area may include

- finding new approaches to teaching,

- learning a new skill that would be useful,

- getting instructional support from other teachers,

- asking the student to assume responsibility for some teaching, and

- using the student's strengths as activity reinforcers.

When working with a student who has a strong logical-mathematical intelligence, for example, an O&M specialist who lacks confidence in this area may need to consider a more analytical approach to teaching the student, one in which questions are asked and answers are discovered within the travel environment. O&M specialists can try to enhance their teaching by learning a new skill (for instance, learning beginning braille on their own) or getting help from someone else to incorporate braille materials within lessons. If the O&M specialist has a weak spatial intelligence, perhaps another O&M specialist can help make maps. Asking a student to help the O&M specialist can be effective and motivating to the student as well. For instance, a student may be more knowledgeable about adaptive computer software than the O&M specialist and can demonstrate how the software is used for making maps or recording information. An O&M specialist can also give a student time at the end of a lesson to enjoy an activity in which the student excels as a reinforcer or reward for a job well done. For example, if the O&M specialist is weak in linguistic intelligence, he or she can give a highly linguistic student time at the end of a class to braille or tape-record in an O&M journal or design an O&M newsletter for the school newspaper.

Weak-Weak Match

Areas in which both the O&M specialist and student are weak still need to be addressed. If it is a skill or concept area that the student needs to know or practice, genuine attempts to teach and learn the skill or concept must be made even if it is uncomfortable for both the student and the specialist. To address these areas of weakness, the O&M specialist needs to explain clearly to the student why the skill or concept is important and how it is relevant to independent travel or important life skills. Then he or she has three options: to make an agreement with the student that they will learn the new skill together, to collaborate with another professional to coteach the skill; or to come up with an alternative approach to teach the skill. For example, if both the O&M specialist and the student are weak in bodily-kinesthetic intelligence and the specialist needs to teach a particular cane skill such as three-point touch that requires a high degree of coordination, he or she can do one or more of the following: (1) practice the skill along with the student; (2) find another student or instructor to demonstrate the skill; or (3) use another intelligence (such as verbal or musical) to teach the skill.

A student who has weak bodily-kinesthetic intelligence and becomes bored easily when practicing cane skills or focusing a monocular still needs to learn how to travel safely using these mobility aids. As was just noted, it is necessary to discuss with the student why a particular skill is needed, even though the skill may be difficult to learn or tedious to practice. For example, Figure 5.3 presents a lesson plan in which the O&M specialist and student are both weak in bodily-kinesthetic intelligence. Rather than use demonstration, drill, and practice to remediate the student's cane skills, the O&M specialist incorporates musical and logical-mathematical strategies (such as singing and measuring) to create a highly motivating lesson in which the student practices cane skills correctly.

On occasion, it may prove useful for O&M specialists to tell students about the learning challenges they experienced, either during school or when they were undergoing sleepshade (blindfold) training. By doing so, the O&M specialists can exhibit empathy and be supportive of the students' efforts to learn difficult skills or concepts. In addition, students and O&M specialists can agree to learn the new skill together (for example, using computer technology to generate large-print maps of a training area if both are weak in logical-mathematical intelligence).

Collaborating with other O&M specialists is another way of teaching an area that is particularly challenging. O&M specialists may chose to do a "student swap" for a period of training, so they can give their students the benefit of learning a skill from another O&M specialist who is strong in a particular area. Alternatively, they may be able to find the

Lesson Plan

Student: _Zach (3rd-grade student with low vision)_

Instructor: _Adam_

Date: _October 17_

Time: _10:30 A.M._

Lesson Location: _the block surrounding the elementary school_

Goal: _To improve orientation skills and expand concept development_

Lesson Objectives:
1. _To examine three objects along the west side of a given block_
2. _To identify the functions of the three objects that are found_
3. _To record information about objects on a tactile map_

Instructional Materials: _"scout pouch" with mapmaking materials inside, tactile map, student's baseball cap_

Methodology/Instructional Strategies:

1. Introduce the lesson by reviewing the east and north sides of the tactile map that Zach created in previous lessons. Let Zach know that he will explore a third side (west) today and have him check the scout pouch to see if he has all the materials he will need (measuring tape, safety scissors, Wikki Stix, magnifier, talking compass, masking tape, small notepad, and pencil).
2. Recite the "Scoutin' Song" while leaving the school:

    We will go a scoutin', my scout pouch 'n me.
    We will go a scoutin', to see what we can see.
    Snip, snip, cut 'n paste, magnifier as well.
    Let's measure all the things we find, so we can go 'n tell.

3. Ask Zach if he thinks the same things found on the east and north sides of the map will be found along the west side of the block. Remind him to use his best cane skills.
4. Along the west side of the block, prompt Zach to the move to the inside or outside of the shoreline, depending on what is there, anticipating that Zach will select the large tree, unusual retaining wall, and mailbox.
5. Encourage Zach to explore the tree. Zach should use tape to measure the diameter of the tree and record information on the notepad. Discuss the functions of the tree (like shade) and have Zach take notes. Zach may chose to cut a leaf or piece of bark to attach to his map.
6. Repeat step 5 for the retaining wall—measuring its height at its tallest point.
7. Repeat step 5 for the mailbox.
8. Return to the class reciting the "Scoutin' Song" and comparing what was found today with what was found in previous lessons. Preview the next lesson on the south side of the block.

Daily Notes:
Zach is strong in musical and logical-mathematical intelligences, so he enjoyed the lesson activities. He is still having trouble staying in step with his cane (he really struggles with the bodily-kinesthetic tasks), but was more willing to work on his cane skills because he was doing so well with the other lesson objectives. Continue to teach to Zach's strengths, but push for more and more attention to cane skills in future lessons. Perhaps he would enjoy measuring his cane arc and gait.

Figure 5.3

Incorporating Musical and Logical-Mathematical Strategies into a Lesson to Improve Cane Skills and Expand Concept Development

time to coteach a series of lessons, thereby giving their students the advantage of learning from both specialists' strengths and allowing the specialists to learn from one another.

Although individual learning and teaching styles provide a way to look at a range of teaching options for students who are blind or visually impaired, when planning instruction, O&M specialists also need to take into consideration all the other personal characteristics that influence a student's ability to learn and participate in lessons, including the student's gender, age, cultural background, and additional disabilities (if any). These factors are discussed in the next section.

ADDITIONAL CONSIDERATIONS

Although it is believed that all individuals have various degrees of potential in each of the eight intelligences (Gardner, 1993), there are additional considerations that may influence how individuals learn and the ultimate effectiveness of various teaching practices. Gender, culture, age, and the presence of additional disabilities can be important factors to consider when developing appropriate instructional programming and the types of teaching activities that O&M specialists may design or select.

Gender

By recognizing the typical gender interests and preferences of same-sex peers, the O&M specialist can explore a range of activities that may be motivating if they are incorporated into O&M lessons. For example, it is common for young men in our culture—including those who are blind or have low vision—to be interested in cars and motorcycles, even when they do not or cannot drive. Therefore, traveling to a used-car lot to compare prices and specifications as part of an O&M lesson could be highly motivating for a young man who likes cars. However, O&M specialists should avoid adopting rigid gender stereotypes in lesson planning, since, for example, young women may also be interested in cars. In addition to interests, O&M specialists should not assume certain capabilities of students that are based on traditional gender stereotypes. Not all male students are gifted in math and science, nor are all female students strong in verbal and interpersonal skills. Not all teenage girls are preoccupied with clothing and makeup, nor are all teenage boys naturally independent and unwilling to ask for assistance. Nevertheless, exploring typical gender-based interests may be a starting point for designing

O&M lessons, including interesting destinations for travel, career roles for exploration, and teaching strategies that will be effective. By recognizing the uniqueness of each student, O&M specialists can judge the degree to which gender-related activities will be motivating to individual students.

Culture

Although it is important to understand and appreciate cultural differences, O&M specialists should not assume that students will behave a certain way if they are from a specific culture. A balance is needed between recognizing and respecting cultural differences and avoiding inappropriate generalizations. For example, in some traditional cultures, families may be protective of their daughters and may not want them to have independent travel experiences at a given age, yet individual families in these cultural groups may not necessarily feel the same way. Talking with a student and her family will enable the O&M specialist to develop an appropriate travel curriculum.

Taking the time to explore each person's unique culture can provide O&M specialists with a source of ideas for O&M lessons that are both motivating and respectful of family values. For example, traveling to a specialty ethnic market in a student's home community may be more motivating and relevant for a child whose family members pride themselves in preparing traditional food than going to a large supermarket. Even reinforcement strategies can be influenced by a student's culture. Some cultures may value group success more than individual achievements, and a student who has been raised with such values may not believe that being singled out for a particular accomplishment is rewarding. In contrast, other students may excel in lessons in which there is competition among peers.

The value attached to any given area of intelligence and resulting product can vary by culture (Gardner, 1993). If a society values skills that stem from one of the intelligences, it will encourage those who are naturally talented in that area, provide them with special training, and encourage them to excel in the field. By determining the skills and products that may be of greatest importance to a student's culture, O&M specialists may be able to assist a student in achieving skills that would complement the family's values and, in turn, bolster his or her self-esteem. For example, if a family's culture highly values scientific achievement, a student who is proficient in planning and using public transportation may gain respect from his family members by planning to travel to an important science exposition.

With thorough planning, awareness of different cultures and appreciation of diversity can be introduced as a by-product of O&M. Independent travel experiences in the community, such as the following, can help to broaden a student's exposure to cultures that are different from his or her own.

- A student with low vision may be able to use a monocular to locate signs written in other languages.

- Exploring a range of ethnic markets or boutiques may increase a student's curiosity about the food or dress traditions of another culture and provide ideas and motivation for future travel destinations.

- Interesting resources on the traditional customs of different cultures obtained through travel to a library or bookstore can be shared with classmates.

- Comparing the architectural styles in different ethnic neighborhoods traveled during O&M lessons may be interesting to some students who have low vision.

Interpersonal skills will assist O&M specialists in understanding and appreciating cultural differences among students who are blind or visually impaired. Cultural differences may even influence a family's acceptance of, coping with, and expectations for a son or daughter who has a disability. These differences also affect how students learn and progress in their O&M skills and may have an impact on the type of follow-through that will be provided in the home for skills that are learned. For example, if a family of a particular cultural group values musical skills and abilities, then independent travel may seem more culturally relevant if it is tied to getting to a music lesson or music store, and family members may be enthusiastic about practicing an O&M route that leads to such a destination. Sensitivity to diversity should be taken into account when selecting teaching strategies and developing O&M curricula that will ultimately be culturally relevant.

Age

Age is often a determining factor in selecting an appropriate O&M curriculum for students. Although there can be wide variations in the selection of various aspects of the curriculum, it is common to teach the following aspects to the following age groups:

- Preschool age: body awareness, basic skills, and school orientation

- Elementary age: residential environmental concepts and related travel skills

- Teenagers: independent travel in light business areas, the independent use of public transportation, and the use of good interpersonal skills in asking for assistance in shopping and business areas

- Adults with acquired vision loss: the entire O&M curriculum in sequence or selected areas based on critical needs

- Elderly people: travel in the home neighborhood, the use of public transportation and paratransit options, and critical skills necessary to remain independent or semi-independent in the home.

These portions of the O&M curriculum are only general parameters and were selected to illustrate how age differences may affect teaching. Program planning and expectations should be based on individual students' abilities and readiness for learning experiences.

As was stated earlier, identifying a student's learning style or styles is helpful in finding teaching approaches and activities that are motivating. Pairing this information with considerations of the age appropriateness of various activities often results in greater success. Gardner (1993) identified different learning formats that are typical for three specific age groups:

- Young children tend to learn through repetitive experiences and are able to copy or imitate certain patterns or abilities within the intelligences. For example, they can copy a rhythm from a song that they are familiar with.

- School-age children start to formalize the use of symbols and are increasingly exposed to and successful with notational systems.

- Adolescent and adult learning is typically oriented toward career exploration and development.

Additional Disabilities

Many students who are blind or visually impaired have additional disabilities, ranging from mild to moderate to severe. An additional disability may be secondary to the visual impairment or the primary disability that presents more significant challenges than the visual impairment. It may be present at birth or may develop later, either as a temporary or permanent condition, and may be stable or change over time. Some additional disabilities affect individuals' sensory and motor channels, but not necessarily their ability to reason or to communicate, whereas others, in which the brain has been affected, have an impact on the way students move, their ability to orient themselves, and their ability to express themselves and interact with others.

When considering teaching approaches for students with additional disabilities, O&M specialists need to use the most appropriate sensory and learning channels. Blind or visually impaired students with additional sensory or motor impairments should be taught according to their strongest intelligences. For example, in working with a gifted student with low vision who uses a walker for mobility, an O&M specialist can use linguistic, logical-mathematical, spatial, musical, intrapersonal, and interpersonal intelligences to teach spatial orientation, visual efficiency skills, the use of low vision aids, skills for information gathering and interacting with the public, and understanding of traffic patterns.

If one sensory channel, like hearing, cannot be used, others can be substituted. For example, as Gardner (1993) noted, Helen Keller, who was unable to use her vision or hearing, was taught primarily through her sense of touch. Her linguistic intelligence was expressed not through aural speech but through finger spelling—signing the letters of the manual alphabet and recognizing and decoding the signs when they were pressed into her palm—her bodily-kinesthetic intelligence. Gardner identified Keller's teacher, Anne Sullivan, as being particularly gifted in interpersonal intelligence because of her ability to understand Keller's moods, motivations, intentions, and desires without a shared spoken language. This sensitivity enabled Sullivan to seek the most effective methods for communicating with Keller from the beginning. O&M specialists may commonly work with students who have dual sensory impairments or expressive language limitations. These students may use sign language, finger spelling, tactile signing, gestures, object cues, tangible symbol systems, written or pictorial forms of communication, or electronic communication boards of various kinds. Communicating information about a destination or route ahead of time may involve written, taped, or pictorial cues, as well as gestures.

A wheelchair user typically receives less bodily-kinesthetic input, especially if an assistant manually operates the wheelchair. A visually impaired individual who uses a wheelchair may gain additional bodily-kinesthetic feedback by using a long cane (as appropriate) to clear the surface immediately beyond the wheelchair and to examine the environment. Turns can be perceived more accurately by the individual who is being pushed in a wheelchair if he or she places a hand on the turning wheel or if the assistant exaggerates the movement of turns.

Physical prompting may be necessary to assist some students in learning specific routes. For some students who have limited expressive and receptive language, teaching a rote route may be done primarily through their bodily-kinesthetic and musical intelligences. Students may learn best if they are physically prompted through a route many times while "cue words" of familiar landmarks (such as "bumpy tiles," "breezeway," or "west wing") along the route are repeated in a consistent manner. Familiar objects (tactile cues) that are easily associated with a travel destination (like a milk carton associated with the route to the cafeteria) or a series of tactile cues found along a route can also be presented to the student in the order in which they will be found, like a map (Joffee & Rikhye, 1991). Sounds, especially if they are consistently present, should be pointed out to the student while traveling. Other cues, like changes in texture, a gradient (ramps or stairs), or olfactory landmarks (smells from a cafeteria or photocopying room) are important to point out to the student as well. Frequent physical repetition of a route, along with these other cues, may foster some students' motor memory and ability to learn specific independent routes. When possible, other teachers, staff, and students should be encouraged to reinforce route skills to promote independence, rather than to enable dependence by guiding students along routes they can complete themselves. If students can execute a route but are unable to solve problems through the use of their linguistic, logical-mathematical, and spatial intelligences when they become disoriented, they may require verbal or physical prompts. Students who are semi-independent route travelers need to be monitored by someone else as they travel along a route by themselves or as part of a group. Figure 5.4 is an example of a lesson plan that makes use of interpersonal strategies, such as describing landmarks to classmates,

Lesson Plan

Student: _Daisy (age 21, low vision with cognitive delays)_

Instructor: _Bryan_

Date: _January 19_

Time: _11:15 A.M._

Lesson Location: _familiar residential and light business areas_

Goal: _To improve semi-independent travel skills and community awareness_

Lesson Objectives:
1. _To identify and describe three given landmarks along a familiar route_
2. _To request sighted assistance at street crossings without the O&M specialist's prompting_
3. _To use money appropriately to make a purchase_

Instructional Materials: _recipe box with mobility terms, tape recorder and tape, student's wallet, hat and tints for glare_

Daily Notes:

Daisy isn't usually very observant of her surroundings (she's weak in the naturalist area), and so having her describe landmarks to classmates was very effective (met this objective). Daisy is very strong in interpersonal intelligence and loves to talk. She enjoyed the tape recording. She needed a prompt to ask for assistance at the second crossing. At the store, she allowed the clerk to take the money from her hand and did not pay much attention. Need to address this issue in the next individual lesson.

Methodology/Instructional Strategies:

1. _Come early to Daisy's community-based instruction (CBI) class to review the lesson objectives. Review Daisy's purchase items by listening to the tape recording that she made of her teacher requesting items for a bake sale. Tell her we will tape-record her at the end of the lesson telling what she was able to purchase and how much it cost._
2. _Role-play the use of money to make a purchase as a review._
3. _Ask Daisy if she is ready for the class trip (cane, hat, tints)._
4. _Ask Daisy to find the "landmark" file from the O&M recipe box of mobility terms. Have her pull out four cards (such as size, shape, texture, and color) and read them. Daisy can select one of the four cards. This is the way she must describe each of the three landmarks along the route. Tell her she can describe them to a classmate who will guess what the landmark is._
5. _Review expectations for street crossings and how Daisy will ask for assistance from a teacher or assistant._
6. _Check with the CBI teacher to see if there are any concerns for the class trip._
7. _Allow Daisy to walk with her classmates and monitor her cane skills from a distance. Move closer at intersections. Monitor Daisy's interactions at the store from a close distance._
8. _Note how Daisy describes landmarks to her classmate._
9. _At the end of the class, tape-record her presentation to the class of the items that she purchased (items purchased, how much they cost, and the change that she received)._
10. _Save the tape to listen to at the next individual O&M lesson._
11. _Say good-bye to Daisy and thank the CBI teacher for helping with the objectives._

Figure 5.4

Using Interpersonal Strategies to Improve Semi-independent Travel Skills and Community Awareness for a Student with Cognitive Delays

to reinforce travel skills and community awareness of a student with low vision and cognitive delays. The O&M specialist works collaboratively with this student's teacher to reinforce the student's semi-independent travel skills and to increase her community awareness.

When considering approaches for teaching students who are blind or visually impaired and have additional disabilities, O&M specialists should use the most appropriate learning channels when possible.

Once O&M specialists have assessed their students' curricular needs and learning styles and planned teaching strategies that will best motivate their students and help them learn as thoroughly as possible, they need to consider another important factor: where to teach the students. The next chapter considers ways of finding the most appropriate training environments.

Descriptions of O&M Activities, Sample Forms, and Materials Categorized According to the Eight Intelligences

This appendix presents a sample of activities, forms, and materials that capitalize on each of Gardner's eight intelligences to teach a variety of O&M skills and concepts. Although the activities are categorized according to the intelligences that they focus on, many of them can be used in more than one area of intelligence. Activities and samples can be adapted for use with a variety of students who are blind or visually impaired, including those who have additional disabilities. The following is a list of the activities in this appendix; additional activities are listed throughout the book and can be found in the Index of Activities at the end of this book.

Linguistic
Rhymes and Poems for Cane Skills
O&M Recipe Box
Book in a Bag

Musical
The Parallel Nearside Song
Cheers and Chants about Monocular Skills
Tape-Recorded Verbal Maps
Address Rap

Logical-Mathematical
How to Find a Specific Destination
Treasure Hunt
Danger Points and Traffic Pattern Quizzes

Spatial
Address Grid
Pictures of Traffic Light Housings
Cardboard Shoe Organizer

Bodily-Kinesthetic
Stair Travel Warm-ups
Interactive Models
Grip Cane and Wrist Practice

Interpersonal
"Guess Who?" Game
Intersection Analysis
Bus Travel Trivia
Mobility Rap Group

Intrapersonal
"And How Do You Cross?" Game
Monocular Quiz
Bus Information Forms

Naturalist
O&M Scrapbook
Identifying Tape-Recorded Natural and Man-made Sounds
Mobility Adventures with Sherlock Holmes

LINGUISTIC APPROACH

Rhymes and Poems for Cane Skills

Ages: Preschool to early elementary school; students with multiple disabilities

Description: For the rhymes and poems indicated in this section, recite with or without your own invented tune, or choose a song you like and invent words for it to help teach a skill. If the tunes are difficult for you, add variety without singing by speaking softly and then more loudly, slowly and then more quickly, or with exaggerated inflection. Use rhythms often as you teach and physically prompt the skills and as the child demonstrates them in practice without physical prompting. Tape-record the child saying the rhymes and send the tape home or share it with the child's class.

Learning about the Cane

THIS IS THE CANE THAT _____ HAS

(adapted from "This Is the House that Jack Built"; substitute the child's name for "Jack")

This is the *cane* that _____ has.
Here's the *elastic*, so thick and long, that goes on the cane
    that _____ has.
Here's the *grip* you find and feel, that surrounds the elastic,
    so thick and long, that goes on the cane that _____ has.
Here's the *shaft* so smooth and strong, that touches the grip
    you find and feel, that surrounds the elastic, so thick
    and long, that goes on the cane that _____ has.
Here's the *tip*, all red and white, that holds the shaft, so
    smooth and strong, that touches the grip you find and
    feel, that surrounds the elastic, so thick and long, that
    goes on the cane that _____ has.
This is the cane. This is the cane. *This is the cane that* _____ *has!*

Keeping the Cane Down on the Ground

KEEPING THE TIP DOWN

Tip down, touch the ground.
Tip down, touch the ground.

Down, down, down on the ground.
Cane tip, cane tip, down on the ground.

Centering Hand and Cane

CENTERING THE CANE

Buckle, buckle, *belt* buckle.
Center your hand on the *belt* buckle.
Buckle, buckle, *belt* buckle.

Cane out front by the *belt* buckle.
Buckle, buckle, *belt* buckle.

Center my cane, center my cane,
Center my cane by the *belt* buckle!

Maintaining the Arc

MAKING THE ARC

Shoulder to shoulder, shoulder to shoulder.
That's where my [your] arc should go.
Shoulder to shoulder, shoulder to shoulder.
My [your] arc goes to and fro!

Constant-Contact Technique

CONSTANT CONTACT CANE

Sweep, sweep, sweep [the, my, your] cane
From side to side we go.
Keep the cane in front of you,
Tip on the ground so low!
[or, Down on the ground so low!]

Two-Point-Touch Technique

TWO-POINT-TOUCH CANE

Tap, tap, tippity tap
My cane tip is tapping.
(repeat)

Tippity, tippity, tippity, tapping, tappity, tappity, tip!

Variations: Similar rhymes can be created for learning protective techniques, trailing, and any number of body and spatial concepts.

O&M Recipe Box

Ages: Elementary and middle school; students with multiple disabilities

Description: This is a large recipe box (one that takes 5 X 7-inch index cards is a good size) with dividers that can be arranged in any order. Section dividers are labeled according to the O&M curriculum and skills:

Orientation, Mobility, Basic Travel Skills, Information Gathering, Types of Signs, Types of Maps, and so forth. Each section contains cards with specific information from the O&M curriculum. Each card has one piece of information written and brailled on it. More recipe cards can be added to or taken away from the files at any time, depending on a student's needs. These cards can be used when new information is being introduced, explained, or reinforced or new skills are being practiced. The O&M Recipe Box is portable, so the O&M specialist can share it with students in several locations.

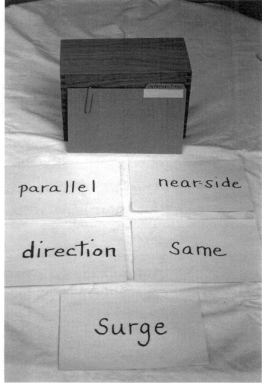

Photo 5.1

In the recipe box (*left*) activity cards containing one piece of information are placed behind each divider in random order. New dividers and cards can be added at any time. The file section shown here (*right*) is Intersections. Each of the file cards has one word describing a concept used when teaching and learning about street crossings at traffic light-controlled intersections. Students may be asked to put this group of cards in a logical order when analyzing an intersection.

Examples of the Section Contents

Orientation File Cards

Body references

Spatial references

Environmental references

Route shapes

Landmarks

Cardinal compass directions

Street names

Basic information from the address system

Questions for soliciting assistance

Mobility File Cards

Names of street and traffic hardware

Traffic pattern terminology

Different kinds of stop sign-control intersections (with 1-, 2-, 3-, and 4-way tactile stop sign shapes)

Different kinds of traffic light shapes (tactile cutouts can be made for traffic lights with 3, 4, 5, and 6 lights) and tactile intersection shapes

Information-Gathering File Cards

Questions like

"Please tell me what . . . ?"

"How . . . ?"

"When . . . ?"

"Where . . . ?"

"Who . . . ?"

Variations: Any of the information on these cards can be presented in pictorial form, with the picture on one side and the word on the other side. A similar format with an emphasis on organizing route directions, bus routes, or travel-related phone numbers could be used with adults and seniors.

Examples of the Ways These Cards Can Be Used

1. The students select several cards from the Orientation file by reading them or selecting them "unseen" (these are references that they have used before). The O&M instructor gives the route for that lesson using these references only.

2. The students select a section and choose several cards from that file. The purpose of the lesson is to find the items on each card, learn about them, and discuss why they are important.

3. Use the cards at the beginning, middle, or end of the lesson to remind the students of the focus of the lesson.

4. Use the files as a curricular guide. The students study all the cards of a particular section (for instance, all the characteristics of a landmark) before they move to the next, more advanced file (such as using compass cardinal directions).

Book in a Bag

Ages: Elementary school; students with multiple disabilities

Description: This activity uses a series of tactile "pages" made of foamboard with layers of tagboard and LEGO pieces glued on top to portray a landscape. The changes in the successive pages suggest a story line about the growth of a city, based on a script the O&M specialist and student have improvised. (The "pages" are kept in order in a bag, hence "Book in a Bag.") As the LEGO city becomes progressively more developed, the improvised story can be used to teach the concepts of blocks, streets, and intersections and their interrelationships. The "book" also teaches beginning map-reading skills, since it begins with a blank "page," and each page adds one or more tactile pieces of information. The following description of the pages shows how the O&M specialist can help the student improvise a story while teaching the requisite concepts:

Page 1. The story starts a long time ago (with a blank page). The student imagines and can act out what it is like to travel through four different environments (the northwest part is a

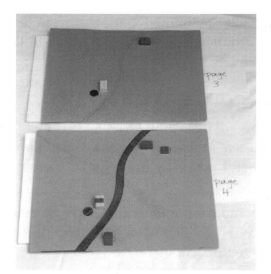

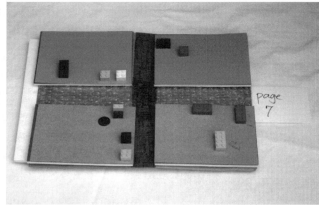

Photo 5.2

A "Book in a Bag," consisting of foamboard "pages," with tagboard, LEGOs, and other materials glued on to make tactile illustrations, is used to teach concepts of blocks, streets, and intersections and beginning map-reading skills. Early pages (*left*) show the beginnings of a small community with only a few houses and one small crooked footpath. As the story progresses to page 7 (*top right*), the community has grown. At the end of the story (*bottom right*), a metropolitan city has risen with numerous intersections and blocks and a freeway.

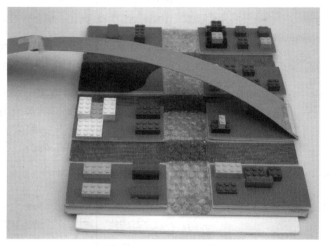

small mountain, the northeast part is a forest, the southwest part has a pond, and the southeast part is an open field). The student is "alone" to enjoy all the adventures of the country.

Page 2. The student "builds" a small house (a yellow 6-dot LEGO) and a wishing well (a penny) while continuing to roam around the "page" hiking, climbing, swimming, and running. At the end of each page, the student might like to repeat the refrain:

"And then it was time to go to bed. ——— [student's name] tossed a penny in the wishing well and made a silent wish [student makes a wish] and climbed into bed. And the days went by, and the days went by, and the days went by, and then, one day . . . "

Page 3. A friend comes to this special place and builds a cabin in the woods. The two run back and forth between their houses, forming a tiny, crooked north–south footpath.

Pages 4–6. The story continues, with more friends and more buildings of various kinds, horses or bicycles giving way to carriages and cars as the village grows.

Page 7. The two crooked intersecting streets are straightened out—some of the buildings have to be taken down for this—and four rectangular blocks are formed. The tactile streets are made of plastic screening and plastic bubble wrap.

Page 8. As the city grows, more streets are made, and finally one sees part of a busy city. There is now a park where the forest once was, a high school complex where the field was, a hospital near the pond, and high-rise apartments on the mountain. The historic well [penny] has been in the same place since page 2, but this landmark is now covered over on page 8 to build more streets.

Page 9. The last page shows part of a metropolitan city with numerous intersections and blocks. A freeway bridge is built of tagboard, and the houses are torn down. Only the original "historic" house (the yellow 6-dot LEGO) is saved by the Historical Society, preserved for the community.

Prompt the student to find new items on each page, noting how the landscape has stayed the same or changed. Review the location of the streets and how they have changed over "the years" owing to increased traffic. Encourage the student to make up reasons why and how the various changes on each page have taken place. Remind the student that this story illustrates how many cities are formed.

Variations: In order to teach young students the concepts of street, block, and intersection, it is best to start the story with a path that eventually widens with use into a road, an intersecting path that also becomes a road, and the addition of more parallel streets and the gradual straightening of the streets to form rectangular blocks. However, students and instructor can create their own landmarks, place any sort of objects on the blocks to represent buildings and other structures, and imagine their own history. The Book in a Bag format can also be used to teach the real history of a specific area.

MUSICAL APPROACH

The Parallel Nearside Song

Ages: Elementary school

Description: Students who like to sing will enjoy this song to help learn about the concept of parallel near-side traffic and how to use this traffic when crossing at traffic light-controlled intersections.

THE PARALLEL NEARSIDE

(sung to the tune of "K . . . K . . . K . . . Katie")

The parallel nearside
is my choice of car,
Helps protect me from the traffic near and far.
The parallel nearside
makes a special "wall,"
When I cross no cars at all will make me fall!

The parallel nearside
is my choice you see,
Gives me time to cross as safely as can be.
The parallel nearside
is what I wait for,
That great big surge I hope I'll hear to cross once more!

Variations: Students can add their own verses about parallel farside or perpendicular traffic patterns to the same tune or to another one. The information in the songs needs to be accurate, since it helps them recall what they need to know when preparing to cross at a traffic light-controlled intersection.

Cheers and Chants about Monocular Skills

Ages: Elementary to middle school

Description: Cheerleading-style chants can help students remember their focusing, tracing, and scanning monocular skills.

For Tracing Horizontally Sideways, Left to Right

MONOCULAR TRACING CHEER NUMBER 1

Trace, trace!
Keep the pace!
Moving left, moving right.
Keep it focused and fight team fight!

For Tracing Horizontally Lengthwise, Near to Far

MONOCULAR TRACING CHEER NUMBER 2

Forward and back
Keep on track!
Forward and back
You got the knack!
Fight team fight and lead the pack!

For Scanning in Either Direction

MONOCULAR SCANNING CHEER NUMBER 3

Scan man, yes you can!
Scan man, yes you can!
Sweep, turn, sweep some more
C'mon team, increase that score!

Variations: Encourage the students to make up their own chants-cheers using monocular terms based on the names of their schools or various activities they like. Similar cheers, chants, songs, and raps can be developed to reinforce other skills.

Tape-Recorded Verbal Maps

Ages: Any age

Description: Students who are strong in musical intelligence may also have keen auditory skills and enjoy listening to different sounds. A tape-recorded verbal map can be made with a combination of verbal directions and information and tape recordings of various sounds commonly found at specific points along the way. The students can create their own maps and share them with others to see if the directions are clear enough to follow. They can guess what the auditory cues may be along the way. The students can also use verbal maps to review routes prior to travel.

Address Rap

Ages: Junior high and high school

Description: Students who listen to contemporary rap music will enjoy learning about the address system by making up their own address rap, as in this example. (See Lesson 7 in Chapter 2 for an example of a lesson in which a rap is used.)

FIRST AND MAIN RAP*

(to the beat of Queen: "We Will We Will Rock You")

Come on everybody let's go downtown
Where the beginning of the address system can be found
You can walk, you can wheel, or you can use your cane
'Till you find the intersection of First and Main.

First and Main, First and Main, First and Main,
     First and Main
"Are you insane?" It's just First and Main.
I said, "Are you insane?" It's just First and Main.
What's so special 'bout First and Main?

You've got 100 North, 100 South, 100 East, and 100 West
100 North Main, 100 South Main, 100 East 1st, 100 West 1st

You see there's nothin' plain about First and Main
There's nothin' plain about First and Main
It all starts here at First and Main
It all starts here at First and Main
First and Main, First and Main, First and Main,
     First and Main.

[fade out]

Source: By Bryan C. Klinesteker, O&M specialist, Los Angeles Unified School District, © 1997. Reproduced with permission.

LOGICAL-MATHEMATICAL APPROACH

How to Find a Specific Destination

Ages: Middle school, high school, and adults

Description: Students need to know what kinds of questions to ask friends, relatives, or other individuals to find an unfamiliar destination. It is helpful for them to learn these questions during O&M lessons when they can practice with their O&M specialists. The How to Find a Specific Destination Form (see Figure 5A.1) helps students learn what a destination is, what it looks like, and where it is located. To find the information to fill out the form, a student can ask (1) the O&M specialist, (2) another O&M student during the lesson, or (3) friends and family members (about the home neighborhood). The student should record the information in the most appropriate medium. Students can ask a clerk, business owner, or cashier for business cards to attach to the form. The information can also be put into an address book to be shared by all the students. This form is a helpful organizer for students when they are working in light business areas.

When they first use the destination form, the students are at the destination and read from the form. They request information about the location and appearance of the destination and how to use cars or public transportation to reach the destination. Students tape-record or braille (using a slate and stylus or Braille Lite) what is being said to them by the person they are questioning. If the students have low vision, they can write down the information on a large card or sheet of paper. They can then go inside the destination, if it is a business or public building like a library, to look around, make a purchase, or talk to the staff. The students should be encouraged to collect business cards, menus, notices, advertisements or other pertinent information from the destinations they find. This type of information, along with the completed form with answers, can be put in individual three-ring clear plastic sheet protectors and kept in the student's O&M notebook or portfolio. If the student uses braille, the sheet protector itself can be inserted into the brailler and all the taped information can be brailled directly onto it.

Variations: The students can put their plastic sheet protectors with the information into a common address book and share their information this way.

How to Find a Specific Destination

Name of destination (ask for a business card): _____

Address: _____

_____

Telephone number: _____

Hours: _____

Description (size, shape, color, doorways, landscaping, stairways, gradient changes):

_____

_____

Location (if midblock):
(next to …, across the street from …, above/below …, nearby landmarks are …)

_____

_____

Location (if near the corner):
(next to …, intersection name, type of intersection, cardinal compass directions)

_____

_____

Traveling by Car
(general area of the city, name and cardinal compass directions of the nearest intersection, cardinal compass directions of the side of the street where located, parking locations):

_____

_____

_____

Traveling by Public Transportation
(bus or route number nearest the destination, street traveled on, location of bus stop, distance from bus stop to the destination, how to get to the destination from the bus stop):

_____

_____

_____

Figure 5A.1

How to Find a Specific Destination

Treasure Hunt

Ages: Elementary school; students with multiple disabilities; can be adapted for adults

Description: In Treasure Hunt, the student has to figure out a secret message to find a treasure (such as a toy, markers, Wikki-Stix, a blank tape or music tape, batteries for a tape recorder or CD player, a fancy hair clip, a McDonald's coupon for lunch, or an envelope with a few dollars in it to spend during the next O&M lesson, depending on the student's age and interests). The secret message can be anything to indicate where the treasure is. There are two versions of the Treasure Hunt: Version A, for young students who are blind or have low vision, who will simply be given directions to follow, and Version B, for older students with low vision who can read. Adults and seniors who enjoy crossword puzzles may also like activities similar to this one. Version A reinforces listening skills, simple spatial concepts and orientation skills, and basic cane skills, such as grip and arc. Version B facilitates practice of monocular skills and reinforces knowledge of environmental hardware and spatial concepts.

Version A

The student receives a brief letter each lesson from a mythical person (the O&M specialist) with commands to help the student find a surprise located somewhere along a route. The O&M specialist can read the messages to the student in a robot voice or other mysterious manner or can use a walkie-talkie to read the letter or even to give commands along the route. Letters include reminders about mobility skills as well as information on orientation, as in the following example:

> Commander X indicates that you are to trail past the second wall and then turn left. She is selecting students who have good cane arc skills to locate her Gem Treasures. Be alert! Be aware! Don't be square!

The surprise hidden along the way or at the end of the route may be jacks, marbles, baseball cards, LEGOs, beads, or anything the student likes, can collect, and/or share with the class. (The original idea was given to Mark Winnick, 1995, and adapted by him.)

Version B

The student is given a Treasure Hunt card with blank spaces corresponding to a secret message (as in the game Hangman), which, when completed, tells the student in a phrase or short sentence where to find a prize or treasure. (Each blank is labeled with the number of the corresponding clue.) At each lesson, the student gets another card containing directions for a specific route and instructions to locate a specific sign at the destination. This card also contains one or more numbers, and the student is directed to find the letters in the sign that correspond to those numbers. Then the student uses these letters to fill in the blanks on the Treasure Hunt card and begins to decipher the secret message. Over several lessons, the student is asked to gather more letters from various street, parking, or store signs and fill them in on the rest of the blank lines to complete the secret message. The goal of the last lesson is for the student to find, play with, and share the treasure as appropriate.

For example, suppose the treasure is located above one of the file cabinets in the main office of the school. In the first lesson of Treasure Hunt, the student receives two cards. The first one gives instructions to go to a certain corner along a given route and locate the street name-sign using a monocular. The number on the card is 2, so the student finds the second letter on the sign. The street name is "LAPEND DRIVE" so the letter is "A." The student fills in the letter "A" in the corresponding spots on the Treasure Hunt card above the number 1.

The second card contains the letter 5, so the student finds the fifth letter of the same street sign and fills in this letter, "E" above the 2 on the Treasure Hunt Card, as in the following example:

A __ __ __ E   __ __ __ E   __ A __ __ __ E __
1 5 10 11 2   7 3 8 2   6 1 5 4 4 2 9

At the beginning of the second lesson, the student is assigned a route and uses a monocular to find and read a PARKING IN BACK sign painted on the side of a building. Card number 3 instructs the student to fill in the fifth letter of the sign above 3, the "I." The next card asks the student to find and fill in the entire second word in the sign, "IN," above 4. The fifth card asks for the first letter of the last word in the sign above 5, the "B," and the last card asks for the third letter of the last word in the sign above 6, the "C." During the next lesson, the student travels a route to a fast-food restaurant, goes inside, and uses the monocular to locate menu words. The O&M specialist assists the student to find FRENCH FRIES on an overhead menu board ("the third word from the top in the center section under the LUNCH menu"). The O&M specialist tells the student to find the first letter of the first word and fill the letter in above 7 on the Treasure Hunt card, the "F." The O&M specialist orders a drink for the student and asks him or her to sit down at the table to scan some more. The O&M specialist prompts the student to use the monocular while seated at the table to find the letter "L." The student reads the word (Lunch Menu), and fills in "L" above 8 on the card. Then the student finds the DRINKS part of the overhead menu to read the word "T" and finds the letter "T." This letter goes above the 9 on the card, so the Treasure Hunt card now reads:

```
A B _ _ E   F I L E   C A B I N E T
1 5     2   7 3 8 2   6 1 5 4 4  2 9
```

The words "file cabinet" are now complete. The O&M specialist prompts the student, if needed, to guess what "A B _ _ E" is and asks the student to complete the Treasure Hunt card with the letters "O" and "V." The O&M specialist then brainstorms with the student about the secret message and where the "file cabinet" may be located.

In the fourth and final lesson, the student finds the treasure. Before the beginning of the next lesson, the O&M specialist explains to the office staff what the lesson will be and hides the treasure. The O&M specialist then takes the student to the main office and prompts the student to ask questions to find the treasure using the secret message "above file cabinet." The O&M specialist gives the student time to tell his or her friends about the treasure (if appropriate) or discusses when the student will enjoy the treasure. If the treasure is money, the O&M specialist and student discuss where to go for the next O&M lesson so that the student can spend the money.

Variations: For Version B, the student with low vision can work together with a student who is functionally blind to find the treasure together. The student with low vision uses the monocular while the student who is functionally blind is in charge of the route and/or filling in the blank letters on the Treasure Hunt card using a slate and stylus.

Danger Points and Traffic Pattern Quizzes

Ages: Upper elementary, middle school, high school, and adults

Description: A simple diagram of a basic plus-shaped intersection of streets with two lanes and with four clearly identified corners can be used to create quizzes in which students are asked to mark the diagram to show their understanding of various related concepts, such as the sequence of "danger points" encountered when crossing streets in a clockwise or counterclockwise direction or to show the direction of vehicles in various traffic patterns (T. Fields, personal communication, 1992). Each quiz uses a separate diagram. Directions could be as follows:

Danger Point Quiz

A. Draw in the four danger points encountered when only crossing clockwise. Number them 1 through 4. Use an arrow to show the direction in which you are crossing.
B. Draw in the four danger points encountered when only crossing counterclockwise. Number them 1 through 4. Use arrows to show the direction in which you are crossing.

Traffic Pattern Quiz

Draw in four cars at this intersection, all going in a different direction. Use arrows to show the direction in which each car might go. (Make sure students turn the cars into the correct lanes.)

Variations: The quizzes can be completed as a small group or in teams, providing students with opportunities to explain to one another why they think they may be correct.

SPATIAL APPROACH

Address Grid

Ages: Middle school, high school, and adults

Description: A tactile/low vision aid to teach the address system. Students begin with an 18 x 24-inch corkboard and tape pieces of string or yarn at the edges of the board to form the two center dividing streets of the address system. They then put in four rectangles of different textures to represent the four quadrants formed by the center dividing streets. Students with low vision recognize these quadrants because they are two different

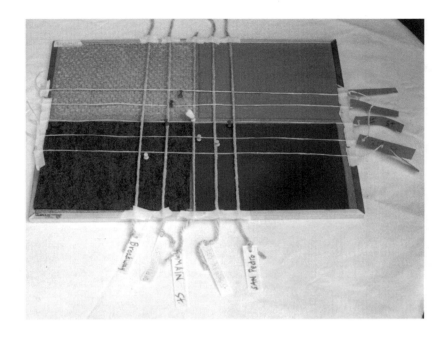

Photo 5.3

A tactile address grid, made with simple materials by the student and O&M specialist, can be used to teach the address system to students who are blind or have low vision.

colors (green and beige) and two different textures (rough and smooth). For students who are functionally blind, the top of the board, (where "north" is) can be placed on a book, so that it is slightly raised and higher than the lower "south" part of the board. The students then recognize the quadrants because of the two different textures and the higher and lower levels of the board. In succeeding lessons, more string or yarn is added to form surrounding streets, and push pins are used to indicate various locations (specific blocks like the 200 or 300 block; the beginning, middle, or end of a certain block; even and odd sides of the street; or individual address numbers). Each street has its name written or brailled on a card that is attached to one of the ends of the string or yarn.

Variations: O&M specialists can plan a field trip to the center of the city or town where they are working with their students. They can prepare a series of small cards with information learned from the corkboard, so the students have tactile/visual aids as they are crossing the center dividing streets and learning about how the address system works.

Pictures of Traffic Light Housings

Ages: Elementary school through adults

Description: Students with low vision recognize the shapes of traffic light housings more quickly and easily if they know ahead of time what

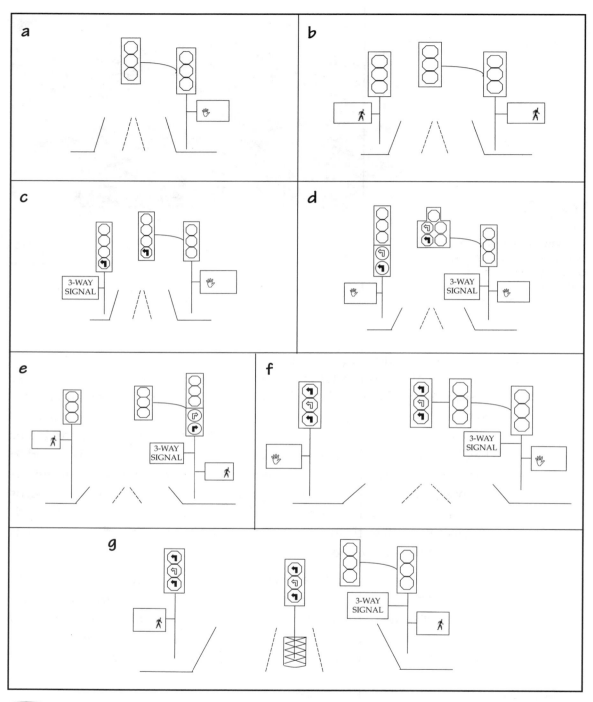

Figure 5A.2

Types of Traffic Light Housings

These illustrations of various types of traffic light housings can be enlarged and used to teach students to recognize the shapes they will see before they encounter them in real traffic situations.

to look for. Understanding the variety of traffic lights and how they work helps them learn about traffic patterns and when to cross intersections. Students can use the accompanying diagrams (see Figure 5A.2) to compare the shape, size, and positioning of the simpler traffic lights ("triplets" have three lights) with the ones that have left/right turn arrows ("quads" with four, "fivers" with five, and "six packs" with six lights either together or in two housings next to each other). They can focus, scan, or trace with their monoculars more efficiently having seen on the samples where the traffic lights are in relation to the corner and intersecting streets (on a vertical or horizontal pole; to the right, center, or left of the intersection; or on a center island).

Variations: Adapt the pictures by enlarging them and using them as samples to make the individual traffic light housings and their lights tactile. A "triplet" would be a rectangle with three circles, with one of them (the red, for example) the thickest; the yellow, less thick; and the green, the thinnest. Arrows can be indicated on the circles with glue or another form of raised line. Students who are unable to see the traffic lights can use these tactile samples when learning about different types of intersections, their traffic patterns, and when to cross. Pedestrian signals and their boxes can also be illustrated in the same tactile manner.

Cardboard Shoe Organizer

Ages: Elementary school; students with multiple disabilities

Description: The O&M specialist purchases a cardboard shoe organizer and assembles it so there are a series of cubicles, each one intended for one shoe. A variety of interesting objects can be placed in and removed from selected cubicles by the O&M specialist or student, one at a time, depending on the particular body concept or spatial concept being taught or practiced (above, below, to the right of, in the center/middle, or diagonal). If right and left were being practiced, for example, an object would be placed in a cubicle to the far right and far left in the box. The student would be asked to find the object to the right, remove it, and describe it or demonstrate how it is used. He or she would follow the same procedure with the object on the left side of the box. The types of objects used will depend on the ages and interests of the students and may include familiar objects from the kitchen and bathroom; objects that make noise; action figures, dolls, and animal toys (dinosaurs are popular); puzzle or LEGO pieces to assemble; audiotapes; different geometric two- and three-dimensional shapes; and Play-Doh or other pliable material (N. Pouliot, personal communication, 1999).

Variations: The box can be presented empty, and the student can place objects in relation to other objects in specific cubicles, practicing several spatial concepts at the same time.

BODILY-KINESTHETIC APPROACH

Stair Travel Warm-ups

Ages: Elementary, middle school, and elderly people; students with orthopedic disabilities, only as appropriate and with consultation from a physical therapist

Description: Some O&M students have weak sensory motor skills, overall poor tone and coordination, and/or weak ankles and use their feet incorrectly. These students often have difficulty descending or ascending stairs efficiently, preferring a step-together-step sequence, rather than alternating their feet on each step. In addition, they often slide their heels down along the riser at the back of each step, thereby scuffing the backs of their shoes and landing on each step with a flat foot. They may have difficulty continuing to move their support arm forward along the railing as they are ascending or descending. They often have difficulty coordinating the movement and timing of the cane as they move their legs. These warm-ups are intended to make the students more aware of the various body parts needed for efficient stair travel and to strengthen certain parts of the leg. Once the students become stronger, they are usually better able to coordinate their arms, legs, and torso for smoother, safer stair travel.

The following exercises can be done standing in the classroom or by the stairs, depending on the degree of privacy desired. Music can be used if it makes the warm-ups more motivating. The "support" leg carries the weight; the other leg carries no weight and is free to move in various positions.

Leg Swings

Position: Standing sideways to the wall, one hand on the wall for support and the other hand on the hip bone of the free leg; the student

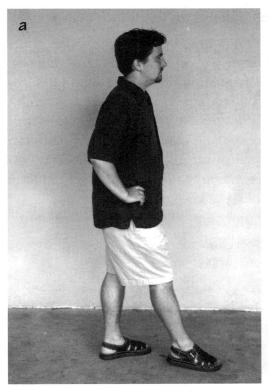

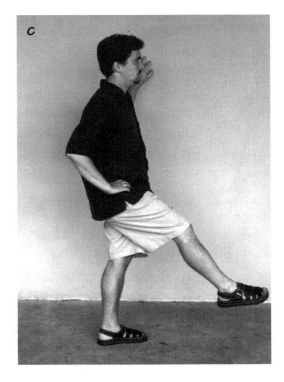

Photo 5.4

In the leg-swing warm-up for stair travel, emphasis is on movement of the leg at the hip joint, while the rest of the body is held still, so that the leg can swing freely.

stands "tall" (or "pulls up") on the support leg, rather than sinks down into the support hip.

Action: The student moves the free leg, so the toe touches in front and then in back of the body. Both hips should stay still while the free leg moves freely below the hip. The student then increases the size of the swing, so the free leg is now lifted off the floor and swinging forward and backward from the hip socket (the student can pretend that he or she is kicking a soccer ball or performing a routine as a dancer, gymnast, or ice skater). Make sure the leg swing is at the same height in the back as it is in the front, no higher than the knee of the supporting leg (about 45°); repeat the exercise on the other leg.

Explain: Legs need to swing freely to ascend and descend stairs safely and smoothly, even though the swing is small.

Variations: The student sits sideways on a chair with the seated leg in front of the body and the free leg loose at the side. She or he moves the free leg forward and backward while holding onto the back of the chair. The swing is easier to do if the leg swings and crosses over the "seated" leg and then swings behind while the student leans forward.

Mini Knee Bends and Lifts

Position: The student stands with his or her back and hips against the wall in a "square off" position; the heels are placed about one shoe's distance from the wall, and the legs are extended.

Action: The student bends slightly just at the knees, getting a bit shorter as he or she slides down the wall a few inches, holding this position for a few seconds to feel the thigh muscles working (the student can place his or her hands on the thighs to feel the muscles.) The student then slowly returns to the standing position, so legs are extended, and rises on the tips of the toes (ball of the foot and toes) for a few seconds, feeling the calf muscles working. These movements are then repeated with a slight bend, standing "straight," lifting onto ball and toes, then straight, then bending, and so on.

Explain: Mini knee bends and lifts are good warm-ups for stair travel because they strengthen the feet and legs and improve balance. The knee bend is not very big—*not* a squat, but a demiplie.

Variations: Once the student knows the exercise, the entire sequence can be done with the student facing the wall and holding onto the wall with

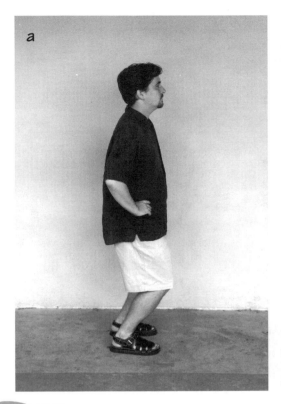
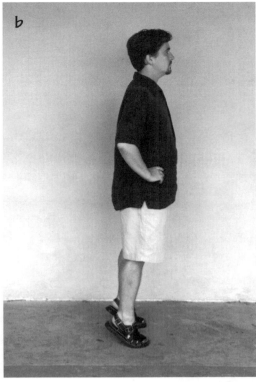

Photo 5.5

Mini knee bends and lifts are good warm-ups for stair travel because they strengthen the legs and improve balance.

both hands or holding onto the wall with one hand while standing sideways to the wall.

Foot Exercises

Position: The student sits in a chair with his or her legs parallel.

Action: This student lifts the heels slightly, resting the feet on the balls of the feet and toes; then places the feet flat on the floor; lifts the toes and balls of the feet off the floor with the weight on just the heels; then places the feet flat on the floor; and repeats this sequence.

Explain: Explain that movements of the ankle and foot are important for "taking off" and "landing" on each step of stairs. A flexible foot absorbs the shock of landing on each step by letting the body weight pass from the toes to the ball of the foot and then to the heel. When the student uses the ankle, foot, and toes correctly, he or she will not have to scrape each

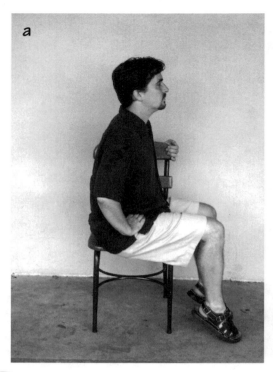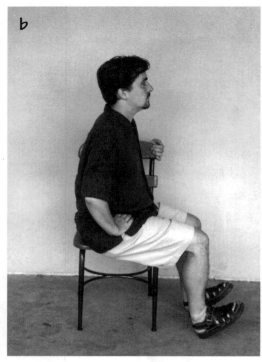

Photo 5.6

This seated variation of a stair travel warm-up requires the student to lift the heels and then rise on the balls of the feet in a slow rocking motion. It helps make the feet more flexible for proper liftoffs and landings on stairs.

heel against a riser or land awkwardly on a flat foot. Point out that basketball players, volleyball players, and ballet dancers use their legs this way, to reach taller or as a preparation for a jump.

Variations: The student repeats this sequence in a continuous "rocking" motion forward and backward.

Ankle Circles

Position: While seated, the student crosses or rests one leg on the other, so the free foot is near the supporting knee.

Action: The student circles the foot at the ankle clockwise several times and then counterclockwise while keeping the leg still.

Explain: Moving the foot at the ankle of the free leg increases the foot's flexibility and strength; stronger and more flexible feet help the student with overall coordination and balance as he or she travels up and down stairs.

Variations: The exercise can be done without shoes; the student can identify by touch various parts of the foot: toes, ball of the foot, main arch, instep, ankle bones, heel, Achilles' tendon.

Stair Practice

Position and action ascending: The student holds the cane correctly to the stairs, moves the support arm forward along the railing with each upward step; each leg swings forward at the hip to find the next upward step (like part of the leg swing exercise), bends and extends at the knee (like the mini knee bend exercise), and pushes off and lands using the foot (like the foot exercises).

Position and action descending: The student moves the cane correctly in rhythm with each step, moves the support hand forward along the railing as he or she is going down. Each leg swings forward at the hip to find the next downward step, extends and bends at the knee, lands with the free foot toe-ball-heel with control, absorbing the landing.

Explain: The use of various parts of the leg (as well as the torso and arms) helps control and coordinate movements for safer and more graceful (smoother) stair travel; landing on a flat foot or on the heel while scraping the back of the shoe on a riser is stressful to the foot and leg and awkward, providing less overall control and balance.

Interactive Models

Ages: Elementary through high school

Description: Interactive models involve large props or materials with which a student or students interact physically, moving their entire bodies in certain ways to learn a concept. The activities presented here illustrate how these models can be used to teach the address system and the concept of a block.

Address System

Students who do not understand the address system when it is explained on paper may have a better chance of understanding the concepts involved if they act out the address system through movement. O&M specialists can use the interactive model with individual students or several students together and probably need to present the address-system sequence over a period of several lessons. Two lengths of rope (a clothesline, thick yarn, or plastic tape work well) can be fastened to chairs or furniture along the sides of a room at about waist height (or use tape taped on the floor). These ropes form two long perpendicular "streets," representing the two center dividing streets of the address system. Individual compass cardinal directions can be printed or brailled on cards at the "end" of the streets, so the students know what direction they are traveling (holding onto the rope and walking north, they will see or touch the "north" sign at the end of the rope, for example). This setup can be used to teach the following concepts:

1. Identifying the traveling direction: The students travel along the two intersecting streets (rope or tape) in different directions, each calling out the particular direction in which he or she is moving (for instance, "I am traveling north").

2. Identifying sides of streets: The students review the compass cardinal direction sides of the two streets (that is, the north–south street has east and west sides). Traveling north or south, they call out that they are on the east or west side, as well as the direction they are walking (for example, "I am traveling south on the west side") and then repeat the exercise on the east–west street.

3. Identifying sections of the city: The students review the fact that the north–south street also divides the entire city into east and west sides or sections. As they travel on the north–south street, they can let go of the rope (or step off the tape) and walk around the east or west "side of town." Discuss what they may find there. Repeat with the east–west street.

4. Identifying the four quadrants of city: The students review that the east and north sides of the two streets form the northeast quadrant of the city, another way of referring to a section or part of town. They can walk around the northeast quadrant, again mentioning real or imaginary locations. Repeat the exercise with the other three quadrants.

5. Identifying block numbers: The students place (tape, tie, or clip on) street-sign cards (braille or large-print cards with"100 N," "100 E," "100 S," "100 W") in the correct corner positions where the two ropes intersect. They review that the address system begins with street signs starting at "100." Taking two or three steps north, they place a "200 N" card in position, signifying a cross street and beginning of a new block. They continue this procedure so that there are four or five cross streets/blocks on the north side. They can now travel north or south on the east or west side of a particular block or meet at one of the intersection corners of the north–south street and a cross street. Repeat the same procedure on the south side. Next, the students travel farther along the main north–south street, locating blocks on the north or the south side, counting the number of intersections "crossed" (for example, from the 300 south block to the 200 north block, the students will cross four intersections). Repeat the entire procedure along the east–west street, adding cross streets on the east and west sides. Finally, the students travel in various directions on the north–south and east–west streets, locating blocks along the way on either main street.

6. Identifying an address location within a block: The students review that lower numbers in a block are usually, but not always, near the beginning of the block; middle numbers are often near the middle of the block; and higher numbers are near the end of the block. They use destination cards with block numbers (such as 210 N, 351 S, 190 E, and 407 W) to travel to these locations on the interactive model. They can invent what they think these destinations may be.

7. Identifying even- or odd-number address locations: The students review the mnemonics *NOW* and *SEE* that help them determine on which side of the street a particular address is located. They use the same cards to locate their destinations with more accuracy, since they are now on the correct side of the street, as well as near the beginning, middle, or end of the block. More cards can be made to practice finding destinations, and students can invent what they think these destinations are.

8. Giving routes: The students give routes to one another on how to travel from one destination to another using all the references practiced in steps 1–7. They also correct one another's mistakes.

Neighborhood Block Concept

Some young students who are congenitally blind have a limited understanding of the concept of a residential block, since they can feel only parts of a parkway, sidewalk, fence, or building line. They are often confused about the interior of a block and what is located there. Understanding the basic concept of a block is easier for these students if they can act out traveling around and "into" a residential block within the smaller dimensions of a 9 by 12-foot rug. They can discover what is typically found along the perimeter of a block (the sidewalk area and fronts of houses) and what is typically "inside" the block (the backyards and fences between neighbors' properties). This rug block can be a "fantasy" block or based on a real block with which they are familiar. Actual landmarks that students have located while traveling can also be represented on the rug block. This interactive model takes about six lessons to complete, and the setup time before each lesson increases, since there are more items to put into place. The rug needs to be free of furniture and completely accessible to build and move within the model. The "houses" or "buildings" placed on the rug can be made of cardboard and assembled (three-dimensional boxes about 1 1/2 feet long by 1 foot wide and about 6 inches high) or cut from tagboard to make rectangular two-dimensional cutouts. Lessons using the rug "block" proceed as follows:

1. The student *reviews the definition of a basic "block"* and understands that the rug represents a block. He or she walks along the edge of the rug using the touch-and-drag cane technique or confirming the edge with stocking feet. The O&M specialist reviews the names of the streets on each side, noting that there are two long sides and two short sides to the block (making up street names if this is an invented block). The street names can be written/brailled on large cards and placed at each block side for reference.

2. The student *reviews that a block has north, east, south, and west sides.*

3. The student *places buildings* (cutouts or boxes) *on one side of the block,* adding props as appropriate. These are fantasy houses or ones the student has found during lessons (for instance, the real house near the corner with a large flower garden can be represented by a box with paper flowers, pipe cleaners, and perfume).

4. The student repeats this procedure until the *four block sides are finished* and each side has several buildings on it. In addition to landmarks of various kinds, address numbers can be added to some of the houses or buildings.

5. Various routes are given to the student to *find different locations around the block,* so that he or she practices route shapes, body references, street names, landmarks, address numbers, and cardinal directions as appropriate. The student also gives routes to the O&M specialist. Role-play inviting each other for a pizza party, birthday party, dinner, and so forth.

6. The student and O&M specialist each *choose a house* on opposite sides of the block, so their backyards are facing each other. Discuss with the student what kinds of things may be in "the back" of houses—what is in the backyard.

7. With assistance, the student tapes laundry rope or thick yarn onto the rug to represent the shape (three borders) of the student's and O&M specialist's backyards, noting that there are *two "backyards"* with a common "back fence." The student examines the shape of his or her backyard and the adjoining backyard of the O&M specialist's house. The student uses cardinal direction references, as well as positional and directional references, while describing the two backyards.

8. Continue the *role-play* of inviting each other over and having a party in each other's backyards (there will not be much room!). The student can visit by walking around the block on the sidewalk to the front of the "house" or stepping over the "back fence" (rope). Offer each other something to drink and eat. Stand in the two backyards and talk over the "back fence." Add things to the backyards (like a mirror for a pool, telephones for calling, miniature doll chairs and tables, plastic turf for grass, and a spray water bottle for the sprinkler system).

9. Add a business building to the "block" (if it is a "fantasy" block) with a side driveway and entrance and a back parking lot. Compare this "back" area with the backyards of the houses.

10. Continue to *give and follow routes* to places along the rug block using body, spatial, cardinal directional, and/or address system references. The students review that the rug block is a small re-creation of a real block and all the associated concepts.

Grip Cane and Wrist Practice

Ages: Early elementary school; students with additional disabilities; students of any age who are just learning cane skills

Description: This is a physical warm-up (or remediation) to practice the correct use of a cane. Make a "grip" cane out of an unusable folding cane

Photo 5.7

The O&M specialist is using a "grip cane"—made from the grip of a cane with a marshmallow tip on the end—to demonstrate wrist movement warm-ups for the two-point-touch cane technique.

by cutting the elastic, keeping the grip section, and attaching a marshmallow tip to the metal shaft at the end of the grip. The cane becomes a grip with a tip. Students sit with their cane arm positioned correctly out in front of them resting on a table. They hold the cane with the correct grasp, keeping the cane arm from moving back and forth by holding their forearm with their free hand. In this position, they can practice the constant-contact, two-point-touch, or flagging technique used before street crossings. Emphasize that the movement of the cane comes from the wrist, not the swinging movement of the arm, and that the cane is positioned directly in front of them, not to their side.

The purpose of the exercise is to help students perceive kinesthetically the correct positioning of the cane and the wrist movements necessary for moving the cane in an arc. Music or a metronome can be used for interest and to assist with the rhythm of the cane. O&M instructors can vary the tempo of the cane arc for interest or use different pieces of texture taped to the table that the cane will hit as it taps back and forth.

Repeat the exercise after adding another part of the shaft to the grip, so that the cane is longer and harder to move.

This exercise should not take more than 10 minutes and is helpful to do at the beginning of a class, to make the students more aware of how they should use their canes when they travel later during the lesson. The advantage of this warm-up exercise is that the students are seated, so they are more relaxed and better able to concentrate on the specific wrist movements they are doing. In addition, the cane is lightweight and easier to use since it is short.

Variations: The students may want to color (paint) the grip cane, wrap it with ribbon or another texture, or use stickers and decals to decorate it. Another object, like a piece of wooden dowel, that is lighter weight can be used instead of a cane.

INTERPERSONAL APPROACH

"Guess Who?" Game

Ages: Elementary and middle school

Description: Students with low vision who like to socialize with their peers, as well as those who need practice with interactive skills, will enjoy playing Guess Who? The Mystery Face Game, a widely available commerical board game (manufactured by Milton Bradley) that is designed for two players. In addition to interactive skills, students will practice the visual skills of identification, comparison, and discrimination. The game contains two sets of 24 picture cards of faces. The object of the game is to determine which cards the opponent has picked by asking yes-and-no questions related to the appearance of the person on the card. The different types and ages of the faces, including a variety of extras like makeup, facial hair, eyeglasses, hairstyles, and hats, make the game fun and visually challenging.

Variations: Instead of just two players, more students can play, divided into two teams. After the students play the game, encourage them to talk about the similarities and differences in the way people look. Also encourage them to look around the classroom and describe what they see in detail, comparing objects by noting their similarities and differences.

Intersection Analysis

PLEASE TELL ME ABOUT:

Intersection Configuration

1. street names?
2. shape of intersection?   "+"   "X"   "T"   "Y"   "offset"   "multiple legs"
3. size?   width of street   number of traffic lanes
                               parking lanes (hours)   bicycle lanes
4. types of corners?   aligned or offset   wheelchair ramps   blended
5. any left-turn lanes?   any right-turn-only lanes?
6. any one-way streets?
7. any islands or medians?
   location   shape
   Is there a pedestrian control button?   Do I have to stop and wait on the island?

Traffic Controls

1. type?   stop sign (1-, 2-, 3-, or 4-way)   traffic light (3, 4, 5, or 6 lights)
2. timing of traffic lights?   timed   semiactuated   full actuated
3. pedestrian crosswalk lines? location   color
4. pedestrian control buttons? none   regular   auditory   tactile
5. traffic light arrows?   left turns   right turns   straight ahead

Traffic Patterns

1. volume on each street?   low   medium   high
2. volume variations?   peak hours   off-peak hours
3. speed on each street?   slow   medium   fast
4. any unusual features?

Other Concerns

1. visibility?   hazards   obstacles
2. right turners?   volume   peak hours
3. left turners?   volume   peak hours
4. surge?   adequate   inadequate
5. noise level?   quiet   too noisy to detect surge

The answers to these questions can be used to determine the following:

1. Is it safe to cross at this intersection?
2. Is it safer to cross going clockwise or counterclockwise?
3. Does the parallel nearside surge start with the beginning of the WALK signal, as expected? If not, can I still cross with the parallel nearside surge?
4. Are there alternate crossings that would be safer?
5. Should I ask for assistance in making this crossing?

Figure 5A.3

Intersection Analysis Form

Intersection Analysis

Ages: High school and adults

Description: This activity uses an intersection analysis form (see Figure 5A.3) to increase students' awareness of different types and features of intersections prior to working on actual street crossings with the O&M specialist. It takes advantage of interpersonal intelligence by encouraging students to ask questions about potential travel environments. Students can be asked to analyze a particular intersection and to complete the form by (1) asking questions of the O&M specialist; (2) asking another student during the O&M lesson; or (3) asking friends or relatives in their neighborhood as homework. Students should record information in the most appropriate media such as braille, large print, or audio. The activity also relies heavily on logical mathematical intelligence for environmental analysis.

Variations: This form can be modified as appropriate to make it simpler for use with younger students or for use in less complex environments

Bus Travel Trivia

Ages: Middle school, high school, and adults

Description: Students who are learning to use public transportation may enjoy playing bus travel trivia in small groups or in teams with larger groups. The format can be patterned after popular game shows. The following is a sample list of trivia questions. The O&M specialist can ask students to think of more questions as well.

1. What is the acronym and full name of your local bus/rapid transit company?

2. What is a layover?

3. Where are bus stops typically located?

4. A bus driving west stops at an intersection to let people off. Where are two possible street corners at the intersection where this stop may be located: northwest, northeast, southwest, or southeast?

5. A bus driving south stops at an intersection to let people off. Where are two possible street corners at the intersection where this stop may be located: northwest, northeast, southwest, or southeast?

6. Where is the individual identification bus number located on the outside of the bus?

7. Describe two kinds of railings found on the inside of a bus.

8. Describe three ways that bus seats can be different.

9. Give two reasons why you should sit directly across from the bus driver.

10. Which door of the bus should you exit from and why?

11. Describe common things that you may see at a bus stop.

12. What will you always see at a bus stop?

13. What should you ask the bus driver before entering the bus?

14. Why is it important to have a watch while traveling on a bus?

15. Give three reasons why you should use your cane while traveling on a bus.

16. Describe four fixtures that you find inside a bus.

17. Can buses with different route numbers stop at the same bus stop?

18. Describe three ways that you can let the bus driver know that you want to get off the bus.

19. Describe four ways that you can recognize a route while on the bus.

20. When the bus stops at the "nearside," what does that mean?

Variations: Students can design their own trivia questions for one another.

Mobility Rap Group

Ages: Middle school, high school, and adults

Description: In a group setting, students are encouraged to talk about their independent travel and other related experiences and have an opportunity to learn by sharing experiences, feelings, and strategies with one another. The group can be facilitated by the O&M specialist, a counselor, or by the students themselves. Topics may include frustrations with public transportation, strategies for dating as nondrivers, dealing with the public, or getting ready for graduation.

Variations: Students can take turns hosting a monthly meeting. Guest speakers can be invited to talk on applicable topics.

INTRAPERSONAL APPROACH: ACTIVITIES

"And How Do You Cross?" Game

Ages: Middle school to adults

Description: Students with low vision who are strong in the intrapersonal intelligence and enjoy analyzing intersections may also like to independently analyze how certain pedestrians cross at large intersections. Observing if these people push the pedestrian buttons or scan, noting when these people step off the curb to cross, and how they walk through the intersection helps O&M students learn what skills are safe or unsafe. It is also fun when observing pedestrians to categorize them in a humorous way. After categorizing various pedestrians, students can also decide if they themselves are similar or dissimilar to any of the pedestrians they have observed. Here is a list of "traveler types" that the students can use to describe the pedestrians they see:

> Mr. or Ms. Speed Demon No Matter What
>
> Mr. or Ms. Better Get Outta My Way
>
> Mr. or Ms. Button, What Button?
>
> Mr. or Ms. Do I Really Have to Turn My Head to Scan?
>
> Mr. or Ms. Daydream Right Off the Curb
>
> Mr. or Ms. I Forgot My Monocular
>
> Mr. or Ms. Run at the End of the Cycle
>
> Mr. or Ms. It's Too Noisy/Hot/Cold/Wet/Dirty to Cross the Street
>
> Mr. or Ms. Oops! I Always Forget about the Turners
>
> Mr. or Ms. I Will Wait for the Perfect Surge.

After using the descriptions, students can briefly discuss the possible advantages and disadvantages of the travel characteristics of these pedestrian "types."

Variations: Students can make up their own categories when observing pedestrians or when describing types of drivers.

Monocular Quiz

Ages: Elementary through high school, adults and elderly people

Description: After students learn to identify the parts of the monocular and their functions, they can take a simple test. For example, they can

Monocular Quiz

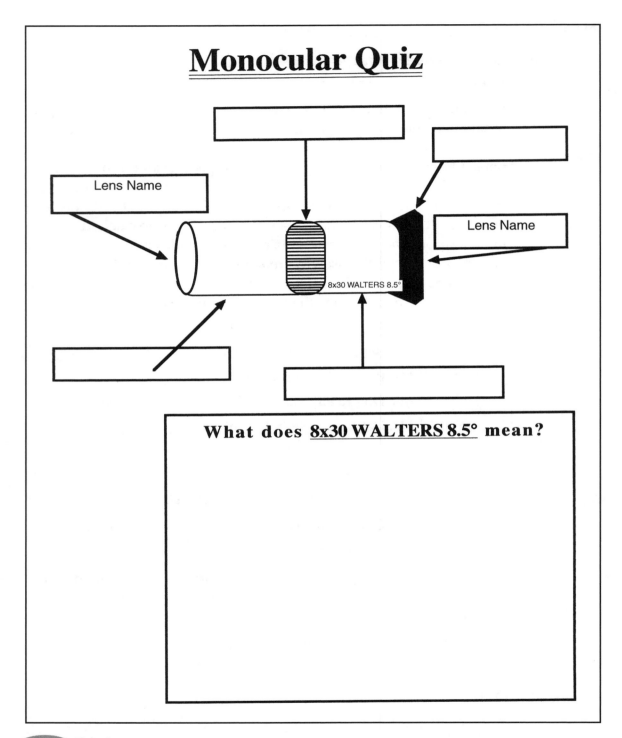

Lens Name

Lens Name

8x30 WALTERS 8.5°

What does <u>8x30 WALTERS 8.5°</u> mean?

Figure 5A.4

Monocular Quiz

be asked to label and explain a simple diagram of a monocular (see Figure 5A.4) and answer such questions as "What is the meaning of the inscription '8X30 Walters 8.5°' on the monocular?" Students who are stronger in the intrapersonal intelligence may enjoy this type of independent activity in which they can evaluate their own grasp of the material (T. Fields, personal communication, 1994).

Variations: Students can be given tests on other parts of the O&M curriculum. Tests can be made easier or more complex, depending on the student.

Bus Information Forms

Ages: Middle school, high school, and adults

Description: Students can be given forms on which to independently record bus-schedule information. These forms may start with the starting and ending points of the route and the day and time they are planning to travel. They can have spaces for students to record information about the bus route as they obtain it, such as the

- bus number,
- approximate time the bus would arrive at a particular stop,
- intersection where they catch the bus,
- any intersections where they need to transfer,
- intersection where they get off,
- how often the bus runs, and
- length of the trip.

Completed bus-route forms can be kept in an O&M notebook or portfolio.

NATURALIST APPROACH: ACTIVITIES

O&M Scrapbook

Ages: Any age

Description: Students who are participating in residential travel may enjoy maintaining a scrapbook collection of the various types of leaves, grass, or flowers they found while they were traveling. Students can collect leaves or snippets of grass that they would like to include or spend time at a library or bookstore to locate pictures or descriptions of flowers, bushes, and hedges to include in their book. The scrapbook can be divided up into specific streets in which these items were found. O&M terms should be used, when possible, to identify locations.

Variations: A similar scrapbook can be created for travel in a light business area. Students can collect business cards, take-out menus, and advertisements from local shops and businesses along their routes. These items can be organized in the O&M scrapbook using street names and addresses.

Identifying Tape-Recorded Natural and Man-made Sounds

Ages: Any age

Description: Students who enjoy classifying various sounds can practice their auditory identification skills when listening to tape-recorded natural and man-made sounds. The level of difficulty will be based on the individual student's ability and travel experience.

Variations: Students can create their own tape recordings and allow other students or the O&M specialist to guess what the sounds are. Sounds can be categorized as natural, man-made, or animal.

Mobility Adventures with Sherlock Holmes

Ages: Upper elementary or middle school students with low vision

Description: A series of lessons can be developed around a Sherlock Holmes theme. The unit can be started by reading Sherlock Holmes tales (at an age-appropriate level) to pique the student's interest in the characters. The O&M specialist can read to the student, the student can read to the O&M specialist, or the two can take turns. Emphasize the magnifying-glass aspect of the stories. Give the student a magnifier and/or monocular that can be worn on a chain or carried in a pocket to take on travel routes during the mobility adventures. Create a mystery story with the student using the magnifier to investigate and collect clues to solve the mystery. Combine scanning and focusing activities with the use of landmarks and clues along designed routes of travel.

Variations: A similar series of lessons can be conducted with a small group of students. Functionally blind students can investigate the environment by exploring tactilely or by listening to auditory clues along the route.

Multiple Intelligences Inventory

Instructions: There are two sections to complete for each of the eight intelligences. In the first section, circle each sentence that describes you most of the time. The number of sentences circled is the score for that section. In the second section, rate, on a scale of 1 to 5, how much the description provided describes you; that is the score for the second section. The two scores should be added together to get a total score for each area. The total score should fit into a range of low, medium, or high to represent your strength in that particular intelligence.

Linguistic Intelligence

Circle the sentence or sentences that describe you and the activities you like most of the time:

   a. I am good at writing and know how to spell.

   b. I enjoy reading, including reading out loud.

   c. I have a good memory for names, places, dates, and trivia.

   d. I learn best by reading or listening.

   e. I enjoy puns, nonsense rhythms, tongue twisters, and word games like Scrabble.

Score: _____

Linguistic people have excellent listening skills and recall what is said to them. They hear words when they are thinking. They have well-developed vocabularies and express their creativity (imagination) through talking or writing. They are comfortable talking in a group.

Source: Adapted from J. Bishop, Developing effective learning skills—Application of Gardner's multiple intelligences theory, April 3, 1998; B. Campbell, The building tool room—The Naturalist intelligence, The Toolroom [On-line]. Available: www.newhorizon.org/article_eightintel.html; S. Teele & A. Bivo, The Renaissance Project, University of California at Riverside (1990); and L. O. Wilson, The eighth intelligence: Naturalist intelligence [On-line]. Available: http://www.uwsp.edu/acad/edu/lwilson/learning/natintel.htm.

Circle the number below according to how accurately this describes you:

1 (not like me)   2   3   4   5 (just like me)

Score: _____

Linguistic Intelligence Total Score: _____
(1–3 = low, 4–7 = medium, 8–10 = high)

Musical Intelligence

Circle the sentence or sentences that describe you and the activities you like most of the time:

   a. I often listen to the radio, tapes, CDs and/or television.

   b. I can hear when a note is off-key.

   c. I easily remember the melody of a song.

   d. I can keep time accurately to the beat of music I hear.

   e. I prefer listening to music when I study or read.

Score: _____

Musical people recognize and appreciate pitch, rhythm, and timbre and enjoy listening to music. They may enjoy singing, playing a musical instrument, and/or composing (or improvising) music. They notice background noise and may be more sensitive than other people to sounds in their environment.

Circle the number below according to how accurately this describes you:

1 (not at all)   2   3   4   5 (just like me)

Score: _____

Musical Intelligence Total Score: _____
(1–3 = low, 4–7 = medium, 8–10 = high)

Logical-Mathematical Intelligence

Circle the sentence or sentences that describe you and the activities you like most of the time:

   a. I reason things out logically.

   b. I look for patterns, categories, or relationships in things.

    c. I like to know how and why things work.

    d. I enjoy math and/or science.

    e. I enjoy and am good at chess, checkers, and other kinds of strategy games.

Score: _____

Logical-mathematical people enjoy doing activities in a sequential order and approach problems in an organized and logical way. They like to experiment to test things they do not understand and enjoy using a computer. They compute arithmetic problems quickly in their heads.

Circle the number below according to how accurately this describes you:

1 (not at all)   2   3   4   5 (just like me)

Score: _____

Logical-Mathematical Intelligence Total Score: _____
(1–3 = low, 4–7 = medium, 8–10 = high)

Spatial Intelligence

Circle the sentence or sentences that describe you and the activities you like most of the time:

    a. I think in spatial images and/or pictures.

    b. I prefer maps to written directions.

    c. I am good at knowing what is around me and where things are.

    d. I enjoy jigsaw puzzles and/or making three-dimensional structures/sculptures (using Play-Doh, LEGOS, clay, and so forth).

    e. I describe representations of things and/or people accurately.

Score: _____

Spatial people are able to visualize images when thinking, reading, or talking about things. They orient themselves easily to new surroundings and are able to give accurate directions to given locations. They like to draw (doodle) and enjoy using a camera. They remember words and numbers by seeing them.

Circle the number below according to how accurately this describes you:

1 (not at all)   2   3   4   5 (just like me)

Score: _____

Spatial Intelligence Total Score: _____
(1–3 = low, 4–7 = medium, 8–10 = high)

Bodily-Kinesthetic Intelligence

Circle the sentence or sentences that describe you and the activities you like most of the time:

    a. I like activities that involve movement.

    b. I enjoy swings, slides, and/or rides at amusement parks.

    c. I am well coordinated.

    d. I learn a skill by doing it.

    e. I write things down to remember them.

Score: _____

Bodily-kinesthetic people have expressive body language and use gestures as they talk. They process and internalize information by touching, manipulating, moving, or acting things out. They use their bodies or hands in skilled ways and enjoy being physically active.

Circle the number below according to how accurately this describes you:

1 (not at all)   2   3   4   5 (just like me)

Score: _____

Bodily-Kinesthetic Intelligence Total Score: _____
(1–3 = low, 4–7 = medium, 8–10 = high)

Interpersonal Intelligence

Circle the sentence or sentences that describe you and the activities you like most of the time:

    a. I enjoy being with people.

    b. I prefer group activities to ones I do alone.

    c. I am aware of other people's feelings.

      d. I like to organize people and often lead activities.

      e. I belong to groups, clubs, and/or various organizations.

Score: _____

People with strong interpersonal skills are good communicators and enjoy relating to and cooperating with other people. They have many close friends and are able to empathize with others. They learn best in a cooperative group setting and are skilled at teaching a skill or activity to other people.

Circle the number below according to how accurately this describes you:

1 (not at all)   2   3   4   5 (just like me)

Score: _____

Interpersonal Total Intelligence Score: _____
(1–3 = low, 4–7 = medium, 8–10 = high)

Intrapersonal Intelligence

Circle the sentence or sentences that describe you and the activities you like most of the time:

      a. I like (need) to spend time alone.

      b. I am self-motivated and independent.

      c. I often set goals to reach.

      d. I rarely ask for help with a personal problem.

      e. I am intuitive.

Score: _____

People with strong intrapersonal skills are aware of their own inner strengths and weaknesses and have a deep sense of self-confidence. They have a strong will and are able to motivate themselves to do well on independent projects. They prefer working on their own to working in a group.

Circle the number below according to how accurately this describes you:

1 (not at all)   2   3   4   5 (just like me)

Score: _____

Intrapersonal Intelligence Total Score: _____
(1–3 = low, 4–7 = medium, 8–10 = high)

Naturalist Intelligence

Circle the sentence or sentences that describe you and the activities you like most of the time:

  a. I enjoy learning about plants, animals, and the environment.

  b. I like to be outside whenever I can.

  c. When I am feeling stressed, I want to be out in nature.

  d. I like to collect and organize things.

  e. I have always been interested in television shows, videos, books, and magazines about science, nature, and animals.

Score: _____

People who are high in naturalist intelligence enjoy observing, understanding, sorting, and organizing what they see in the natural environment. Naturalists are able to recognize and classify types of plants, animals, and natural phenomena. They are sensitive to changes in their surroundings and have a heightened level of sensory perception. They enjoy collecting and classifying things from nature (butterflies, shells, rocks, and the like).

Circle the number below according to how accurately this describes you:

1 (not at all)   2   3   4   5 (just like me)

Score: _____

Naturalist Intelligence Total Score: _____
(1–3 = low, 4–7 = medium, 8–10 = high)

6

Selecting Training Environments: Sites for Different Students

CHAPTER PREVIEW

Searching for and Selecting Training Environments
  Environments for the Traditional O&M Sequence
  Environments by Demand
  Imperfect Environments
  Scouting Unfamiliar Environments

Organizing Environments by Shape
  The Plus
  The Block or Perimeter
  The Strip
  Scattered Locations
  Adding on with Ls

Organizing the Environment by Typical Destinations
  Small Shopping Plaza
  Supermarket, Department Store, or Discount Store
  Shopping Mall

Environmental Considerations for Students with Special Needs

TEACHING LESSONS in a variety of environments enables O&M specialists to present different kinds of lessons, choosing locations where specific strategies are most effective. Chapter 6 explains ways to search for, select, and organize appropriate environments in which to instruct and reinforce O&M skills. Once the O&M specialist has found the appropriate environments, the area can be visualized in terms of certain shapes, depending on the type of area, what is located there, and the objectives of the lessons to be taught there. Lessons can then be organized according to how the environment is visualized.

SEARCHING FOR AND SELECTING TRAINING ENVIRONMENTS

Once O&M specialists have assessed students' curricular needs and learning styles, they are ready to find training areas that will best suit their students. For students who have similar needs and are in the same area (the same school or agency), O&M specialists would look for a training environment nearby where these particular needs could be met (intersections to teach advanced street crossing skills or a light business area with many shops to practice interacting with the public). For students who are at the same site but have different levels of ability and experience, O&M specialists would select an "all-purpose" area (such as a residential area near a light business area) in which both basic and more advanced skills could be taught and practiced. In both cases, planning ahead ensures that the training area is appropriate for the skills being taught. In addition, it is more efficient to spend time initially searching for a training area than to select different locations before individual lessons week after week.

There are other advantages to finding a training site ahead of time. If O&M specialists spend time researching an area thoroughly and writing down relevant information before they teach students, they will not only know where to teach but will

- *know when* they will be able to teach specific skills (for example, when shops are open),

- be able to *plan lessons units* more easily and with more continuity, rather than teach one lesson at a time,

- *not forget specific details* needed for lessons (such as where and when to park, where the blended curb is, which street had unusual sidewalks), and

- be able to *spend more time planning lessons*, thinking of appropriate teaching strategies, and making teaching materials.

Selecting areas for training ahead of time is beneficial to students as well. Familiarity with an area helps students develop their cognitive mapping skills (their ability to organize the physical environment mentally, which is discussed in detail in Chapter 7) more accurately and easily. Lesson units that are contained within a certain area also help students

- form their own awareness of spatial relationships, so they can develop their route-planning skills more effectively;

- learn to plan the kinds of routes that mimic real-life situations, in which people travel routes in a given area to run errands, for example;

- become familiar with what a community is by learning what is in it; and

- generalize their knowledge when traveling to unfamiliar communities.

The learning that results from this type of advanced planning of teaching environments is therefore more effective than the more fragmented learning that takes place from training in random, unrelated areas in successive lessons.

Sometimes the O&M specialist is familiar with a travel area, sometimes not. A travel area may be requested by a student for an immediate need or chosen to teach several O&M students the full O&M curriculum. In either case, there are some basic procedures to follow to organize lessons into a unit (a more cohesive whole) by using the characteristics of various training environments.

Environments for the Traditional O&M Sequence

O&M specialists who teach the full O&M curriculum to many students need to look for general travel environments in which both basic and more complex skills can be taught and that fit the needs of several or many students who are in the same geographic area. These students have different travel needs, depending on their age and abilities, but all follow the general O&M curriculum. The environments should have a place where indoor mobility skills can be taught and an overlapping residential and light business area that is located within a reasonable driving distance.

Indoor Training Areas

Indoor training sites can be located within a school building, an office building, a public building like a library, or a shopping mall. Features that are needed to teach indoor travel skills include

- long hallways with good lighting and recessed doors (or doors that are generally closed at certain times to prevent injury to beginning students who are learning to trail),

- intersecting hallways,

- multiple floors (for teaching stair travel),

- hallways that are not crowded, and

- different types of doors and doorknobs.

Variety can be added by taking students to indoor areas that have carpeting or different floor treatments. Selecting interesting places where students can rest or have a break can be helpful (such as sitting in a library and looking at a magazine or using the sighted (human) guide technique to take them into a store in a mall).

Residential Training Areas

Both O&M students who are beginning travelers and those who are more experienced travelers benefit from travel within residential areas to learn or refine cane skills, line-of-travel skills, concepts skills, and orientation skills. The area selected should be about four to eight contiguous blocks so the students can practice these skills over time. O&M specialists need to look for the following when scouting for a basic residential training area:

- equal-sized blocks that are rectangular;

- intersections with 2-, 3-, and 4-way stop-sign controls;

- intersections that are plus shaped and T shaped;

- sidewalks that lead directly to the corner, so students are lined up correctly to cross;

- relatively smooth sidewalks with a minimal amount of cracks and holes;

- walkways; driveways; and sidewalks with grassy strips

- a variety of landscaping along the edge of the sidewalk (fences, walls, grass, flower beds); and

- an area that is free from loose dogs and relatively safe during the training time.

If more advanced students are learning how to maintain their line of travel when they find an unusual curb cut, odd-shaped intersections, and corners would also be appropriate as part of the overall residential training site. For students who have low vision and those who are practicing monocular skills, neighborhoods with different kinds of houses and apartments allow for a greater variety of objects for practicing spotting, tracing, and scanning skills. Some advanced residential areas also have blocks with alleys, schools, churches, fire stations, or small corner stores that students can use as landmarks or visit during a lesson to practice their speaking skills.

Light Business Training Areas

For more advanced students, O&M specialists need to look for a location that has

- timed and volume traffic light intersections (plus and T shaped),

- boulevard stop-sign controlled intersections, which may also be offset, that is, not directly across from one another,

- wheelchair ramps and a variety of traffic signal hardware near the intersection corners,

- bus stops,

- public telephones,

- sidewalks without a strip of grass next to the street and with street hardware (such as telephone poles, parking meters, newspaper stands, traffic signs, or outdoor café furniture),

- midblock driveways,

- gas stations or L-shaped plazas located at the corners of blocks,

- a variety of businesses and opportunities for interacting with the public (such as a bank, post office, library, police station, Chamber of Commerce, and recreation center), and

- an area that is relatively safe during training time.

Some students need to learn how to travel in more challenging environments. It is always helpful, then, if O&M specialists find any of the following features within or near an all-purpose training area:

- subway system;

- railroad tracks (also a train station);

- changes in elevation, like steep outdoor stairways;

- elevators and escalators; or

- skewed-shaped intersections and ones with multiple legs.

Figure 6.1 shows the configurations of both basic and complex intersections.

Having found an area in which basic curricular skills can be taught and reinforced, O&M specialists can develop lesson units in which beginning travelers can walk from a residential section to a light business shopping area as they practice sighted guide skills or purchase items of interest. Advanced students can start their routes in a residential area on their way to a light business area in order to refine their residential street crossing skills. The order can be reversed for both types of students as well, with the lesson beginning in a light business area and ending in a residential section. Both types of students benefit from lesson units that take advantage of this variety of environments. Not only can they learn and practice needed skills, but they will also be more motivated by the variety of stimuli offered to them.

When students are learning about a new neighborhood, the O&M specialist can have them use an information-gathering form, such as the one presented in Figure 6.2. Completing this kind of form helps familiarize students with a travel area, and the information learned can be generalized to anticipate the kinds of business and services they might typically find in a similar neighborhood. It also allows students to share the responsibility for learning about a new community. Students can answer the questions on the form, filling in the names of businesses and possibly other information such as addresses or descriptions, by asking the O&M specialist. They can ask another student during the O&M lesson, or they can ask friends and relatives to help them fill out the form about their own neighborhood for homework. Students who are blind can read a braille version of the form while they are traveling in the neighborhood and tape record their answers. Then they can braille the responses later when they are back in the classroom. Students with low vision use a large-print form and can practice using a monocular to search for the various types of stores. Teaching Tips for Environments for the Traditional O&M Sequence includes additional ideas for pre-

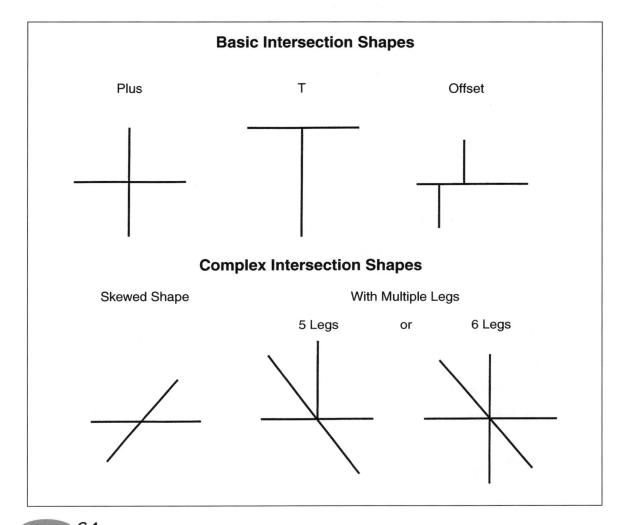

Figure 6.1

Basic and Complex Intersection Shapes

senting routes or environments to motivate students within the traditional O&M curriculum.

Environments by Demand

Sometimes students need to learn specific routes. These are lessons "by demand" (see Chapter 2) because the travel environment is determined by a student's needs. For students who are in elementary school, high school, or college, these environments may include

Learning about a Neighborhood

Student _____ Instructor _____ Date _____

WHERE ARE WE?

(name and area of town, name of street walking along, direction walking, which side of the street, and so forth)

_____

_____

WHAT DO YOU SEE?

1. market (super, small, specialty) _____

2. restaurant (fast food, sit down) _____

3. convenience store/pharmacy _____

4. pet store _____

5. repair (appliance, electronics, shoe) _____

6. clothing store (type) _____

7. laundromat/drycleaner _____

8. gas station/auto repair _____

9. hair, nail salon/barber shop _____

10. furniture store (type) _____

11. electronics store _____

12. large discount store _____

13. recreation (book store, music store, video rental) _____

14. post office _____

15. bank/ATM _____

16. medical office (general, dentistry, optometry) _____

17. other (specify) _____

Figure 6.2

Learning about a Neighborhood

TEACHING TIPS FOR ENVIRONMENTS FOR THE TRADITIONAL O&M SEQUENCE

- Focus lessons one day a week on orientation skills and the other day on mobility skills and integrate the two in the third lesson.

- Plan for students who share a training area to build a map together of that environment.

- Have the students match "career cards" (cards with individual types of careers written or brailled on them) to various businesses found in a new training area (students may enjoy role-playing careers of interest).

- Ask the students to make a list of questions that they could ask when traveling in familiar and unfamiliar environments, such as "What types of businesses are found along this block?" or "Can you tell me if there is a crosswalk at this crossing?"

- learning the locations of general buildings,

- learning the locations of recreational areas (a physical education field, running track, swimming (pool, gymnasium, stadium, and the like),

- learning the locations of specific destinations (such as classrooms, rest rooms, the cafeteria, library, and auditorium), and

- learning routes between relevant parts of the campus.

A similar need to learn and practice routes would apply to O&M students who are traveling within a new workplace, traveling to this new site from their home, and traveling from the site back home at the end of the day. Other students may need to learn how to negotiate safely within a new home, apartment complex, or care facility. They may also need instruction on weekly or monthly routes to medical appointments; art, dance, or music lessons or rehearsals; meetings of clubs or social groups; cultural programs and religious services; and sporting events and sports activities.

All these types of students need to learn indoor and outdoor routes to specific destinations in school, at work, or in their home neighborhoods. The O&M specialist, along with the students, chooses the most appropriate way for the students to reach these needed destinations as independently as possible, given their needs and abilities. To do so, the O&M specialist first visits these places ahead of time to determine the safest and most efficient route and then recommends this route to the student in the first lesson. Instruction takes place as the O&M specialist and student work together on this route or select another route that is better for the student. The total number of lessons needed to learn a route or several routes depends on the student's ability and motivation and the complexity of the travel environment. For some students on these kinds of routes, motivation is high because of the immediate relevance, but for others, the necessary route repetition may be tedious. For students who tire easily, become bored, or lack motivation, teaching a route using reverse (backward) chaining may be effective (see Chapter 3 for a complete description). Since the end of the route is reached each time with this strategy, learning a route in this way can be more motivating for students than learning it from the beginning point. Tips for Teaching Environments by Demand presents additional suggestions for presenting such routes or embellishing lessons to help students who are not highly motivated. (See Chapter 5 for suggestions on matching instruction to students' learning styles.)

Imperfect Environments

Sometimes O&M specialists who are itinerant and travel from place to place are required to train in an area that is not ideal for teaching specific O&M skills. O&M specialists are challenged when there is only one kind of environment in which they pick up their students—which may be considered an environment without choice—or there is not enough time to travel to a better or more varied training location. If the school district is in a rural or semirural area, for example, it is difficult for O&M specialists to teach how to analyze and cross at complex traffic light-controlled intersections. Similarly, if the training area is in a suburb, where there are long residential blocks, it is difficult for students to practice more than one street crossing in each lesson. In both rural and suburban areas, it may be difficult to find little shopping areas where students can practice interacting with the public and making purchases in a variety of shops. If these goals are appropriate for their students, O&M specialists need to plan a series of special field trips to more urban areas. Time is a crucial factor in making such trips, since the O&M specialist and the student need more time to travel to the new location and complete the

TIPS FOR TEACHING
ENVIRONMENTS BY DEMAND

- Let the students choose which route to practice first when there are several routes to accomplish.

- Make progress charts with the students to keep track of how they are doing.

- Use the sighted (human) guide technique for parts of routes to reduce fatigue.

- Allow time for short breaks as needed.

- Provide reward time for young students when they have spent a long time learning a given route.

- Reverse roles and let the students teach routes to the O&M specialist or other students.

- Play word games, landmark searches, or other challenges while practicing routes.

- Incorporate the use of students' stronger learning styles as a motivation for learning routes.

lesson. Since it may be difficult to plan such trips during the school year and during the week, O&M specialists should consider planning such trips during summer school, when scheduling demands are less rigid, or on weekends. Teaching Tips for Imperfect Environments presents additional suggestions for making the most of existing environments.

Another drawback may be that the neighborhood in which students live, work, or go to school may be unsafe. For example, there may be only certain times of day when it is wise to travel in a neighborhood, or there may be areas in the neighborhood to avoid. Furthermore, in some cases, it may be safer to teach lessons accompanied by a family member or an escort. This is yet another reason why it is important to familiarize oneself with an area before one plans lessons.

Scouting Unfamiliar Environments

When O&M specialists look for training areas in unfamiliar locations or communities, it may be advisable to ask people who know a particular area well what locations may be good for training. The criteria mentioned

TEACHING TIPS FOR IMPERFECT ENVIRONMENTS

- Plan O&M field trips for longer lessons outside the training area to teach necessary skills in ideal environments, such as a trip to an urban or downtown area to learn how to use revolving doors.

- Teach several O&M students together on O&M field trips or outings.

- Use libraries, videos, the Internet, and guest speakers to teach concepts related to unavailable environments, such as a comparison of mass transit options from region to region.

- Consult with the local police for information on a specific area, including the best times of day to work there, the types of clothing that should not be worn, and additional safety considerations.

- Use maps and models, including interactive ones, to introduce intersection concepts to students from rural areas.

earlier should be considered when talking to school staff, personnel at a work site, or family members. If certain locations or streets are mentioned, O&M specialists can visit them to see if they are appropriate for training.

Another efficient approach is to use a map to find a potential all-purpose training area for teaching all basic skills. In looking at a map, an O&M specialist can select areas depicted by heavier and lighter lines arranged in a gridlike pattern, rather than curved, winding lines or areas with few lines. Heavier lines in a grid pattern on a map generally indicate major streets, typically within light business areas, whose intersections are probably controlled by traffic lights. The lighter lines usually indicate smaller, less-congested streets whose intersections may be controlled by traffic lights or stop signs. A training area with a combination of major and smaller streets, commonly found in advanced residential and light business areas, gives the O&M specialist the kind of variety needed for teaching both beginning and more advanced students. The grid-pattern arrangements of parallel and perpendicular streets usually involve basic shaped intersections, with right-angle corners that are the simplest type of corner for lining up before crossing.

These kinds of corners are more appropriate for teaching and reinforcing basic street-crossing skills than odd-shaped corners or corners that are offset, both of which are often found in areas with curved streets.

For teaching students rural travel skills or familiarizing them with more unusual travel environments, the O&M specialist may choose areas of the map with curved lines. These environments may be hilly and have no sidewalks. They may also contain odd-shaped intersections that require learning and practicing more complex street-crossing skills (such as challenging lining-up skills needed for corners where veering is more common). There may be cul-de-sacs and other forms of dead-end streets to show students. The following are some unique challenges to consider with these kinds of travel areas:

- It may be more difficult to arrange lessons during which students can practice route-planning skills because of the complex shape of the streets.

- Hilly areas may be tiring for many students.

- Streets without sidewalks may be dangerous for pedestrians.

- Areas with few lines or lines that are far apart make it harder to practice more than one intersection crossing in a given lesson owing to time constraints.

If instruction in rural or hilly areas is needed, but there is not enough time to do so during a lesson, O&M specialists may consider choosing these environments during a summer school O&M lesson, a field trip for a group of O&M students, or a specially designed extra long O&M lesson.

As was already mentioned, it is important for an O&M specialist to travel to potential training areas ahead of time and to make notes or diagrams to remember where certain unusual features (such as cul-de-sacs) are located that may be needed for instruction at a later date. Knowing about these features ahead of time helps the O&M specialist to plan lessons for students with a variety of needs. Figure 6.3 and Table 6.1 present two formats for recording information that may be important for planning lessons in a chosen area. The O&M specialist can create a map, such as the one depicted in Figure 6.3 to use as a quick visual reference when surveying a potential training area. The O&M specialist would include information on the map about the area that is important in designing lessons, such as types of intersection controls, the address system, and the location of major landmarks. A table, such as the one

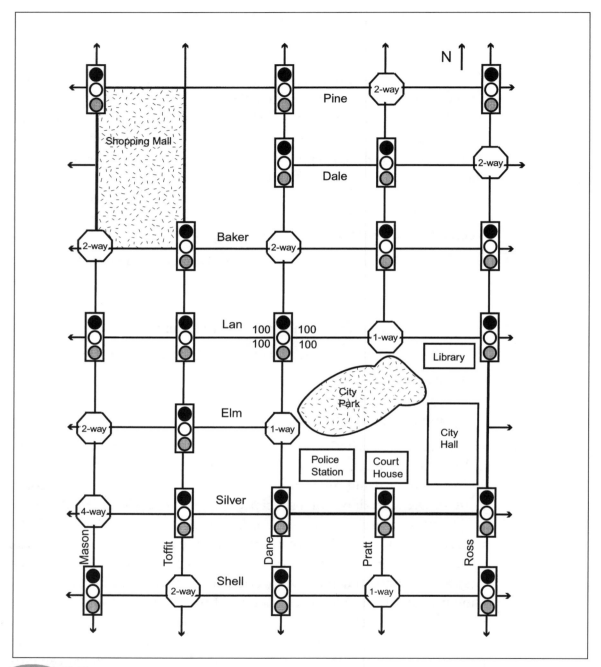

Figure 6.3

Map of a Training Area

An O&M specialist could use a map, like this one of a typical advanced residential–light business training area, to plan lessons to be conducted there. The O&M specialist includes important information, such as the types of intersection control, the address system, and location of major landmarks.

Table 6.1 Sample Training Area Destinations

Street Name	Address	Destination	Hours	Comments
Baker	151 East	Market Place Drug Store	Monday to Friday, 8 A.M.–6 P.M. Saturday, 10 A.M.–5 P.M.	Nice clerks; cheap educational and personal care items to buy *Cannot cross at Dane
Silver	290 West	Solly's Music Store	Monday to Saturday, 10 A.M.–7 P.M.	New and used records, tapes, and CDs; interesting posters on the wall *Poor lighting
Toffit	312 South	Bab's Bagelry	Monday to Friday, 7 A.M.–10 P.M.	*Look out for low overhang! *May be good place for a student's job?
Ross	237 North	Grrr & Purr Pet Palace	Monday to Saturday, 9:30 A.M.–5:30 P.M.	Pet grooming fun to watch; can hold reptiles; owner has dog guide pup.

depicted in Table 6.1, can then be used to record greater detail regarding specific businesses and other possible destinations that can be found in that same area.

In addition, it is helpful for O&M specialists to visit the training site at the times of day instruction or actual travel will take place. These visits provide an opportunity to observe vehicular and pedestrian traffic patterns. For some students, it may be safer or easier to train at certain intersections or businesses in the midmorning or early afternoon when there is less congestion. Other students may need the experience of traveling at peak travel times (rush hour), such as early morning or late afternoon. With these considerations in mind, lesson times can then be planned accordingly.

Once O&M specialists have written down, drawn, or charted relevant information about the training areas they have visited and selected, much of their general lesson planning can be done at the office. It is still important, however, for them to check the specific training areas before lessons are conducted to see if unexpected construction or other kinds of activities may affect their lesson plans.

ORGANIZING ENVIRONMENTS BY SHAPE

After selecting a training area, it may helpful to visualize it in terms of a shape and then introduce the area to students in terms of this shape. (For more information on this topic, see the discussion of cognitive mapping in Chapter 7.) Perceiving a new travel area at first in terms of a simple shape often helps O&M specialists and students understand more quickly and thoroughly how to relate to it. The shape acts as an organizer for them to package the particular content of a specific learning unit. When doing so, they may find a tactile or visual map helpful as appropriate (see Figure 6.4). This approach may be especially useful for students who are strong in spatial intelligence.

Since route directions are often based on shapes (I, L, U, and step), introducing a new training area this way is not unfamiliar to students. Once students have learned how to use shapes as an orientation guide or organizer in one area, they can then generalize this skill to another unfamiliar area while learning their way and planning new routes. Students can learn about how a particular city or a part of a city is formed by envisioning certain locations and their relationships by shape. For example, the address system (at the center of a city) is based on a plus shape, with its grid system starting at a center "plus" point. Students may also learn about a city by understanding the types of neighborhoods located along one main thoroughfare, recognizing how the environment changes as they travel in a particular direction along this street (a strip or straight line).

The Plus

An O&M specialist may select a plus-shaped intersection that would be good for training both orientation and mobility skills. He or she visualizes a large plus shape, centered directly on top of this intersection and continuing a distance of about five or six blocks in each direction. Units of three or four lessons each could then be oriented around this center point. Looking at a map of this area, the O&M specialist would highlight the two intersecting streets of this intersection on the map and then visualize the blocks and streets spatially in relation to this center

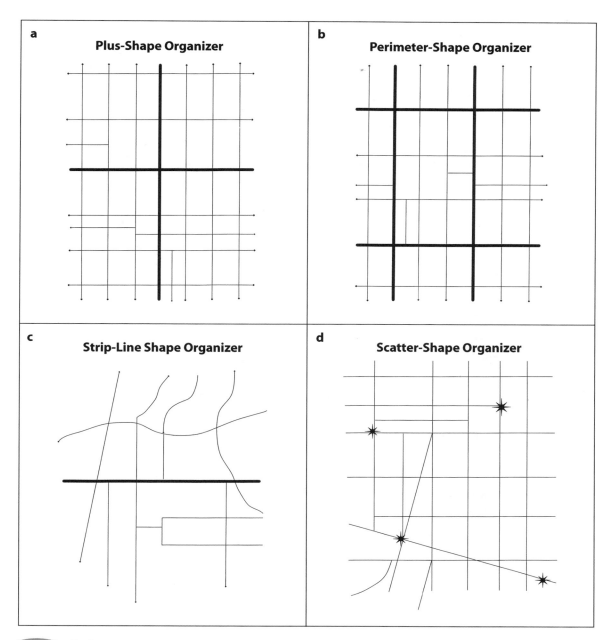

Figure 6.4

Organizing Environments by Shape

Using shapes to organize the training environment helps the O&M specialist and student to visualize the training area more clearly. (a) A plus-shape organizer can be used when a plus-shaped intersection is selected as the center of a training area. (b) When one block or several parallel and perpendicular streets are selected as the center of a training area, a perimeter-shape organizer can be used. (c) When one central street is the center of a training area, a strip-line organizer is used. (d) A scatter-shape organizer helps to visualize a large area where several different unrelated training sites have been selected.

intersection. In presenting this new area to a student, the O&M special-ist would describe only this simple plus shape (the center intersection) first, rather than include all the streets in the training area. The student would recognize that the intersection itself, the center of the plus, was also the center of the training area (see Figure 6.4). In short, the O&M specialist would present a simple focal point at which to begin, which is easier for a student's orientation, rather than ask the student to com-prehend the relationship of all the blocks and streets on the map at once.

The four areas on each side of this superimposed plus shape would be training quadrants. Lessons could be designed to start at the center of the plus (the center intersection) and move away from it in I-, L-, or U-shaped routes. Lessons could move through the center intersection from one quadrant into another or begin in one quadrant and then move to the others for comparison.

If this center intersection is in an urban light business area, it would be a simple or more complex traffic light-controlled intersection, with a variety of businesses and shops along the two main streets. Lessons could be planned to visit these locations (such as a bank, public library, medical center, or community center). The extended quadrant areas would probably have basic or advanced residential areas with stop sign-controlled intersections, where students could pretend to live. Students could focus their route-design skills on traveling from their "homes" into the business area and back, simulating the types of travel activities that people typically engage in during the week (like running errands, shopping, and visiting friends) (V. Fazzi, personal communication, May 1986).

A plus-shape organizer can also be used in a residential area with the same format. Typically, lessons start at the central point where the two selected streets intersect, usually a plus-shaped intersection with four stop signs (an "all-way" stop-controlled intersection). The various streets intersecting these two "main" streets may be 2- or 4-way stops or 1- or 3-way stops if they are T shaped. Within the quadrants of this area, students will find a variety of types of homes (duplexes, apartments, and so forth), as well as different kinds of landscaping, sidewalks, and curb treatments.

The Block or Perimeter

O&M specialists can select a particular block whose shape can be visu-alized as a rectangle. Working within one block can provide many opportunities for the development of concepts and orientation skills and the refinement of cane techniques before street crossings are introduced. This type of lesson unit works well for teaching students of various ages the general O&M curriculum, especially when it involves walking around the block of their school, agency, or home. There is little need for a car to transport students with this type of unit or, if there is, the driving time will only be a few minutes. This location is time efficient for young children or older adults whose lesson time may be short and who may tire if they walk long distances.

Lessons that progress in a certain direction around the block help young students who are congenitally blind learn about concrete spatial and environmental concepts, such as laterality and the function and location of sidewalks and driveways, as well as more abstract spatial concepts like blocks and streets. Such lessons are also useful in teaching orientation skills. Students are learning to know where their schools or homes are located and what these buildings look like. Basic mobility skills, to teach or reinforce, include different midblock cane techniques, trailing, straight line of travel, and recovery from veering. Students can be encouraged to make maps of the block and to share these maps with their classmates at the end of the unit.

O&M specialists can also visualize a training area by looking on a map for several large intersecting boulevards that are near one another. They can choose four streets that form a square or rectangular perimeter. The training area is the square or rectangle shape that is bordered by and includes these four larger streets (see Figure 6.4). The inner area surrounded by the four larger streets may be residential.

If the area surrounded by the larger perimeter streets is residential, lessons can include residential routes that move outward to one of the larger perimeter streets. In this way, the students can review residential street-crossing skills and travel in a light business area in the same lesson. This kind of training area is good for both beginning and advanced students, who are either learning or reviewing skills. Each of the four larger intersections should have traffic light hardware for students to practice more advanced mobility skills. Students can learn to compare these four traffic light-controlled intersections in terms of traffic patterns, types of corners, and hardware (timed-controlled traffic lights whose timing is set versus volume-controlled traffic lights whose timing varies with the amount of traffic present). Lessons can also be designed for travel along the perimeter streets, where there are businesses and a variety of light business hardware in the middle of the block, such as parking signs, parking meters, cement benches, trash cans, planters, and the like. Lesson routes along these busier streets are appropriate for more advanced students who do not need to review residential travel skills (Hector Copado, personal communication, July 1986).

The Strip

A lesson unit can also be designed along a strip, using one street (see Figure 6.4). The O&M specialist may train in an area that has only one main street, and there is little choice but to use it as a basic I shape. A strip training area may also be chosen because of the variety of interesting destinations found along both sides of the street. Using a strip-shape organizer can work well in either residential or light business areas. Routes are designed along the main street (the strip) and all the streets that branch off from this main thoroughfare. All the types of intersections found along this street can be analyzed, and L-, U-, and stair-shaped routes can be designed that cross the main street. In addition, students can be asked to note the changing neighborhoods as they travel in a particular direction along this main street. There may be an end destination, which will take four to eight lessons or more to reach, or the intent may simply be to travel along a particular street to see what is there. Perhaps the history of a town can be learned by traveling along its main street. Sometimes, as was mentioned before, there is little choice in training areas, and the environment has only one main street along which to travel. All mobility training that needs to be given, then, has to be presented along this one route. Field trips may have to be arranged for students to experience other travel environments if this is part of their curriculum.

Scattered Locations

There are times when O&M specialists need to teach certain mobility skills involving hardware that is not readily available (learning to travel on escalators, in elevators, through revolving doors, or on the subway) or involving crossing unique kinds of intersections (three-way signal intersections or intersections with multiple legs). O&M specialists may need to teach certain orientation skills (such as learning and applying the address system or negotiating around gas stations or through parking lots) that are not located in any particular location. Lessons introducing three-way signals, for example, may involve traveling from an intersection in one part of town to a similar intersection in another part of town (see Figure 6.4). Perhaps one lesson will be in one area and the next lesson in another area simply because the goal is to teach general elevator skills and the elevators are located in different locations. A student who is practicing scanning skills at boulevard two-way stop intersections, may enjoy the variety of practicing these skills along several different boulevards in different areas of the city.

Lessons that are scattered throughout the training area in unrelated parts of town have some disadvantages in terms of students' ability to develop both orientation and mobility skills. If the training area changes with each lesson, for example, students may be overloaded with information as they try to learn about a new area each week. They may respond by becoming overly nervous in an effort to "learn everything" or in response to being disoriented. Because this weekly change is tiring, other students may lose track of the goal of the lesson or start to tune out and assume less responsibility for learning about where they are. Instead of becoming active learners who seek information about new areas, some students may instead become more passive or indifferent to these new experiences. Students' overall mobility skills may suffer if they are unfamiliar with what a particular area looks like. If students are generally curious about the new places where they are traveling, they will naturally focus more on orienting themselves to new textures, sounds, and changes in levels, for example, than on mobility skills like their grip or being in step. Thus, teaching or reinforcing cane skills in unfamiliar locations with these types of students may be less effective. Therefore, these "scatter" types of classes should be kept to a minimum and perhaps presented between units that take place in specific locations.

Adding on with Ls

O&M specialists can use an "adding-on" arrangement based on a route shape when they teach students skills from the general O&M curriculum. This type of organizer can be a fun twist for well-oriented students. In this scenario, the students learn or practice skills while they travel along a beginning L-shaped route. They continue to practice or learn skills while traveling a second L-shaped route that leads off the first, and then do so on a third L-shaped route that leads off the second, and so on.

Students who have limited orientation skills can be successful with simple L-shaped routes. The completion of each L may give the student a sense of accomplishment. For example, the first route taught to a student may emphasize mobility skills at an intersection nearest the student's home, school, or work site. Since the route is L-shaped, it involves only one turn to reach the intersection or one change of facing at the intersection itself prior to crossing the street. Completing the route may take several lessons, since the student is working on turning and lining-up skills. Once this route is completed, the student continues to travel on the next L-shaped route.

If the goal on the first route is to work on orientation skills instead, the O&M specialist may provide a tactile or large-print map for the students to see where their training area and the beginning L-shaped route are on the map. The O&M specialist would plan one or two lessons for the students to practice map-reading skills (compass cardinal directions and understanding the names and sequence of streets to be crossed) and to execute this first route correctly. The unit plan would then evolve from this intersection area to another one nearby, reached by traveling a second L-shaped route. One or two lessons would be planned for this second intersection, with the students then traveling another L-shaped route from there to a third intersection. The unit plan, then, consists of a series of intersection lessons all joined by L-shaped routes. The overall shape visualized by the O&M specialist evolves as a series of Ls joined together, moving in any direction within the overall training area, depending on which intersections are chosen (see Figure 6.5).

The O&M specialist will have traveled to the general training area ahead of time to locate interesting intersections and to design the various L-shaped routes that connect the intersections. There may be choices to travel from one intersection to another, and some students may be given the opportunity, if appropriate, to choose from among the recommended L-shaped routes or to make up new ones. The final intersection studied will be far from the original one, and the overall floor pattern of this type of unit will appear rambling, since any of the L-shaped routes can lead in any direction away from a particular intersection.

ORGANIZING THE ENVIRONMENT BY TYPICAL DESTINATIONS

Another way of organizing the training environment is by destinations that students may need to visit, such as various types of businesses, facilities, or services. Different areas, such as shopping plazas, different

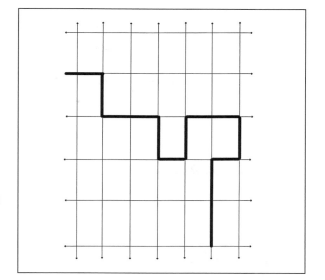

Figure 6.5

Adding on with Ls

A series of L-shaped routes is visualized over a training area. When students complete the first L-shaped route independently, they learn a second route connected to the first one at an intersection and can continue to travel in any direction until the unit is completed.

types of stores, and shopping malls, have unusual features that may be useful for students to practice various skills. They are also environments that students need to negotiate in the course of daily life and, in the case of shopping malls, may be an attraction in themselves for young students. Other destinations that would be useful for students to visit include a public library, airport, train or bus station, post office, and bank.

Small Shopping Plaza

Small shopping plazas are common in advanced residential–light business transition areas. These plazas typically have one or more fast-food restaurants and other small businesses like video stores, hair salons, Laundromats, small grocery stores, liquor stores, and specialty shops. These L-shaped plazas are commonly located at the corner of large intersections. The plaza is set back from the main sidewalk by a parking lot and has driveways leading in and out of this parking area from each street (see Figure 6.6 for a diagram of an L-shaped plaza). The plaza usually has smaller walkways next to the building line, with access from either one or both of the street sidewalks. Another location for a plaza is midblock. The midblock plaza is usually I shaped and does not have its own access walkway from the main sidewalk. Pedestrian access is typically through the parking lot.

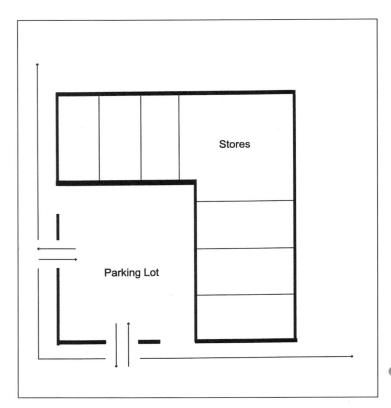

Stores

Parking Lot

Figure 6.6

Diagram of an L-Shaped Plaza

Different kinds of minilesson units can be planned for these kinds of environments as part of the general O&M curriculum. Students can be familiarized with the basic types of plazas and learn how to travel safely to the stores within them. They can locate where the plaza walkway intersects the main sidewalk and practice locating various businesses. Beginning students can review basic cane skills to locate and navigate these walkways. More advanced students can practice maintaining a straight line of travel along the main sidewalk or recovery from veering into the parking lot. Traveling to and shopping in a plaza is good for students who need to learn or review outdoor and indoor sighted (human) guide skills. Students with low vision can practice their monocular skills while scanning and focusing on the large overhead sign at the corner of the plaza and along the storefronts. Orientation skills may include an adaptation of room orientation skills to learn about the interior of a particular store or noticing the address numbers of the plaza's businesses. Sometimes these addresses correspond to the address numbers of one of the streets, or the plaza has its own separate address system based on letters or numbers. Students can learn how to find the safest routes when the plaza has no walkway leading from the main sidewalk. All students can practice interacting with the public to gather information or to make purchases. Often these corner locations have bus stops and bus benches, mailboxes, and newspaper stands—parts of the environment that all O&M students, both beginning and advanced, need to learn about and use.

Supermarket, Department Store, or Discount Store

Learning how to travel in a supermarket, department store, and discount store is a necessary skill for O&M students, whether they shop independently or with assistance from a store clerk, family member, or friend. (See Figure 6.7 for a layout of a typical grocery store.) For this reason, training in these stores is an important part of the general O&M curriculum. These large indoor environments are particularly useful locations in which to teach when it is too wet, too cold, or too hot to practice O&M skills outdoors. Therefore, it is useful to have a minilesson unit on hand for these occasions, lessons that are useful for any level of student. Skills that can be introduced, practiced, or refined include

- room orientation using the perimeter walls and inner aisles;

- mapmaking;

- basic cane skills;

- auditory skills for negotiating aisles;

- monocular skills;

- basic spatial and directional skills, including route shapes;

- verbal and listening skills to describe or follow a route in the store;

- interacting with the public; and

- handling money, making purchases, and using general organizational skills.

Items can be found with assistance or independently once the student is familiar with the store. These units are often fun when some lessons include small groups of O&M students or when students are making purchases for their class at school.

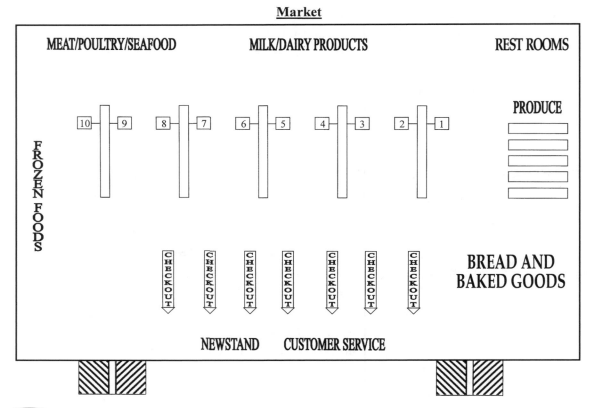

Figure 6.7

Typical Grocery Store Layout

Shopping Mall

Since shopping malls are common environments in most urban and sub-urban areas, it is important to design a lesson unit that teaches students to travel effectively within them. (See Figure 6.8 for a sample layout of a shopping mall.) For a student who wants to get a job in a shopping mall or who needs to shop there frequently, this unit may be a unit "by demand," and the particular shopping mall may be designated by the student. Therefore, it is important for the O&M specialist to travel to the mall ahead of time and locate where the public bus and taxi or minibus stops are, as well as the parking areas for people with disabilities.

The O&M specialist can obtain a map of the mall and transfer this information into a tactile or large-print format, so the student can easily see the names and locations of the anchor department stores and how they are arranged in relation to one another. Sometimes a mall has a plus,

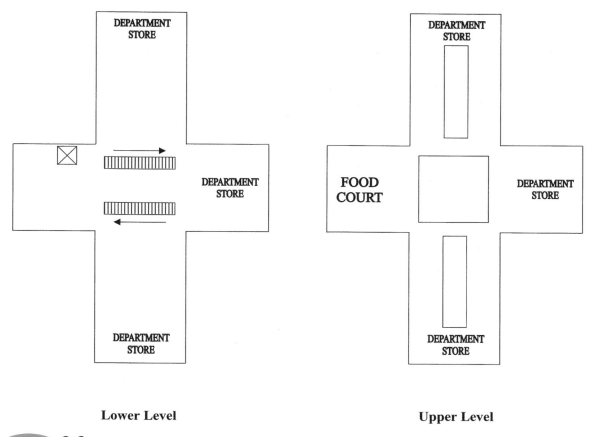

Lower Level   Upper Level

Figure 6.8

Typical Shopping Mall Layout

L, or grid shape in relation to these department stores, and understanding this general shape can assist with basic orientation. As the lessons evolve, the student and O&M specialist determine which entrances are best, as well as the locations of the rest rooms and telephones nearest to this entrance. It may be important to know where the central information desk is and how to get there from the entrance. Students can then ask for assistance, if necessary, to do their shopping. Students who have low vision can be taught to use the large colored maps and directories often located in display cases near the entrances. Many of the skills mentioned under Supermarket, Department Store, or Discount Store apply to travel in a shopping mall as well, since they are typically enclosed. Because the malls are larger, however, students may need to learn rote routes at first to find the stores they need efficiently before they can design routes on their own.

ENVIRONMENTAL CONSIDERATIONS FOR STUDENTS WITH SPECIAL NEEDS

Although all the environments mentioned in this chapter can be used for lessons with students with special needs, training areas for students with multiple disabilities are more typically in environments that are dictated by circumstances—"by demand" or "without choice." For example, students who have difficulty recalling routes and need supervision while traveling may need to learn indoor rote routes so they can travel as independently as possible within their everyday environments—to the rest rooms of their sheltered workshop, for instance, or the dining hall and recreation room of their school or assisted care facility. Some students may also have orthopedic disabilities or poor stamina that make it difficult for them to travel on stairs or for long distances. O&M specialists need to consider the following factors as they determine the easiest and safest route for their students to learn within indoor environments:

- overall length of the route;
- places to stop for rests en route;
- shape of the route and number of turns needed;
- landmarks to use and obstacles to avoid;
- pedestrian traffic patterns at the time of travel;
- noise-sound factors; and
- texture, gradient, and level changes along the route.

Although these considerations are important when instructing all O&M students in indoor travel, they are particularly important to keep in mind for students with additional disabilities. Travel aids may include setting up a buddy system for traveling with another student or expecting the student to travel alone on only part of the route. Orientation aids may include adding extra landmarks along the way for the student to use or making a tape the student can listen to that provides auditory cues.

If the students are hard of hearing, it is important to select training environments that are quiet, like a small residential area, or that have definite identifiable auditory cues, such as a business area with clearcut traffic patterns and minimal background noise. If the students are wheelchair users, O&M specialists need to select environments with accessible routes that have as many wheelchair ramps as possible for crossing intersections safely. If these students are learning bus travel, O&M specialists need to select environments with bus routes that accommodate wheelchairs. If these students need to get to a specific location (environment by demand), they have to learn how to research the bus routes and find the ones that have kneeling buses.

The overall abilities of a particular student may affect where the lessons take place. Certain students, for example, may be motivated to learn but may be restricted by their lack of stamina or specific orthopedic problems. Because they tire easily or cannot walk far, they may be able to train only near or at their schools, homes, or workplaces, even though they need exposure to a greater variety of spatial and environmental concepts. Often these students are better served more frequently but for a shorter amount of time per lesson. They can be driven or transported in their wheelchairs for part of a lesson, even if it is a short distance, to learn certain environmental concepts. It may be appropriate to take a folding chair so that a student can rest often while traveling on lessons. The scheduling of the lesson may also be important. Students with special needs may have more energy earlier in the day, for example, so lessons may need to be scheduled at that time, rather than later in the day. For additional suggestions, see Teaching Tips for Students with Special Needs.

O&M specialists will benefit from taking the time to modify their lessons when working with students with special needs. The physical layout of the training area, the length of the lesson, and when the lesson is held are just a few of the factors that are important to consider when teaching these students.

O&M specialists who spend time investigating training areas for teaching the O&M curriculum know ahead of time the best places to teach or reinforce specific skills like midblock basic cane skills, residential and light business street-crossing skills, concept skills, route-planning skills, auditory training, and practicing the address system and interacting with the public. Even when the training area is "by demand" because of a student's unique needs, an O&M specialist needs to review the area and determine the safest and most efficient way to travel to and from the desired locations. Organizing training environments by shapes

TEACHING TIPS FOR STUDENTS WITH SPECIAL NEEDS

- Consider the weather when planning lessons, since some students are adversely affected by extremely hot, cold, or wet conditions.

- Bring water, juice, or small snacks for students who frequently need these items when exercising.

- Consult with students who are diabetic or have other health conditions to determine the most appropriate time to schedule O&M lessons. (Medical personnel can also be consulted when necessary.)

- Allow adequate time to complete routes with students who have orthopedic disabilities and may travel slowly.

- Instruct teaching assistants and health care workers in the proper use of the sighted (human) guide technique.

- Select the most relevant travel routes from a student's daily routine to teach first.

- Prepare written notes for students who are deaf-blind to use when communicating with others while using public transportation.

and specific areas helps the O&M specialist develop lesson units that have continuity and allows more time to develop creative and motivating teaching strategies. The initial time it takes to research where to teach saves time later on and enables O&M specialists to present more organized and interesting lessons.

7

Choosing Teaching Materials:
Maps, Models, Manipulatives, and More

CHAPTER PREVIEW

The Uses of Maps, Models, and Manipulatives

Theory of Cognitive Mapping
Definitions of Maps, Models, and Manipulatives
Maps, Models, and Manipulatives in the O&M Curriculum

Types of Maps

Visual Maps
Tactile Maps
Verbal Maps
Interactive Models
Maps for Students Who Have Additional Disabilities

Teaching Map Skills

Introducing Map Skills
Making Maps Ahead of Time
Making Maps with the Student

Planning and Organizing Maps, Models, and Manipulatives

Making Instructional Materials Portable and Durable
Making Instructional Materials Practical
Where and How to Store Instructional Materials

Appendix

7.A   O&M Recipes: Preparing and Using Maps, Models,
       Manipulatives, and More

THE SELECTION and creation of instructional materials to support students learning of O&M skills and concepts is an important part of each O&M specialist's work routine. Unlike other areas of teaching, in which there may be an abundance of commercially available materials to assist professionals with instruction, O&M specialists frequently need to develop their own resources for creating maps, models, and other instructional tools to use with a range of students.

This chapter briefly reviews theories of cognitive mapping and stresses the importance of incorporating the use of maps, models, and other instructional materials within O&M lessons. It also presents examples of different types of tactile and visual maps and models and suggestions for how to make and present a variety of maps, models, graphics, and manipulatives with students of different ages and abilities. The chapter's Appendix contains "recipes" for making a variety of instructional materials that can be used to teach orientation concepts and mobility skills.

THE USES OF MAPS, MODELS, AND MANIPULATIVES

Depending on the needs of their students, O&M specialists spend time selecting curricula, planning lessons, and (as described in Chapter 6) finding training sites that are appropriate for teaching relevant concepts and skills. Once they have done so, they then need to determine the best way to present lessons and describe training sites to individual students. The most effective presentation style varies according to students' strongest modes of learning. Students with strong linguistic skills, for example, may prefer to have their lessons, training environments, and routes described in words. Sentences that include relevant spatial and environmental concepts are effective for giving these students information that they can readily understand. Other students with strong spatial skills may want to use models to understand the concept of a stairway or may find large-print or tactile maps effective in learning where various streets and landmarks are located near their schools or workplaces. Students with strong musical skills may enjoy listening to a tape of certain unique sounds that are typical of the training area as an introduction before they travel there. Students who enjoy practicing skills in an interactive group would enjoy using manipulatives or tactile diagrams to learn more about a certain area (for example, a table game to match pictures of landmarks with the words that describe them).

Selecting and creating instructional materials that are the most useful for a particular student or group of students is an ongoing challenge and an excellent opportunity to explore creative possibilities.

Theory of Cognitive Mapping

The purpose of orienting students to a particular training environment is to begin the process of forming a cognitive map. *Cognitive mapping* describes how individuals perceive and mentally organize their physical environment. For those who have low vision or are functionally blind, cognitive mapping describes the way in which they perceive the relative distance and spatial relationship between objects in a given area and between themselves and these objects (Bentzen, 1997). Depending on their ability to form an accurate cognitive map, people who are blind or visually impaired can use their internal "visualization" system effectively to learn about given environments and then travel within them more easily, to follow simple routes, and to plan a variety of new routes within familiar or unfamiliar areas.

Cognitive mapping skills also enable students to update their changing position relative to the various objects in their environment while they are traveling any given route (*spatial updating*). For example, students who practice room-orientation skills to learn about their classrooms are developing cognitive maps of these particular environments. Through tactile examination, locomotor movement, and dialogue with the O&M specialist, they form a picture of where various objects are along the perimeter and inner part of the room. They review this information as they repeat various routes within the room, confirming the presence or absence of objects. Their cognitive map builds as they reconfirm orientation information about the room through movement, identifying more accurately the relative distance and position of objects to one another (what is behind, in front of, or to the side of something.) As their cognitive map becomes more precise, they are able to locate any part of the room from any other location within the room, no longer dependent on set routes. In addition, if there is a change in the room, they are able to recognize it and make adjustments in their route travel so they are still able to travel efficiently within the environment.

Cognitive mapping at the "route level" involves learning and demonstrating knowledge of rote routes within a familiar area (Bentzen, 1997), whereas the more complex "survey level" of mapping enables travelers to make up new and different routes within a familiar area (see

Chapter 6 for more information on mapping routes). At this more advanced level, students are able to understand the position of all fixed objects (including their own positions) within an environment, and hence to recover from veering and detours as needed.

Tactile maps and models are effective in helping students form cognitive maps at both the route and survey levels, enabling them to understand the general arrangement of objects and to point to them accurately (Bentzen, 1997). Cognitive mapping skills are aided and reinforced by the use of maps and models as students learn about unfamiliar places, especially places that are large and therefore difficult or impossible to examine through exploration alone. Maps (like a cutout map of the United States or a globe of the world) enable students to comprehend these large spatial environments relatively quickly and safely while seated in their classrooms (Bentzen, 1997).

Definitions of Maps, Models, and Manipulatives

A *map* is a representation of a generic or specific place or area, like a representation of a classroom or room at home, college campus, workplace, specific residential or light business neighborhood, or city. Maps are two-dimensional, but tactile maps have a slightly three-dimensional aspect so that the reader who is blind or visually impaired can identify various significant features by touch.

A *model* is a three-dimensional representation of a place or object, such as a shopping center, historic park, building, intersection, or elevator or staircase. Models can represent the same environment as a map, but give the user a better idea of the dimensions and the relative size of the various objects or buildings located there.

Tactile diagrams are two-dimensional tactile drawings that may illustrate the different shapes of intersections, sizes of doors, shapes of traffic signs, or types of corners found in travel environments. Tactile diagrams are typically more effective if they are portable and can be used on location when traveling. For example, when students are learning about the corners of a block and are examining a particular corner, they may be given a raised-shaped diagram of this type of corner. The diagram would have the same-shaped corner cut and same bordering grassline shape as the real corner they were seeing or touching. As the students were exposed to other kinds of corners with different shapes and borders, they would be presented with tactile diagrams corresponding to these new features, so they could compare the various diagrams and types of corners. Tactile and large-print diagrams can be used to represent generic parts of the environment or help explain features specific to a given area.

Manipulatives are teaching tools that involve students in different kinds of gross- or fine-motor movements to help them understand spatial or environmental concepts more thoroughly. Examples of manipulatives include miniature cars for simulating traffic patterns, blocks for counting or building, traffic cones to negotiate around while practicing cane skills, carpet squares used to represent blocks for sitting on and walking around, and costumes or props for role-playing.

Manipulatives may be small, such as LEGOs, which can be positioned on a table; large wooden blocks to arrange on a carpet; or toys that represent larger real objects (like a toy construction backhoe for digging dirt or a toy three-story parking garage for parking toy cars). The O&M specialist may bring larger stationary manipulatives, including traffic cones, or use those that are part of the environment, such as tables or chairs. Manipulatives may be handled by students while standing in place (for instance, tossing beanbags in different directions to learn the four compass cardinal directions) or moving (for example, walking "around" a cone, crawling "through" a box, and jumping on numbered foam squares to learn "even" and "odd"). Other instructional materials or resources may include electronic equipment (such as tape recorders, audible toys, or walkie-talkies) that helps students learn about their environment or gadgets (like a pedometer for measuring a route's distance in steps or a stopwatch to measure the number of seconds a particular traffic light is red or green) that give other information.

Maps, models, tactile diagrams, and manipulatives can be used with individual students or several students together. Each of these teaching aids helps students understand their travel environment more thoroughly and enhances their cognitive mapping skills.

Maps, Models, and Manipulatives in the O&M Curriculum

Maps, models, and manipulatives are essential teaching tools for the O&M curriculum. They can be used for a variety of purposes, including

- reinforcement of body and spatial references for young students,

- mapmaking and reading,

- advanced orientation skills like landmarking and compass cardinal direction skills for planning and following routes,

- exposure to large environments where students cannot travel, or

- assessment of spatial and environmental concepts (for example, using the Chang Kit to ask questions about traffic patterns and controls).

For additional important applications of these materials in the O&M curriculum, see Uses of Maps, Models, and Manipulatives.

Using words to describe information from different types of maps and models improves students' communication skills. As students interact with the O&M specialist, other students, or friends while looking at the map or model, both their expressive and receptive language skills and their social skills are being reinforced. Map-reading experiences often increase students' curiosity about an environment, encourage their questioning skills, and motivate them to explore a new area. As students discuss information from a map or model, their overall awareness or knowledge of travel environments increases, and they become more self-confident as they travel within those places. For some students, discussing a route in words while feeling it tactilely on a map helps them to understand and remember the route better. In addition, a map can be used as a reference to refresh the students' memory if part of the route is forgotten while traveling.

Using a map helps students with their decision-making skills as they plan the fastest or most efficient route to a place, and enhanced decision-making skills help to give students of all ages more independence and self-confidence. Beginning students may plan the simplest straight-line route, whereas advanced travelers may aim for the most complex route shape. In either case, learning how to plan an efficient route to a destination and completing it increases students' memory, recall, and sequencing skills.

Much of the O&M curriculum is based on experiential learning, in which students learn about concepts or environments through movement or interaction with a thing or place. Mapmaking and map reading are important parts of this experiential learning process. Information that may be missing or incomplete because of blindness or low vision can be presented in its entirety using maps or models. Students can use the smaller movements of their hands to read a map of an area where they will be traveling or use full body movements in an interactive model to learn what an intersection is and how the traffic pattern works there. Using words and movements, students can transfer information

> ### USES OF MAPS, MODELS, AND MANIPULATIVES
>
> - Use age-appropriate props (such as a brightly colored rainstick that is moved to various places) to help young children learn spatial concepts, such as in front of, behind, above, and below.
>
> - Use student-made drawings of familiar landmarks or a commercially purchased compass to help older students apply orientation concepts, such as landmarking and basic cardinal compass directions. Students can match the drawings to the real landmarks along the route and use the compass to confirm changes of direction when a route turns.
>
> - Use tactile maps or globes to help students who are congenitally blind to develop an understanding of large geographic areas (states, countries, continents, oceans, and so on).
>
> - Use computer-generated maps to help students begin to plan their own travel routes.
>
> - Use student-made maps to help students execute routes with increasing independence and to problem solve and reorient themselves as needed.
>
> - Use instructor-made graphics and tactile diagrams (like shapes of intersections, basic traffic patterns, and layouts of residential and light business travel areas) to enable O&M specialists to assess students' knowledge of travel environments.

from the smaller scale of a map or model to an actual travel environment, whether they are traveling a route along a specific street or listening to traffic at an intersection. For example, students learn that a route along a certain street (or within a certain area) has odd-shaped intersections and that these intersections correspond to the curved lines of a map of that same area. Once students are able to identify and understand the general features of a map, they can generalize their map-reading skills to learn about unfamiliar travel areas.

TYPES OF MAPS

Maps, models, and manipulatives can be purchased or made. School districts and agencies can order professional mapmaking kits that O&M

specialists can use repeatedly, such as the APH Tactile Graphics Kit, the Chang Kit, thermoform paper and machines, the tactile image enhancer, global positioning systems, and various computer programs (like a talking maps program, Atlas Speaks, by Arkenstone and VisuAide). Although purchased equipment is helpful, it is also expensive. When O&M specialists make their own maps, models, or manipulatives, the materials they use do not have to be expensive and can be purchased within a typical budget allotment. Some materials (such as foam board, acetate, Wikki Stix, grease pencils, highlighters, and puffy paint) can be bought at a stationery, art-supply, or crafts store, and many others (including tape, cardboard, glue, markers, and various sizes of string) can be found at home or in a classroom or office.

Maps need not be limited to the typical pastel-shaded, paper versions, with narrow lines for borders or roads. Visual maps for people with low vision use large print and high-color or black-and-white contrast enhancement. Maps can also be touched, using raised lines and tactile shapes, or manipulated, using objects as sequence cues to represent landmarks. Maps and models that use words are understood through listening, reading, or oral communication with another person. With interactive maps, students can "act out" spatial and environmental concepts to learn them more thoroughly. Students can even make edible maps out of Jell-O or brownies and eat them (see Appendix 4.A for an example). Table 7.1 lists some of the types of maps and models mentioned in this section. Suggestions for ways of using different types of maps appear in Incorporating Different Types of Maps within O&M Lessons.

Visual Maps

Effective low vision maps can be enlargements of professional maps, hand-drawn maps, or a combination of the two. It is important for these types of maps to have high contrast, color highlighting that a student can see well (some students are color deficient in certain shades), clear labeling, and a minimal amount of *visual clutter*—visual information that is unnecessary or confusing).

Maps can be drawn by the O&M specialist, the student, or together. There are a variety of ways to draw maps that can be effective. Drawing surfaces that are useful include dry-erase boards and different sizes and colors of paper and plastics. Dry-erase board drawings and maps are fun to draw and can be copied well on a photocopy machine using ledger-

Table 7.1 Types of Maps

Method of Perceiving	Type of Map	Examples
Hearing	Verbal	Descriptive sequence, word games, global positioning systems used with talking computer programs
Hearing	Taped	Reguar or adapted tape recorder or communication board to follow a route
Reading	Written	Brailled (brailler or electronic aid), large print, handwritten (descriptive sequence, shuffle, diary during and after lesson, poems)
Seeing	Drawn	Symbol sequence, picture sequence, shuffle, hand-drawn large print, enlarged professional maps with overlays or highlighting
Touching	Tactile	Professional kits (Chang Kit, Tactile Graphics), thermoformed maps, tactile image-enhancer maps, a variety of materials for handmade maps, computer programs adapted for tactile medium
Moving (kinesthetic)	Interactive	Use of people and small and large manipulatives
Eating	Edible	Jell-O cake or cookie dough to learn spatial concepts and shapes
Manipulating	Sequential object cues	Presented and manipulated in sequence independently or with assistance

size paper. The O&M specialist can help the student make these into "add-on" maps by gluing on paper cutouts representing different features drawn on the map (see Appendix 7.A for more detailed "recipes" for these and other types of maps).

Maps can vary in size from 8 x 10 inches to several feet long, rolled into a scroll or tube. Depending on the age of the student, the maps can be simple (a few shapes to represent the interior of a room or the school playground) or complex (a series of maps of an intersection, each showing one feature like landmarks, traffic flow, or addresses). "Pop-ups"

INCORPORATING DIFFERENT TYPES OF MAPS WITHIN O&M LESSONS

Verbal Maps

- Play a word game with young children (such as, "I spy something blue that is taller than you") to find a series of landmarks and a hidden treasure at the end of a residential block.

- Have the student listen to a tape-recorded description of a route (produced by the O&M specialist, the student, a classmate, or a family member) to help the student remember a rote route.

Visual Maps

- Shuffle picture cards (either photographs or hand drawn) to help the student practice sequencing landmarks along a route.

- Draw a particular intersection configuration on a dry-erase board, while standing at the corner, to help the student visualize the whole picture.

Tactile Maps

- Adapt a commercially bought highway map with lines of different widths to use with the tactile image enhancer to create a tactile map for a student who is blind.

- Gather tactile landmarks (such as tiny stones, cut leaves, and sticks) while traveling in a new area for the student and O&M specialist to glue on a map.

(items that stand up from the page) are fun to add to large-print maps (see Appendix 7.A).

Students can also be encouraged to draw landmarks, buildings, a shopping plaza, or parts of an intersection during a lesson. These drawings can be on a large surface or on 8 x 10-inch cards, using markers, crayons, or colored pencils. Students can then place these cards in the correct order to indicate that they know a certain travel area, as in the example in Figure 7.1, creating what is known as a "shuffle" map. These drawings are a good way to assess what the students actually perceive when they look at part of their travel environment.

Maps can be enlarged as much as needed for a student with low vision on most copy machines using regular- or ledger-size paper. En-

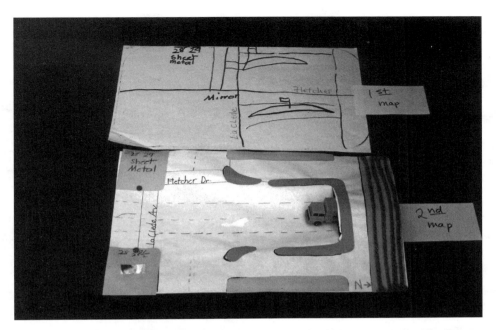

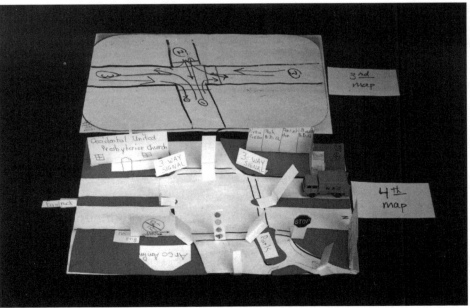

Photo 7.1

Two ways to create a simple map from a student's drawing: *(top)* A student's drawing of an intersection was photocopied from a dry-erase board onto ledger paper. The instructor corrected the accuracy of the map and created paper cutouts for the student to glue on to it. The labels on this map refer to addresses and types of business (a sheet metal shop and a glass and mirror store). *(bottom)* Another simple student-drawn map of a different area was transformed into a pop-up map, with all the landmarks and signs made by the student. The arrows represent traffic patterns.

Figure 7.1

Shuffle Map

Landmark cards such as these can be drawn by the student or O&M specialist and then arranged to form a shuffle map. In this example, the student might explain, "First I go out the door and turn right. When I pass the tree at the corner, I cross the street and walk half a block until I find the tall brick wall. Two houses after that is where John lives."

larged sections of maps on 8 x 11-inch paper can be placed in nonglare plastic sheet protectors so that areas of the map can be highlighted by drawing on top of the plastic with a grease pen. Portions of large maps can be enlarged and pasted together to see the necessary details of a bigger area. Sometimes students enjoy taping the enlargements together in the form of a long scroll that they can carry while traveling along a particular street for a given distance. Any of these enlargements can be marked with highlighters directly on the paper or covered with acetate and then drawn on with grease pencils (see Appendix 7.A). O&M specialists can also trace a few selected features or areas of an enlarged map onto another piece of plain paper, using a thick pen, to make a simpler map for students who are confused by visual clutter.

Students, including adults, who have low vision, can also use a closed-circuit television (CCTV) to enlarge relevant maps or pages from a map book of areas where they want to travel. In this case, the drawing is a detailed professional one, and the students operate the CCTV to focus on the specific area that they want to see. Students can also change the background (white on black) or manipulate other background colors if they wish.

Tactile Maps

There are an infinite number of possibilities for constructing tactile maps. If maps and models are prepared with high-color or black-and-white contrast, as well as large-print and braille labels, they can be used effectively with both students who have low vision and those who are functionally blind.

In general, tactile maps can be divided into two styles: those that have raised lines (such as to represent a street or building line) and those that have raised shapes (such as to represent a block, a building, or a continent) (see Photo 7.2 for samples). Some students may prefer one type to the other because they find it easier to visualize. Others may prefer certain textures used in raised-line maps over those used in raised-shape maps, or vice versa. O&M specialists may chose one style over the other because it is easier or simpler for beginning O&M students to understand or perceive. When traveling in a residential area and practicing beginning map skills, for example, students may understand a raised-shape map more readily than a more abstract raised-line map. Even if students have a preference for one type of map or the other, it is important to teach them how to use both because they will be exposed to both types as they progress in their O&M curriculum and later on when they use premade tactile maps of certain travel areas. Maps that combine raised shapes and raised lines can also be used, but care may be needed to ensure that the combination does not confuse some students.

Students who prefer raised-line maps may be able to use professional mapmaking kits, like the APH Tactile Graphics Kit, to create their own maps during O&M lessons if the 11 x 11-inch size of the APH foil paper is sufficient to meet their needs. O&M specialists also find this kit useful for making tactile maps ahead of time of travel areas their students will use. A thermoform machine, tactile image enhancer, or "hot" pen can be used to produce raised-line maps from regular two-dimensional paper maps that are drawn by hand or made professionally and copied. Glue, puff paint, string, and Wikki Stix are some materials that are useful for making handmade raised-line maps. If the map has been drawn directly on a hard surface, these materials can be used to form the tactile lines. If the map is a paper enlargement, the paper can be glued on a firm surface and then made tactile using the same procedure.

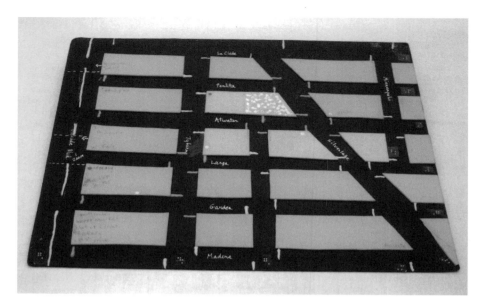

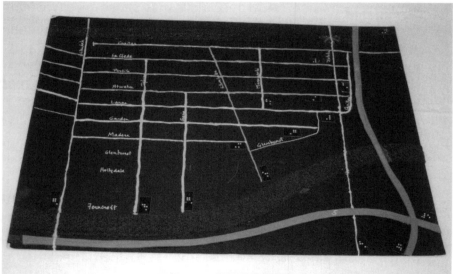

Photo 7.2

Photos of Raised-shape and Raised-line Maps.

These two different types of maps (raised-shape vs. raised-line) of the same training area can be used with different students to teach route planning skills. Some students will be able to perceive spatial concepts more easily on one or the other.

For students who prefer raised-shape maps, O&M specialists can use professional kits like the Chang Kit to teach about blocks, streets, and intersections. The Chang Kit, a commercial teaching aid, can be used as either a tactile or high-color-contrast model to introduce or review spatial and environmental concepts (see Chapter 4 for a photograph). One use of this kit is to teach information about "typical" intersections (like the differences and similarities between a plus-shaped and a T-shaped intersection). It can also be used to teach about a specific intersection, with street names, landmarks and other necessary information added for the student. O&M specialists can make a miniature version of the Chang Kit using an 8 x 11-inch plasttic notepad folder, miniature cars, and some other common materials (see Appendix 7.A), which can be carried easily and used in a lesson when the student is confused about a spatial concept or traffic pattern.

Raised-shape maps can also be made from poster board (or neon-colored poster "glo" board), tagboard, cardboard, foam board, or matte board as the backing. These materials can also be cut to make the various shapes (such as blocks and buildings) used on the map, although softer materials (such as the thin foam sheets of various colors sometimes found in craft or fabric shops) are easier to cut into shapes and adhere well with glue.

Verbal Maps

Another type of map that works well for both students who have low vision and those who are functionally blind is a verbal "map," in which words are used instead of drawings to describe a route or to familiarize a student with an area. These types of maps are used frequently in everyday conversations (to give directions to one's office or house) and are therefore important to understand and practice. For example, students may need to ask directions from a stranger at a street corner or in a department store and hence need to be able to process and recall verbal directions accurately. In addition, they probably need to know how to give their friends and colleagues directions to their schools, offices, or homes.

Verbal maps may include

- route instructions that are written or typed ahead of time on cards by the O&M specialist,

- area descriptions that have been dictated to and recorded by the student in the most appropriate medium,

- directions that are given aurally on a tape,

- information given verbatim as the student is traveling,

- route information given from a distance through a walkie-talkie, or

- orientation information that is word processed by the student on a computer or braille notetaker.

Students can take computer printout instructions or a braille notetaker with them as they travel. Computers are also motivating for students who want to keep a diary of their routes and describe what they found during a lesson or how they traveled at a certain intersection. Other students enjoy using words in the form of poetry or lyrics to a song to follow a route. All these strategies are effective with students who are strong in linguistic intelligence and are motivated by talking and writing.

Interactive Models

Interactive models are another type of map that can be used effectively with both students who are blind and those with low vision. They require students to use full body movements and to incorporate objects and other people as props. To learn how blocks are arranged in relation to one another, for example, students may be asked to walk around the school lunch tables, noting that the tables are parallel to one another, with the longer and shorter sections aligned in the same directions. The four compass cardinal directions could be practiced as well, with one or more students and the O&M specialist moving around the tables as different directions are called out. A detailed description of how to use a similar interactive map consisting of school lunch tables to practice alignment and timing for street crossings is presented in Appendix 7.A.

Large foam jigsaw-puzzle pieces or rug samples arranged in patterns on the floor can help teach the address system. While moving north, students can step (or jump with assistance from the O&M specialist) from one rug piece to another, pretending that these pieces are blocks, such as "100 N," "200 N," "300 N." They can step back and forth between the foam jigsaw-puzzle pieces (the kind with numbers) to practice the even and odd sides of a street (see the unit on the address system in Chapter 2 for a detailed description). Large cardboard boxes, arranged on the floor to represent buildings, can help teach the traffic pattern at a basic plus-shaped intersection. With four cardboard boxes arranged like the corners of an intersection, students can practice "driving" on the correct side of the "street" and turning corners in the correct direction.

Maps for Students Who Have Additional Disabilities

Students who are blind or visually impaired and have other disabilities can also use maps and manipulatives to learn orientation skills or to help them follow specific routes. Some students may need to use communication boards to understand, practice, and review the order of a route on which landmarking and route shapes are indicated by the pictures, words, or codes. Other types of maps may consist of cues, words, or drawings that students can read or interpret in the correct sequence to travel along a prescribed course. These directions typically include landmarks and body references, such as "in front of you," "to your left," or "below," and can be written in large print or braille or drawn on cards. The landmarks represented on these types of maps may be an integral part of the environment (like carpeting, a corner, or an office door) or something added by the O&M specialist to the environment to help travelers (such as visual, tactile, or audible markers on a wall or door). Landmarks that are added to the environment are appropriate for certain places (including the hallways of a nursing home or preschool play area) where travelers have difficulty recalling routes and destinations because of their age or processing problems.

Depending on the student's ability to process and recall, information can be presented with one direction per card, as in "Turn right at the girls' bathroom." An even simpler form of this direction is shown in Figure 7.2; using the letter R as a symbol for "right," the card reads "R at . . . " with a hand-drawn symbol for the girls' bathroom. The cards for each route can be kept on a ring so they are in order and easy to hold. (This is an adaptation of the "shuffle" map shown in Figure 7.1). They can be numbered numerically or have another sequencing code, like color coding or tactile markers of various gradations, to indicate the correct order.

For students who have difficulty recalling routes as they travel independently, turning references and landmarks can be presented in a verbal sequence aurally on an audiotape, as well as in written form. The

Photo 7.3

Jigsaw foam floor pieces can be used to teach basic address-system numbering concepts *(left)*, as well as odd and even numbering-system concepts *(right)* in an interactive way, as students stand on the squares and move from one to another.

students listen to the tape as a reminder while they travel a given route. Other types of sequence cues can be presented in tactile three-dimensional form and carried by the student or given to the student in order (Joffee & Rikhye, 1991). For example, actual objects (such as a toilet paper roll to represent the rest room or milk carton to represent the cafeteria) can also be given to students to help them recall specific landmarks, identify destinations, and sequence routes. Small objects that can be used to symbolize certain travel areas or landmarks can be worn on the wrist (like charms on a bracelet ring or fastened to a plastic wrist keyring holder) or around the neck, hanging on a string necklace. As the student touches these object cues in order, he or she locates the landmarks that these cues represent while traveling on the route (D. Torgersrud, personal communication, November 1998).

Students who cannot recall the entirety of a familiar route and who do not travel independently can be assisted along this route by someone else. The assistant provides verbal and physical reminders and presents

Figure 7.2

Cue Card for a Rote Route

Simple hand-drawn visual cue cards like this one can be used to help students recall landmarks along a rote route.

specific manipulatives or physical cues that represent landmarks at the appropriate time along the route. Symbols of real objects (like a card with three lines to represent Room 3 or a cutout shape of the door of Room 3 with a large print "3" on it) or parts of real objects (such as a faucet handle to represent a bathroom or a spoon to represent the dining hall) can be used. Students are given these objects to recognize particular landmarks along a route that they will locate or to anticipate through touch what their destination will be (the bathroom or the kitchen).

While some students with additional disabilities may use written, brailled, drawn, or tactile cues presented and followed in a sequential form on their own or with the assistance of someone else, other students can read and follow complex large-print or tactile maps independently, as was described earlier. As with other O&M students, students with multiple disabilities can use maps and models while learning the turns and landmarks of a route and as a reminder once the route has been learned. For example, students who travel in wheelchairs and are able to orient themselves well can use a variety of maps to help them learn about a new travel environment. Students who are deaf-blind may be able to use written or brailled cards or object and tactile identifiers to assist them in traveling along routes in a given environment.

O&M specialists have virtually infinite choices of the types of maps they can make and use with their students who are blind or visually impaired. Imagining the various possibilities for mapmaking and developing them as instructional materials for students' lessons is a good starting point for considering how to introduce the various materials and how to teach map-reading skills.

TEACHING MAP SKILLS

There are infinite possibilities for the types of maps that can be made and utilized with students who are visually impaired. Maps can be invaluable when teaching concepts or orienting students to a specific travel environment. Deciding how to introduce maps and how to teach map skills to individual students requires careful thought and planning.

Introducing Map Skills

Prior to introducing maps to students, it is important to determine the kind of map that would be the easiest and most interesting for them to learn first. Considering a student's preferred learning style (see Chapter 5) helps an O&M specialist decide whether a student may prefer a large-print or tactile map (a student who is highly spatial) or a verbal one (a student who is highly linguistic), for example. Students who learn best auditorily may prefer a map given on a tape to one that is drawn, while those with high bodily-kinesthetic abilities may prefer an interactive map to a verbal one. If a student is new, use of the Multiple Intelligences Inventory (see Appendix 5.B) will help the O&M specialist assess the student's stronger and weaker learning styles.

Introducing Maps

Some of the concepts that need to be explained and understood (as appropriate to the student) when defining a map that

- a symbol on a map represents a real object, and its shape on the map is similar to the shape of the real object that is mapped;

- the location on the map represents the actual location in the environment;

- a map represents a view as seen from above (a "bird's-eye view"); and

- directional references on the map correspond to those in the environment (Bentzen, 1997).

An O&M specialist can introduce map skills by asking the student to define the purpose of a map or describe what a map looks like. Depending on the answer, the specialist continues the instruction or adds to the definition of what a map is and shows an example or examples of maps. This explanation depends on the student's age, cognitive level, and visual status; that is, the definition of a map is different for a third grader who is blind, an adventitiously blind young adult, and a high school student who has low vision and cognitive disabilities. The O&M specialist can explain that there are many different kinds of maps, ranging from verbal descriptions and directions to visual and tactile maps, and that some individuals prefer one type over another because of different learning styles. The O&M specialist continues by explaining why the student will be learning about maps and how maps will help the student travel more safely and efficiently. Allowing time for questions and answers enables the O&M specialist to make sure that the student understands the purpose of learning and using map skills.

Environment

It is essential to consider a student's environment when introducing maps skills. Lighting is important, so a student with low vision has enough illumination to see the lines or shapes of a map but is not bothered by undue glare. Seating is important when reading or making maps to avoid confusion. To seat a student properly, align the compass cardinal direction of the map with the same direction as the student is facing; in other words, seat the student so he or she is facing north and the top part of the map is north.

Sequence for Teaching Map Skills

Maps skills are usually taught in a sequential form. Sidebar 7.1 describes a basic map-teaching sequence. This sequence follows the first series of lessons, in which the O&M specialist has described what a map is and why it is important. It can be used for maps that the O&M specialist made ahead of time, as well as for maps that are made during lessons by the student and specialist together. Young students and those with cognitive disabilities will be able to work on the first parts of the sequence.

The student begins or can review this sequence at any point, given

Sidebar 7.1 Map-Teaching Sequence for O&M

The following basic sequence for teaching map skills assumes that the O&M specialist has already introduced the concept of a map and its uses. The sequence specifies that the student will, first with assistance and then independently,

1. Demonstrate a systematic search order to locate a symbol or symbols on the map surface.

2. Locate, discriminate among, and identify symbols, such as shapes, lines, and textural patterns found on a map's surface (for example, identify that the shape is a circle and represents a particular table in the classroom).

3. Identify and/or label north (or a significant landmark) at the top of the map and use compass cardinal directional references (or body or environmental references) as appropriate.

4. Read print or braille labels on shape symbols of a map or numbers referring to these symbols in a map's legend (for instance, the circle shape is labeled "table" or has the number 1 on it, which refers to the number 1 on the legend that indicates "table").

5. Identify the left–right line symbols to the right side of a map by reading the print or braille labels there and top–bottom line symbols to the bottom of the map by reading the print or braille labels there (for example, the left–right line is labeled "Pine Street" to the right of the map depicting the school's neighborhood street).

6. Successfully execute a route given by the O&M specialist using a simple map (such as a map of a small area of the school's neighborhood with only a little detail) along the route to correct himself or herself as necessary.

7. Design and execute his or her own route using information from a simple map.

8. Teach a route to someone else using information from a simple map.

9. Locate, identify, and discriminate symbols of increasing complexity on a map.

10. Read what the symbols represent at the side or bottom of a map or on the legend.

11. Successfully execute a route using maps of increasing complexity (like a map of a college campus with a lot of detail).

12. Design and execute his or her own route using information from a complex map.

13. Teach a route to someone else using information from a complex map.

his or her age, ability, and experience level. For example, elementary school-age students who are congenitally blind would start at the beginning, whereas adventitiously blind adults would not have to learn that a map represents a bird's-eye view. The pacing and timing of this sequencing also depends on the individual student. Students who will use tactile maps only need time to familiarize themselves with each map a portion at a time, since they cannot tactilely perceive all the parts simultaneously. An understanding of the "parts" of the map must then be integrated to form the "whole" concept of the map's representation. Young students who are congenitally blind and some with additional disabilities may need more time to understand conceptually and discriminate tactilely the difference between lines and shapes. Adults who are adventitiously blind already know the difference conceptually and just need time to practice discriminating the difference through touch. In addition, understanding relevant spatial and environmental concepts involves more fine- and gross-motor activity for young students than for adventitiously blind adults.

Students who are too young to begin learning a formal map-skills sequence like the one in Sidebar 7.1 can work on "premap" skills. They need to be presented with as many movement experiences as possible that give them a clear understanding of bodily and spatial concepts. These kinds of activities enable them to learn landmarking after they understand basic two-dimensional and three-dimensional shapes. The students begin to perceive spatial references in relation to themselves and the people and objects around them (laterality and directionality) and to experience the relative size and proportion of people and objects in their environment. When they are older, they will be better able to understand the spatial concepts needed to understand and use maps for route travel.

In general it is easier for students to learn O&M skills or concepts when these elements of the curriculum are presented in the simplest form first (for example, understanding and identifying body parts and relationships are presented before the spatial concepts of in front of or behind). Once students demonstrate an understanding of the basics of a skill or concept, more complex information can be given to them. Building on what they have already learned (for instance, understanding that the cane needs to be positioned farther in front to locate a hazardous drop-off and then demonstrating this cane skill correctly) provides an avenue for teaching more advanced concepts and skills. It is important to use the same approach to learning when teaching map skills. It is easier for students who are first learning about maps to comprehend a map with a small amount of information than to understand a complex, detailed map of the same area. This simple-to-complex approach is also useful for students who have studied mapmaking and map-reading skills but who continue to have spatial and orientation difficulties in general. When there is too much detail, it is difficult to distinguish the general areas or features of the environment that are represented and challenging to interpret and use the map. The simple-to-complex approach to teaching map skills enables the O&M specialist to present units that feature both orientation skills (such as learning about a school campus using a series of maps) and mobility skills (like learning about increasingly complex traffic patterns with the Chang Kit and when to time a crossing).

Once students have been introduced to the concept of maps, there are a variety of ways to begin actual instruction. Instructional approaches can be divided on the basis of whether the maps will be made ahead of time or whether a student will help prepare the maps as part of the lesson sequence.

Making Maps Ahead of Time

The more traditional approach to teaching map skills involves the presentation and examination of maps that are already complete. In this case, O&M specialists prepare maps (raised line, raised shape, large print, or a combination of the three) of various kinds ahead of time for their students. When they make a series of maps of a specific travel environment ahead of time, they can use the simple-to-complex method by beginning with one or two features on the first map; adding one or two new features to the second map, so there are no more than four features to find on the second map; and continuing to add a few new features to each successive map.

The map series involves more work for the O&M specialist since there may be five or six maps to make instead of one. However, it may be easier for certain students to understand when presented in this sequence. For example, it is generally effective to present a series of maps of the highway system of a large metropolitan area or of a school or college campus (or parts of the campus) as the students are oriented to these new areas, rather than try to explain the details of one complete, detailed map. Students are able to absorb small increments of information with each map and are not distracted by too much information all at once.

Making Maps with the Student

Although it may seem simpler to provide premade maps to orient students to new environments, there are many conceptual advantages to involving students in the creation of a variety of maps. If the students each make their own maps or several students who are training in the same area make a shared map, the information put on the map is added over time in stages. As the students find new features (such as intersections, blocks, and landmarks) during their lessons, they add them to their individual or shared maps. In this way, the maps become more and more complex, but the students are familiar with all the details, since they have put each piece of information on their maps individually during a series of lessons. Their map reading skills develop as they participate in building a map from its simple beginnings to its complex completion.

The O&M specialist needs to determine with the students what kind of tactile map they would like to make (raised line or two-dimensional cutout) and have all the appropriate mapmaking materials ready ahead of time. The students need to review their maps and explain to the specialist or other students what is already on the maps before they add the next piece of information. They then add to the maps before they travel on a lesson. This review and explanation reinforces the information on the maps for the students and enables the O&M specialist to assess the students' map-reading skills informally.

There are several ways to involve students in the mapmaking process. One is to take a student to a new travel area and encourage the student to ask questions about what he or she finds during the lesson (like the names of significant streets, types of intersections, type of neighborhood, landmarks, addresses, and unusual features) and to tape-record the information. In the next lesson, the student can begin to make a map on the basis of some of the information found in the previous lesson. This sequence can continue, with lessons "in the field" and then lessons in the classroom to put new information on the map. While traveling during a lesson, for example, a student with low vision could draw an intersection, along with corner landmarks, on a dry-erase board. The drawing would then be transferred to ledger paper using a copy machine. In the following lesson, the student could add details by drawing on the copied paper map, or a student could begin to construct a raised-line map of a new area using foam board on which the O&M specialist has drawn relevant information. After the student travels along a certain street or intersection, he or she could put these areas on the map using Wikki Six or puff paint and add appropriate labels.

Another approach is to give students their partially completed maps (with one or two features such as a raised-line intersection or cutout block) before they travel to a given area. A brief discussion about what the area looks like can precede traveling in the area, so the students feel a bit more familiar with where they are traveling when they begin their routes. As the lessons continue and the students gather more information, they add these new details to their maps.

A more detailed and complete map can be presented to a student who then adds "supporting" information, either on the map or on cards. For example, the map may have all the intersections or blocks on it but no addresses or landmarks. The student would then find this type of information to add more detail to the map.

Finally, if a number of students are involved in building and sharing a map, each student can gather new information for the map, so that all the students help to instruct one another about the travel environment and what they have found. If the map is already complete (a general-area raised-line or raised-shape map made earlier by the O&M specialist or other students), the students can put all the new information they have on 3 x 5-inch cards. Information gathered by the students can be tape-recorded, written using a slate and stylus or Braille Lite, or drawn or handwritten on cards. Card files (labeled with the students' names or color coded) can include local businesses and addresses, landmarks like banks or gas stations, and addresses or descriptions of various houses in residential areas. All the cards can be organized by block number or street names. The students can then compare and share the cards, thereby learning how to describe an environment and understand more about their travel area. The advantage in this approach is that the basic completed map can be used over and over again by many students, since each will put information on his or her own cards, not on the map. The students will still be participating in gathering information about their travel area and thus learning and practicing mapmaking and map-reading skills, albeit in a more indirect way.

PLANNING AND ORGANIZING MAPS, MODELS, AND MANIPULATIVES

Students can become enthusiastic about mapmaking opportunities, and before long O&M specialists may find they have an abundance of maps and mapmaking materials on hand. Therefore, it is a good idea to think about efficient ways to organize these instructional supplies for both the O&M specialist's and students' use. When O&M specialists are designing, making, and storing maps and other tactile teaching aids, they need to consider several factors:

1. They need to make the maps portable and durable, which means constructing them out of the appropriate kinds of materials.

2. When making maps ahead of time, they should design maps that can be used by as many students as possible.

3. They need to consider how to organize maps, models, manipulatives, and tactile diagrams and store them in different locations.

4. They need a plan for saving "master" maps, for adapting other maps, and for filing unused maps so the maps can be located when needed. In addition, they need to know what maps and models they plan to give away to their students.

5. They should sort through their materials periodically to decide what they still need and what can be discarded.

Tips for Constructing Maps for Students with Visual Impairments presents some general suggestions for constructing, organizing, and storing maps, models, and other materials.

Making Instructional Materials Portable and Durable

Maps, models, and other instructional materials need to be planned with portability and durability in mind. The O&M instructor needs to consider such factors as whether a student will take a particular map outside to use in lessons or leave it inside, whether the O&M specialist needs to take a map to another school or facility or leave it at one location, and whether the map is to be used for a long time. If a map or model is too big or heavy to carry, it is appropriate for instruction only inside a classroom and cannot be taken outside to use on a lesson. Maps or diagrams that are intended to be used on location must be portable—that is, light and small enough to grasp easily alone or using a handle or fastening of some kind or in a portfolio or other type of carrier.

If maps are going to be used for a long period, they need to be made of sturdy materials. Sidebar 7.2 lists a variety of mostly inexpensive materials that can be considered, depending on the type of map to be made and the students' specific needs. It is practical to design maps that can be used by as many students as possible. Therefore, when selecting materials, O&M specialists need to consider color, contrast and glare, and a variety of textures.

As was mentioned earlier, it is important for students to be involved in making their own maps. Showing students where to find or buy mapmaking materials can be a part of their overall training. For

TIPS FOR CONSTRUCTING MAPS FOR STUDENTS WITH VISUAL IMPAIRMENTS

- Explore the use of a variety of materials (macaroni, leaves, pebbles, carpet and fabric remnants, shelf liners, rubber backing for throw rugs, foam, buttons, Wikki Stix, foam board, bubble wrap, fine mesh, and so on) for making tactile maps with students.

- Organize mapmaking materials (such as scissors, measuring tape, felt-tip markers, tape, and buttons) in a fanny pack or appropriate container to take along on lessons when constructing maps together along a route.

- Check before the lesson to see if the adhesive (tape, paste, or glue) used is sufficient to keep items on the map while the student explores it tactilely.

- Incorporate high-contrast colors (like white on black or yellow on dark blue) to increase the visibility of visual maps for students with low vision.

- Eliminate unnecessary details from commercially available maps when adapting them for use by students who are blind or have low vision. For example, minor streets can be whited out from a map before it is enlarged on a copy machine if the map is being used to introduce the general layout of an area.

- Cover visual maps with nonglare plastic sheet protectors, so a student can trace routes on them with a grease pencil. In this way, the map can be reused with the same student or other students working in the same area.

- Start a collection of miniature cars and people to use with various maps and models. These simple props add interest to even the most simple maps for students of all ages. It is helpful if miniature cars and people have distinct features that let the students know which is the front and back.

- Find a safe storage place at the school or agency to keep maps that will be used again.

example, lessons can be planned to go to a copy center to enlarge a paper map or to a packaging, stationery, or office supply store to buy various sizes of cardboard or foam board. In this way, students learn where and how to obtain simple materials to use later when they are orienting themselves to a new area with a friend or family member and can be assisted at that time in making a map of a new travel area.

Sidebar 7.2 Materials for Mapmaking

The following are some suggestions for materials that can be useful for making different types of maps or models. In deciding what materials to use for a particular project, O&M specialists need to consider how and where the map will be used, how long it is expected to last, and the visual needs of the students who will be using it.

- *Plywood* may be appropriate, although it is heavy and cannot be used easily by students who are making their own maps.

- *Hard foam board, cardboard, and soft foam* are durable materials for raised-shape and raised-line maps. They are lightweight and can be purchased in a variety of high-contrast and neon colors to assist students with low vision who are using the tactile maps. In addition, they are easy for students to manipulate, cut, and glue with assistance, if necessary,

- *Paper* is less durable but is appropriate for students to use if the maps made of it are kept covered in some way when being filed and transported.

- The *tactile image enhancer* (see the Resources section) creates raised lines through a heating process when a line-drawing is copied onto a special paperlike material and fed through the machine. It is best for making line maps, although these maps are not in color. They are easy to make and recopy, suitable for both visual and tactile learners, and portable (since the maps are made of a paperlike material that folds and is durable).

- *Foam board* is useful for students who have low vision, as well as for those who are functionally blind. It can be purchased in white, gray, and black; plain colors; and selected neon colors. Neon yellow on black, for example, is a high-contrast combination for a tactile map. For students with low vision, foam board has a matte finish that is easy to look at.

- *Gel and acetate overlays* are useful but produce a difficult glare.

- *Textured materials* can be useful, but it is a good idea to practice gluing unusual textures (such as screening or gauze) to see if they will adhere well and not lift off when touched. Some students may not like textures that are too rough, so avoid sandpaper or choose the finest grain available).

- *Nonslip self-adhesive strips* used for bathtubs and nonskid rubber matting used under throw rugs can be useful for mapmaking if they are not too rough.

Making Instructional Materials Practical

If O&M specialists design and make maps and diagrams that can be used for both students who have low vision and those who are functionally blind, they can limit the number of maps and diagrams they need for their caseloads. For example, several students, with different levels of visual functioning, can make a map together of a new school. In this case, O&M specialists need to purchase materials that are tactile (to make raised lines, shapes, and textures) and have high-color or black-and-white contrast and little or no visual clutter in the background (to make high-contrast maps and diagrams with yellow on black, black on pink, black on white, and so on).

Where and How to Store Instructional Materials

Current materials can be stored in a car, at an office, in different locations (schools and the students' homes), and at the O&M specialist's home. Sample materials that are copied or adapted can be kept at home or at an office, labeled so they are easy to find and use when needed. Materials that will be given to students when they are completed do not have to be stored indefinitely. As was mentioned earlier, the O&M specialist periodically sifts through the materials and discards, adapts, or remakes those that are out of date or are too fragile or worn to be perceived tactilely or visually. Sometimes these materials are useful to save "as is" for in-service training programs to show student teachers.

Since O&M is often an "itinerant" occupation, most O&M specialists use their cars frequently and need to store many of their teaching materials in them. O&M specialists can think of their car trunks as giant "resource kits" and hence need to organize their car trunks using various containers with sections that hold a variety of materials they need daily or weekly. Organizing the trunks this way, somewhat like file cabinets, helps O&M specialists find what they need quickly and note if something is missing or misplaced (see Sidebar 7.3).

O&M specialists also need to be creative when storing items at an office or classroom, since space is often at a premium. Maps are bulky, but thin, so they can usually be stored between desks, behind bookshelves, against a wall, or on top of a large cabinet. They can be organized in homemade folders by geographic area (such as residential areas near a school or downtown areas near a workplace), by specific destination or curriculum unit (all maps of a college campus, all bus maps, all advanced intersection maps, and so on), or by individual student. These folders can be separate or have several sections, each labeled at the top, like a large handmade spiral notebook, and should have cloth or string handles to carry them. To help organize and transport maps, various sizes of artist portfolios can be purchased from art-supply stores. These portfolios are usually durable and have multiple dividers and handles for carrying them. Convenient storage and easy ways to

---

Sidebar 7.3 *Organizing Storage in the Trunk of a Car*

O&M specialists frequently need to store and transport many items in their cars, including maps and mapmaking materials, and they need to be able to find quickly just what they need for a specific lesson with a particular student. There are a number of ways to organize the trunk of a car or the backseat of a van:

- Materials can be stored by *size and shape* (smaller items in compartments or drawers of a box and thin, large items in a portfolio folder resting upright against the bumper side of the trunk).

- Materials can be stored together by *function* (all canes together, all low vision aids together, items for teaching spatial concepts together, mapmaking materials together, items for one school together, and so on).

- Materials can be stored by *need* (items used infrequently near the back of the trunk, items used daily near the front for easy access).

- Materials can be stored by *age group* (manipulatives and concept toys in one area for young students and bus schedules, bus tokens and various identification-card application forms in another place for high school aged and adult students).

A trunk can be filled with boxes of various shapes, some of which have smaller boxes, bags, or hanging files within them. The following materials are indispensable for organizing:

- *Hanging files* are essential for filing paperwork and students' files.

- *Boxes with and without handles,* since some will remain in the trunk, while others will be taken out (office supply stores have a variety of plastic boxes with handles).

- *Cloth bags* are useful for storing and transporting a variety of small items from the car to the classroom or for carrying items during a lesson.

- *Plastic sandwich-size bags* are transparent and can be labeled for storing and locating small but essential items (such as bus tokens, batteries, braille and low vision compasses, and small magnifiers). All bags can be folded or tucked within a box.

---

transport materials are important, though often overlooked, factors for O&M specialists to consider as they develop their curriculum, select training sites, write lesson plans, and make teaching materials.

The creation of maps, models, and manipulatives for teaching O&M has benefits for both students and O&M specialists. The appropriate use of such high-quality instructional materials not only enhances learning opportunities for students who are blind or visually impaired, but also makes teaching more fun and efficient.

O&M Recipes: Preparing and Using Maps, Models, Manipulatives, and More

The lessons described in this appendix give O&M specialists some ideas about how to construct maps and other kinds of instructional materials and use them to present O&M concepts. The lessons are presented in recipe form and, like all recipes, can be modified in a variety of ways, depending on the individual student who is learning the material. The six orientation lessons deal primarily with spatial and environmental concepts, while the six mobility lessons address ways to teach concepts needed for mobility skills. Each lesson is conceived of as part of an overall unit, as noted in the description of each lesson.

In each lesson, Selecting the Correct Recipe defines the students for whom the lesson is most appropriate and gives a background of what students have been learning, their skill level, and the goal of the lesson. Of course, the O&M specialist is best qualified to determine the suitability of any lesson for a particular student. Ingredients and Equipment describes the materials that are needed for the lesson. Preparing the Recipe is the heart of the lesson; it explains what the O&M specialist does with the student during the lesson to reach the goal. Recipe Variations describes follow-up ideas for future lessons on the same topic. Adaptations of all these lessons can be made for students who are blind or visually impaired and have additional mild disabilities.

Each lesson plan is intended to be presented in one lesson but may be continued for two lessons, depending on the needs of a particular student. The following is a list of the lessons contained in this appendix:

Orientation Lessons
Large-Print Add-On Map on Paper with Cutouts
Professional Map with Acetate Overlay
Interactive Map to Teach Compass Cardinal Directions

Professional Map Kit, Sequence Maps of Highway
or Interstate System
Corkboard Map for the Address System with Activity
Cards
Object Cues in Sequence

Mobility Lessons
Colored Gels for Scanning a Street in the Correct Order
Portable Tactile Diagram of Four Types of Grassy Strips
Found at Residential Corners
Fantasy Story Written on a Computer to Understand
Traffic Patterns
Rug Squares to Teach Alignment at Different-Shaped
Corners
Interactive Map Using Lunch Tables to Practice Alignment
and Timing for Street Crossings
Mini-Chang Kit to Teach Spatial and Environmental Concepts
at Intersections

ORIENTATION LESSONS

Large-Print Add-On Map on Paper with Cutouts

(presented as part of a classroom Map Unit)

Selecting the Correct Recipe

For elementary school-aged students with low vision; students with additional mild disabilities. This lesson is appropriate for students who are just beginning to learn about maps. The goal is to teach beginning map concepts by making a map of the classroom.

Ingredients and Equipment

- ledger-size paper
- bold black felt-tip pens and highlighters
- glue
- a large clip board or stiff backing, ledger size
- 1-inch x 3-inch prepared pop-up drawings of a blue door and a green bulletin board*
- 3 x 5-inch cards, masking tape, scissors for subsequent lessons

Preparing the Recipe

1. Explain that the student will be making a map of his or her classroom. Ask the student what a map is. Redefine or review if needed, emphasizing the "bird's-eye" view concept.

2. Beginning with the wall of the classroom that has the main exit-entrance (wall 1), ask the student to travel along the perimeter of the classroom, examining and discussing significant objects located along the walls.

3. Ask the student to return to wall 1, prompting him or her to identify each object on or near this wall in more detail (including its name, size, color, and function; whether the student has used it, and whether it makes noise).

4. Seated with the student, draw the perimeter of the classroom on ledger paper with a felt-tip pen, leaving openings for doors and explaining that each line on the map represents one wall of the room (demonstrate the relationship between the line on the map and the wall, if necessary). Ask the student to number the walls on the map, with wall 1 where the main doors are.

---

*To make a pop-up drawing, the items are drawn and colored on 1 or 1½-inch strips cut out of 3 x 5-index cards (the strips can be slightly wider if desired). Each strip is folded at the bottom, and the bent bottom part of the strip is taped onto the map on top of the drawn item. The rest of the strip, containing the picture of the object, will "stand up" ("pop up") on the map. (For a photograph of a pop-up map, see the section on Visual Maps in this chapter.) If the student has trouble drawing a small picture, a larger one can be cut and pasted onto the pop-up backing.

5. Discuss what the student found on or near wall 1 and have him or her choose three or four items, including one of the doors and the bulletin board, to put on the map. The student draws these items along line 1, demonstrating as much as possible correct spatial relationships, proportion, and color.

6. Assist student in gluing pop-up drawing of the blue door and the green bulletin board onto the map in the correct positions.

7. Along with the O&M specialist, the student takes the map (put it on a backing) and walks along wall 1 to review whether the map is correct. Discuss with the student spatial relationships, sizes, colors, and the like. If there is time, the student can make a pop-up of one of the other items he or she drew and glue it in the correct position.

8. End the lesson by asking the student the purpose of the lesson, what the student did well, and what the student needs to continue to work on. Praise the student for at least one skill demonstrated well during the lesson.

Recipe Variations

After all the sides of the room are completed on the map, the student may want to draw items on the map that are located in the center of the room. When all the drawing is completed, the O&M specialist can help the student make pop-ups of these items. Some students may prefer to select more three-dimensional items, such as LEGOS, miniature toy versions of the objects, or little shapes made of balsa wood, to glue on their maps. It may be a good idea to add the shapes at the end of the classroom map unit because it is more difficult to carry the map with taped pop-ups or glued shapes on it.

Professional Map with Acetate Overlay

(presented as part of an Overview of the Metropolitan Area Unit, which teaches the community and highway system near home, school, and work)

Selecting the Correct Recipe

For middle-school or high school-aged students who have low vision; students with additional mild disabilities; adults and older adults. This lesson is appropriate for students who have already seen maps of selected areas taken from an overall map of the city. The goal is to demonstrate how the separate areas of the city and the highways fit together.

Ingredients and Equipment

- a regular-print map (or copy) of the entire travel area used by the student, about 2 feet by 2 feet (called the "big" map)
- a sheet of clear acetate plastic the same size as the map
- grease pencils of different colors with tissues or cloth to erase the lines
- a pen and note paper

Preparing the Recipe

1. In the classroom, the O&M specialist and student place acetate over the big map, viewing the map at whatever angle is needed to avoid glare. All the markings on the map will be done on this protective acetate over sheet.

2. Explain that the purpose of the lesson is to see how all the separate areas of the whole city fit together and where they are in relation to one another on this big map and to see the location and interrelationship of highways. Because the print is small on the map, the student is not expected to read it in any detail. Encourage the student to take notes throughout the lesson as needed.

3. The O&M specialist uses a black grease pencil to make a large circle around the school area, reviewing with the student the names of relevant streets near the school. A few stripes can be drawn inside the circle, so that its shape is easier to see.

4. Ask the student to select another color grease pencil (such as red). Point to the location of the student's home on the map. The student uses the red grease pencil to make a similar-sized circle around his or her home area, adding stripes if needed.

5. Ask or prompt the student for the cardinal compass directional relationships between the two areas circled.

6. A route or routes between these two areas need to be chosen. If the student knows a particular route or routes, the O&M specialist can describe and trace them on the acetate in a third color. If the student does not know a specific route, a route or routes can be designed and drawn over the map by the O&M specialist and the student together. These routes may or may not involve the use of a highway. Street names and compass cardinal directions are reviewed and learned as the routes are drawn.

7. One or two of the detailed area maps the student has been using can be compared to this big map, so the student understands how the enlarging process shows a larger picture, but of a smaller area. (The O&M specialist may wish to explain that a typical map of the state or of the United States is a smaller picture, but depicts a larger overall area.) Routes just designed over the big map can also be pointed out on the smaller detailed maps as appropriate.

8. The second part of the lesson involves pointing out major highways. Erase lines or circles if there are too many of them on the acetate. Trace over the thicker lines on the printed map that indicate highways using a different color pencil. Point out and discuss the names and numbers of the highways, the compass cardinal directions, and the areas to which the highways lead. Select one or two highways that lead to major areas of the city, like public parks and recreational areas, cultural and entertainment centers, and the city hall and other government buildings. Explain or review where the highways interconnect. Point out an example of two interconnecting highways, along with where these two highways exit onto local streets. If the student's routes involve the use of the highways, these routes can be drawn again and reviewed with the student.

9. End the lesson by asking the student the purpose of the lesson, what the student did well, and what the student needs to continue to work on. Praise the student for at least one skill demonstrated well during the lesson.

Recipe Variations

Use this big map with an acetate overlay, along with other smaller, detailed maps of the same area, when pointing out spatial relationships of different travel areas or discussing routes to new travel areas, especially when highways are used. Both types of maps are also useful when teaching the address system.

Interactive Map to Teach Compass Cardinal Directions

(presented as part of an Advanced Spatial Concepts Unit)

Selecting the Correct Recipe

A group lesson for three or four elementary-aged students who are blind or have low vision; students with additional mild disabilities. This lesson is appropriate for students who have been learning compass cardinal directions. The goal is to offer practice in remembering and demonstrating the four directional relationships accurately.

Ingredients and Equipment

- an object that is easy to toss and catch like a large beach ball or a "sockbee" (seven or eight thick socks tied together into a ring and intertwined with bright strips of material for visibility and a few bells if sound is needed)

- four large cards, each with a braille and large-print name of one of the four compass cardinal directions

Preparing the Recipe

1. In the classroom or outdoors, explain that the students will review the names and spatial relationships of the four cardinal directions by playing a tossing game. Each student will represent one of the cardinal directions.

2. Pass out cards that have cardinal directions written on them to the four students. Ask the students to review the directional references.

3. Help the students select who will be north, south, east, and west. (If there are only three students, the O&M specialist will be one direction.)

4. Provide a braille or low vision compass for students to determine north. The "north" student will stand with his or her back to north. The other students will move into correct positions relative to "north," all facing one another in a close square formation.

5. Explain the rules: after catching the object, each student says his or her own direction first and then tosses the object to another student, yelling the direction into which he or she is tossing (for example, "north" student says "north to east " and tosses east, the "east" student says "east to west" and tosses west, and so on). The goal is to say one's own direction correctly before tossing; to toss in the correct direction; and, when receiving, to catch the object. The students must take one small step backward to make the square bigger after each catch, thereby making it harder to toss and catch. If a student drops the object, fails to catch it, or makes a mistake with compass references, he or she must walk around the square saying all the directions correctly and try the game again. (The O&M instructor can increase the tempo of the game as appropriate.)

6. End the lesson by asking the students the purpose of the lesson, what each did well, and what each needs to continue to work on. Praise the students for their accomplishments.

Recipe Variations

Later lessons may include using cardinal compass directional references with an individual student in lessons, either in describing a route or having the student design a route. The O&M specialist could also plan a team lesson with two of the students who played the game. As these two students designed or gave each other a route, they would use cardinal directional references to describe the traveling direction accurately (such as traveling west), the street direction (such as on the east–west street), and the side of the street (such as the north side of the street).

Professional Map Kit, Sequence Maps of Highway or Interstate System

(presented as part of an Overview of the Metropolitan Area Unit, which teaches the community and highway system near home, school, and work)

This lesson is an example of a map-sequence format, in which a new highway is added to each successive map. The sequence might be north–south highways depicted on the first maps, followed by the addition of east–west highways, and then diagonal highways. The sequence could also alternate among the three types of highways with each additional map.

Selecting the Correct Recipe

For middle school- or high school-aged students who are blind or have low vision; students with additional mild disabilities; adults and older adults. This lesson is appropriate for students who are learning about their community and who have traveled on these large roads but do not know where they are. The goal is to learn about the highway system or larger highways surrounding the student's travel area by using a series of maps.

Ingredients and Equipment

- ledger-size paper
- a large-print map of the metropolitan or outlying area where the student travels

- a black felt-tip pen and neon yellow, orange, pink, and blue high-lighters
- clear glue, highway braille labels (made ahead of time or by the student during the lesson)
- an acetate plastic sheet and grease pencils
- extra: miniature highway logos, little cars, LEGO landmarks, circular or oval tagboard shapes with braille labels of general areas of the city

Note: In this lesson, the highway maps are made ahead of time by the O&M specialist by tracing the highways on ledger paper from large-print professional maps. Map 1 will have one highway drawn and raised; Map 2 will have the first highway and another highway; Map 3 will have the first two highways plus a third highway added, and so on, until the final map has all the highways on it together. Use highlighter colors that the student can discriminate well when making the lines (for instance, north–south highways are black, east–west highways are orange or yellow, and diagonal highways are pink or blue). If the student uses tactile cues, groups of highways can be distinguished tactilely; for example, thin clear glue can be placed over the north–south highways, thick glue over the east–west highways, and thin glue dots on the diagonal highways.

Preparing the Recipe

1. In the classroom, explain that the student will see or touch a series of highway maps of his or her community to learn where the highways are. The student will start with a map of just one highway. Present the map and give the name and/or number of the highway, discussing compass cardinal directions and what areas of the city are reached from this highway. Ask the student to write in or glue on the braille label of the name and/or number of this highway. The student then reviews this information while "driving" a miniature car along the highway.

2. Present the second map, showing the student the relationship between the two highways, stating the name and/or number of the second highway, and discussing what areas of the city are reached by this new highway. The student labels this second highway on the map and drives the car on both highways, noting where the two merge and reviewing the names and compass cardinal directions of both.

3. This sequence is repeated with all the maps (there may be five or more maps). The student learns the names and/or numbers of the highways and gradually sees the relationship of the highways and how people travel throughout the city using several different highways to get to certain places.

4. Using the final highway map, take turns with the student playing a game of how to get from one place to another on this map using various highways. Practice using the names and/or numbers of the highways and the correct compass cardinal directions, noting where the highways connect. Determine if there is more than one way to get somewhere using several different highways.

5. Extra: Acetate can be used over the final map so students with low vision can mark where certain important areas or sections of the city are. A grease pencil can be used to make circles or ovals over these areas; circular or oval tagboard shapes can be taped directly on the tactile map to achieve the same effect for blind students. Small shapes (LEGO shapes are the easiest) can be taped on the map as landmarks. If each highway logo has been made ahead of time in miniature, these logos can be taped on the map as well.

6. End the lesson by asking the student the purpose of the lesson, what the student did well, and what the student needs to continue to work on. Praise the student for at least one skill demonstrated well during the lesson.

Recipe Variations

In future lessons, the student will be asked to use highway references such as name, number, and location when describing routes and discussing the large overall-area map. The student will learn which highways are used by family members and friends to reach certain destinations.

Corkboard Map for the Address System with Activity Cards

(presented as part of an Address Unit.)

Selecting the Correct Recipe

For middle school- or high-school aged students who are blind or have low vision; students with additional mild disabilities; adults and older adults. This lesson is appropriate for students who are studying the address system but are confused about the general concept and layout. The goal is to learn how the address system is arranged by constructing a visual-tactile map from scratch.

Ingredients and Equipment

- an 18 x 24-inch rectangular corkboard with a stiff backing with a frame (if the student is functionally blind, raise the north part of the board so it is higher)

- two pieces of thick twine, about 30 inches long (thin enough so a pushpin will go through these two pieces when they are crossed over each other)

- string and yarn of two different thicknesses and colors (such as white string and thick yellow yarn)

- pushpins, masking tape, scissors, a pen, a braille labeler (or machine), and tagboard labels

- four pieces of different types of material, about 7 x 9 inches each, that can provide visual and textural cues to represent the four quadrants—for example, plastic bubble wrap packaging material, beige felt, green outdoor carpeting, and green felt

Preparing the Recipe

1. In the classroom, explain to the student that the purpose of the lesson is to continue learning about the address system by constructing a tactile map, so the center dividing streets of the address system and the quadrants are easier to understand.

2. Place the corkboard on the table, making a label (braille or large print as appropriate) at the top for north.

3. Review the names and alignment of the two streets that intersect at the center of the city (for instance, Main Street is north–south and First Street is east–west) and divide the city into four quadrants.

4. Ask the student to place thick twine in a north–south direction at the midline of the map, taping the two ends onto the cork frame, thus forming Main Street, the north–south dividing street. The student makes a braille or handwritten tagboard label for "Main Street," punches a hole at the end of the label, and fastens the label to the south end of the twine.

5. Review that the corkboard map is now divided into two areas: east and west (Main Street is north–south and cuts the area into east–west sections). The student places two pieces of similar materials (for example, the roughly textured materials on the west sides and the soft, smooth felt on the east sides). Ask the student to move his or her hand north–south on Main Street to review the north–south alignment. Ask the student to review the textural cues of the map: rough equals the western areas of town and smooth equals the eastern areas.

6. The O&M specialist takes a turn, taping thick twine across the midline of the corkboard map, thus forming First Street. This street is the east–west dividing street at the center of the city. Ask the student to help with the label, attaching it on the east side of the map (the label for First Street is on the end of the twine at the east side of the map). The student moves his or her finger along this street, moving in an east–west direction.

7. If the student can use visual cues, he or she will also see that, for example, the lighter colors are on the north side and the darker colors are on the south side. Functionally blind students use gradient cues, sensing that the board is higher on the north side and lower on the south side. Review and discuss that the city is now divided into north and south areas by the east–west street.

8. Ask the student to locate the center intersection (where the two pieces of twine cross) and place a pushpin there. Review the four quadrants from this center point and the four corners of this center intersection, since the references are the same. Review that each corner is numbered 100. Have the student review what has been learned so far with finger movements along the two streets and on the four quadrants.

9. The student adds four east–west streets (using thick yellow yarn for each street), one at a time: two east–west streets south of First Street and two east–west streets north of First Street. Make street labels (brailled or handwritten) together using the real street names and attach them to the ends of the "streets" on the east side of the corkboard.

10. The student places four pushpins at each of these "new" intersections along Main Street. Ask the student to touch each intersection (pushpin) and describe it by name (remind him or her to use the labels if needed). The student then asks the O&M specialist to locate any of these five intersections. The O&M specialist can make mistakes to trick the student, if appropriate.

11. Point out to the student that each pushpin represents an intersection where a new block begins according to the address system. Point out that the areas on the map between the pushpins along the streets represent blocks. Review that each block generally changes by 100 as people travel away from or toward the center intersection (for example, traveling south, the first street south of First Street is the beginning of the 200 block south; the second street south is the beginning of the 300 block south, and so forth). When the student understands this concept, continue with the same explanation for the north side of First Street. Finally, review by asking the student to place a finger on the "200 block south area," "300 block north area," and so on. Take turns, so the student also asks questions of the O&M specialist. Mistakes can be made to trick the student if this is appropriate.

12. Explain that address numbers are generally smaller at the beginning of the block and higher at the end of the block when traveling away from the center intersection (for example, number 102 would be close to the 100 block intersection, while 198 would be farther away and close to next intersection, where the 200 block begins). Ask the student to place pushpins alongside the street at "202 block S," "290 block S," "205 block N," "251 block N," "297 block N", and so on. Take turns, so the student also questions the O&M specialist. (There will now be pushpins on intersections and on blocks next to Main Street.)

Note: The lesson may end here for some students and continue from here in the next lesson after a review. If this is the case, conclude the lesson with item 18 at this point.

13. Add four north–south streets using white string, two on each side of Main Street, with labels on the south end of the map. The maps now have center streets of thick twine, east–west streets of thick yellow yarn, and north–south streets of white string. There is now a small grid of streets on the map.

14. If appropriate for the student, teach or review the "NOW" and "SEE" cue words (the "O" stands for odd numbers, with n = north and w = west; the "E" stands for even numbers, s = south and e = east). Ask the student to point out even and odd sides of the streets on the map, reminding him or her that north–south streets have east–west sides (or sidewalks) and east–west streets have north–south sides (sidewalks).

15. The student now reviews all the concepts of the address system by first locating general and then specific destinations. Prompt the student to move his or her fingers along the streets, describing the direction traveled and the street name (such as "moving south on Main Street"), the area of city (such as "in the south part of the city"), and the block number (such as "along the 200 block south"). Prompt the student to add more specific information, moving his or her fingers to where each block begins (where the streets cross) and to the sides of the streets (on the even or odd side).

16. Ask the student to place pushpins in the correct location on the map for, say, 350 North ———— Street, 283 South ———— Street, 107 West ———— Street, 276 East ———— Street. Take turns with the student, so he or she can ask the O&M specialist to locate destinations as well.

17. If desired, small objects representing houses or businesses can be placed on the map in the correct position. Give the student cards with address and descriptions (like 315 South Pine Street, red house). The student locates the position and puts a red LEGO there, and so on.

18. End the lesson by asking the student the purpose of the lesson, what the student did well, and what the student needs to continue to work on. Praise the student for at least one skill demonstrated well during the lesson.

Recipe Variations

The next lesson or lessons may begin with number 12 and continue to number 17, depending on how much the student knows and how quickly he or she absorbs new information about the address system. After using the corkboard maps as practice, the student can note address references on street signs, houses, stores, and other buildings as he or she travels in residential or light business areas during lessons. Ask the student to locate destinations using the address system. The student can be taken on a field trip to the center of the city where the address system begins if he or she has not been there.

For such a field trip, small portable activity cards can be made ahead of time to use as the student crosses the center intersection and discusses the address system. These cards are miniatures of the big corkboard map. Paste the four quadrant pieces of material on 8 x 10-inch cards to review the quadrants (for instance, "I'm traveling north, crossing from the south side to the north side" or "from the southeast quadrant to the northeast quadrant"). To review the names and direction of the two main dividing streets, one 8 x 10-inch card will have the north–south street twine glued and labeled on it, and a second card will have the east–west street twine glued and labeled on it. The student can use other cards ("block 100 North," " block 200 North," and so forth) as reminders when they confirm the street block numbers on the street signs and discuss directional references at each corner.

Object Cues in Sequence

(presented as part of a Rote Route Unit)

Selecting the Correct Recipe

For students of all ages who are blind or have low vision and additional disabilities. This lesson is appropriate for students who have been practicing a rote route and are aware of at least four landmarks along the route but have trouble recalling landmarks independently and cannot recall the order of the landmarks when traveling in a certain direction. The goal of the lesson is to use object cues to help students remember landmarks.

Ingredients and Equipment

- four object cues that represent landmarks (symbols of real objects or parts of real objects found at the beginning of a route, along the route, and at the destination)

- for later lessons: a fishing vest (with lots of pockets) or a gardening belt (with lots of pouches) to hold object cues during the lesson

Preparing the Recipe

1. Explain to the student that the purpose of the lesson is to locate landmarks along a familiar route (for example, from the classroom to the restroom and back). To make it easier to recall the landmarks, he or she will be given a "reminder" that looks or feels like the landmark. Ask if he or she remembers any landmarks found along the way. Prompt the student with the names of the landmarks as needed. Remind the student that finding landmarks helps people travel routes without getting lost.

2. Show the first object cue to the student, explaining that the cue represents the first landmark found along the route starting at the classroom and will be used as a reminder to help the student remember how to travel the route correctly.

3. Let the student examine the similarities between the object cue and the actual landmark (for instance, three raised dots on a blue card with three similar raised dots on the blue door of the classroom).

4. Ask the student to start the route using the first object cue and assist the student, as needed, to complete the route.

5. Before beginning the return route, have the student examine the first cue again, which the student will find at the end of the route, rather than the beginning. Say, for example, "We will return to Room 3, which has the blue colored door with the three raised dots," and show the cue card that represents the door. At the end of the return route, assist the student, if necessary, to find the three dots on the door of the classroom and compare them with the three dots on the object cue card.

6. End the lesson by asking the student the purpose of the lesson, what the student did well, and what the student needs to continue to work on. Praise the student for at least one skill demonstrated well during the lesson.

Recipe Variations

In the next lesson, orally review the route, landmarks, and first object cue with the student and then present the second object cue. The second cue represents the destination (such as a faucet handle for the restroom). The student puts on the vest or belt to travel the route, storing the object cues in the pockets instead of holding them, matches the first landmark, and then travels the route. At the destination, he or she matches the second object cue with the landmark there. Continue the lesson as noted in the foregoing steps, with the student using two object cues to assist as landmark reminders. In the next few lessons, present two more object cues. (The third object cue may be a piece of rug, and the fourth one may be a small cardboard box, the edge of which represents a corner where the student must turn.) Ask the student to travel the route using the object cues as landmark reminders. All the object cues are stored in the pockets of the vest or belt.

MOBILITY LESSONS

Colored Gels for Scanning a Street in the Correct Order

(presented as part of a Light Business–Basic Traffic Light-Controlled Intersection Unit)

Selecting the Correct Recipe

For upper elementary- through high school-aged students who have low vision; students with additional mild disabilities. This lesson is appropriate for students who are learning where to scan when crossing simple traffic light-controlled plus-shaped intersections and who sometimes confuse the scanning order of stop sign-controlled intersections with simple traffic light-controlled intersections. The goal of the lesson is to learn about the scanning patterns used in crossing intersections safely.

Ingredients and Equipment

All the materials are made ahead of time by the O&M instructor.

- a black-and-white diagram of a basic plus-shaped intersection with four corners, approximately16 inches by 20 inches, made of tagboard

- a piece of clear acetate the same size as the black-and-white diagram, with the traffic lanes, turning lanes, and pedestrian crosswalks drawn with black grease pencil

- transparent plastic of various colors (from file folders or theatrical lighting gels), cut into shapes to represent the movement of typical traffic patterns on the acetate diagram

- miniature cars and LEGO people

Preparing the Recipe

1. In class, review information about scanning by asking the student why it is important to scan at traffic light-controlled intersections. Remind the student, if necessary, that the scanning order is different for stop sign-controlled intersections and traffic light-controlled intersections. Explain that the diagram and colored shaped gels of a plus-shaped basic traffic light-controlled intersection will help him or her to visualize the traffic and scanning patterns more easily. Acting out the traffic patterns enables the student to learn where to scan, the specific order in which to scan, and the timing of when to scan prior to stepping off and while crossing at this kind of intersection. This lesson focuses on counterclockwise crossings, with the parallel street to the left of the LEGO person.

2. Ask the student to place the acetate on the black-and-white diagram of the intersection. Review the location of the four corners of the intersection and the location and names of the three lanes on the parallel and perpendicular streets on the diagram.

3. Ask the student to place the cars in the correct position at the intersection, as if they were all stopped at a red light. There should be a car in the left turning lane (lane 1), a car in the straight-ahead lane (lane 2), and a car in the straight-ahead/right-turn lane (lane 3). The O&M specialist places a LEGO person at the southeast corner facing north, to cross north.

4. Review the movement of parallel cars, including right- and left-turning traffic. Review the movement of perpendicular cars, including farside right-turning traffic. Review that the LEGO person steps off with the parallel nearside surge. The student should be able to demonstrate all these aspects on the diagram without help.

5. Place red-colored gels on the northbound lanes at the southeast corner, with the LEGO person ready to cross north. Cars to look for in the "red zone" are the parallel right-turning cars and the parallel nearside surge of cars. Ask the student to move the cars on top of the gel in these two directional patterns, recognizing that the LEGO person must look left into the "red zone" for these traffic patterns, anticipating the surge with which to cross and possible dangerous right-turning cars.

6. Place the green-colored gel on the perpendicular nearside lanes. This traffic, which has a red light, should not be moving.

7. Place the purple-colored gel on the southbound lanes starting at the left-turn lane. Cars to look for in the "purple" zone are the parallel farside left-turning cars. Ask the student to move the cars on top of the gel from this position, noting that the LEGO person must look diagonally left into the "purple zone" for this traffic pattern, anticipating possible left-turning cars.

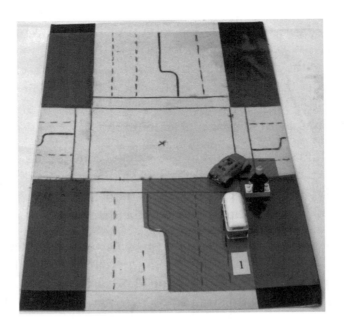

Photo 7.4

The striped section in this diagram is a red gel designating the area of the intersection for nearside parallel same-direction traffic. In the scanning sequence, students are taught to look left into this "red zone" first for right turners prior to stepping into the street.

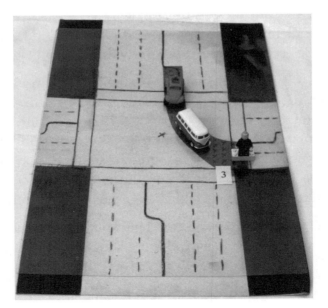

Photo 7.5

The crosshatch section in this diagram is a purple gel designating the area of the intersection for parallel farside cars. In the scanning sequence, students are taught to look left into this "purple zone" for left-turning cars before they reach the midpoint of their crossing.

8. Place the yellow-colored gel on the westbound lanes at the northeast corner. Cars to look for in the "yellow zone" are perpendicular farside right-turning cars. Ask the student to move the cars on top of the gel in this directional pattern. Note that the LEGO person must look right as he or she crosses the center dividing line of the perpendicular street, anticipating possible right-turning cars that may be approaching and hidden from view by perpendicular trucks or buses in lane 2.

9. The diagram now has all four colored gels on it. Review steps 5–8, with the student moving the LEGO person slowly across the street while moving the cars on the different gels and turning his and her head in the correct direction, depending on the traffic patterns. The student is practicing where and when to look as he or she prepares to cross and then crosses the intersection. Make sure that the student is using correct terminology for all traffic patterns.

10. If there is time, take the student to a familiar plus-shaped traffic light-controlled intersection and walk together counterclockwise around the intersection, scanning into the different "colors" (locations) of the intersection in anticipation of specific traffic patterns. In this way, the student is putting into practice exactly what was done on the diagram in class.

11. End the lesson by asking the student the purpose of the lesson, what the student did well, and what the student needs to continue to work on. Praise the student for at least one skill demonstrated well during the lesson.

Recipe Variations

At the next lesson, ask the student to travel a short route to a familiar intersection and cross side by side with the O&M specialist counterclockwise, having the student explain where to look and why. Use the image of the colored zones as a reminder. During the following lessons, which can be at different intersections, repeat the same scanning order, with the student crossing counterclockwise more independently. Re-create the same intersection shape and color-scan shape on one 4 x 6-inch card for the student to carry and use at the intersections prior to crossing.

Portable Tactile Diagrams of Four Types of Grassy Strips Found at Residential Corners

(presented as part of a Residential Block Unit)

Selecting the Correct Recipe

For elementary school- and middle school-aged students who are blind; students with additional mild disabilities; adults and older adults. This lesson is appropriate for students who have completed a unit on residential midblock traveling skills and have walked around the training block clockwise and counterclockwise. They will have just started to cross residential streets on I-shaped routes. Although they have been encouraged to practice a straight line of travel along the sidewalk, they tend to prefer trailing the grassy strips between the sidewalk and the street instead. Because the grassy strips are cut at different angles on the training blocks, students sometimes have had trouble lining up for the street crossings. The goal of the lesson is to learn about the shapes of these grassy strips and to avoid trailing them.

Ingredients and Equipment

- four heavy-cardboard tactile diagrams of typical corners, approximately 8 inches square, each with a different shape of grassy strips made of green felt made by the O&M instructor ahead of time.

Preparing the Recipe

1. In the classroom, explain to the student that he or she has a tendency to trail unnecessarily while traveling along the block and that this habit interferes with recognizing where the corner is and what it looks like. The student has sometimes veered on the street crossings as a result. The tactile diagrams will help the student recognize the different shapes of the grassy strips between the sidewalks and the street and how these shapes influence lining-up procedures. The student will learn in more detail why it is ineffective or misleading to trail the grassy strips along sidewalks.

2. Show the student the first tactile diagram (see Figure 7A.1a). Traveling clockwise, show how the grassy strip is parallel to the student's line of travel until the corner, where it ends and becomes per-a

b

c

d

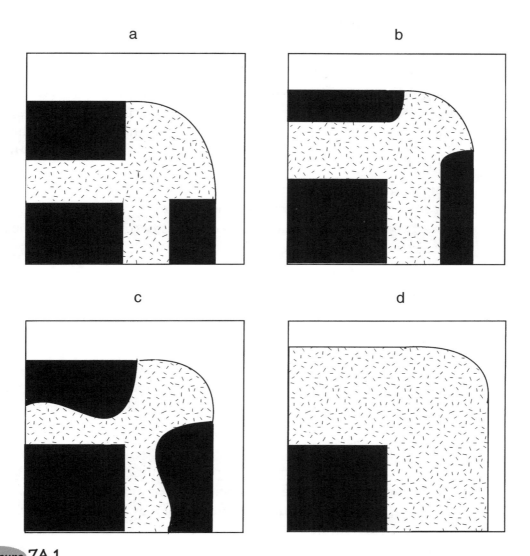

Figure 7A.1

Portable Tactile Diagrams of Four Types of Grassy Strips Found at Residential Corners

Portable tactile diagrams of different-shaped grassy strips found along sidewalks can be taken on lessons for practicing alignment at residential corners. These diagrams are made of heavy layers of cardboard and green felt.

pendicular to the student. The corner angle of the grassy strip is about 90 degrees and can be easily felt by the student's cane because the arc becomes wide all of a sudden on the right side. Remind the student that he or she has recognized this change in other lessons and has realized that he or she is at the corner and can continue walking straight ahead (not trailing) to the curb to cross the street.

3. Show the student the second tactile diagram (see Figure 7A.1b) in which the corner angle of the grassy strip is more on a diagonal and the angle is greater than 90 degrees. Explain that if the student trails along the grass (which he or she has been doing), he or she will probably not recognize the corner angle (because it is not 90 degrees) and will continue trailing it until he or she reaches the curb (which the student has done in earlier lessons). Since the student has not recognized the "corner part" of the grass strip and has not continued walking straight ahead without trailing, he or she has lined up facing out toward the middle of the street because of the cut of the grass strip. This is the reason the student has veered on the street crossings over the past few lessons.

4. Take the student to the training block and have him or her trail the grass on the right about 20 feet from the corner of the parkway that looks like the first tactile diagram. As the student approaches the end of the parallel strip, remind the student to continue trailing to recognize the arc "opening out on the right" at the point where the grassy strip corner is. When the student recognizes this location, ask him or her to stop. Have the student point out on the diagram where he or she is and where the 90-degree grassy strip corner is. Once he is clear about the location ask him or her to continue in a straight line of travel to the curb in front, lined up for a street crossing.

5. Travel with the student, stopping about 20 feet from the grassy strip corner that looks like the second tactile diagram. Show the second diagram and explain that the student may or may not recognize with the cane arc the curvature of the grassy strip at the corner ahead. The cane arc will not "open up" suddenly to the right. Ask the student to walk forward, trailing the grass on the right, and to identify when he or she thinks the grassy strip corner is changing.

6. If the student cannot recognize the grassy strip corner angle, he or she will continue trailing and find the curb. Show the diagram again and point out that to cross the street straight ahead, there should be some traveling distance at the corner where there is no grassy strip. If the student still has the grass on the right and is at the curb, the student has turned with the shape of the grassy strip. If there is sun, the student may be able to perceive the turn but may be unsure where and when to stop trailing the grassy strip and continue using a straight line of travel to reach the curb ahead. Spend some time near and at the corner, as needed, with the diagram, having the student pay attention to the size of the arc as he or she approaches the corner.

7. Discuss with the student the disadvantages of trailing near a corner. Although the corners of some grassy strips are easy to detect, the corners of others are not. There may also be areas where there are odd-shaped parkways or no parkways (see Figure 7A.1c and d), and trailing and lining up would therefore be more difficult.

8. Return to the beginning point of the lesson using the sighted guide technique. Continue to discuss why trailing interferes with the student's ability to travel effectively. Explain to the student that practicing a straight line of travel encourages good cane control and enables the student to perceive through practice how to travel forward along the block and at the corner with little or minimal veering. This skill is needed for street crossings and many other kinds of cane travel where there is nothing to trail or trailing is inappropriate, ineffective, or hazardous.

9. End the lesson by asking the student the purpose of the lesson, what the student did well, and what the student needs to continue to work on. Praise the student for at least one skill demonstrated well during the lesson.

Recipe Variations

Take the student to the same training block and remind him or her not to trail, but to work on cane control through the correct placement and use of the arm and wrist. Provide verbal or physical reinforcement when needed. Have the student line up at the corner using a straight line of travel and cross the street. Continue along the second block and ask the student to trail only when he or she approaches the corner area. Make a friendly "bet" with the student to see if he or she can identify this "new" corner as one of the first two grassy strip shapes.

Fantasy Story Written on a Computer to Understand Traffic Patterns

(presented as part of a Light Business–Street Crossings along Boulevards Unit)

Selecting the Correct Recipe

For middle school- and high school-aged students who have low vision; students with additional mild disabilities. This lesson is appropriate for students who have practiced scanning skills but have poor spatial awareness and are still confused about typical traffic patterns found while walking parallel to a boulevard in a light business area. Because of this confusion, the students' scanning skills are inconsistent. The students have been crossing at boulevard-two-stop intersections (where the smaller street has the stop signs), semiactuated traffic light-controlled intersections (where the smaller street has no pedestrian buttons for crossing, but the boulevard does), and fully actuated intersections (where the larger street and boulevard have pedestrian buttons for crossing in each direction). These students tend to have some difficulty with tactile diagrams and manipulatives like the Chang Kit. The goal of the lesson is to review the basic types of interesections found along a boulevard, the traffic patterns at these intersections, and where to cross safely. This type of lesson is motivating for students who have low vision and who know how to use a computer or have keyboarding skills, are imaginative, and have good verbal-writing skills.

Ingredients and Equipment

- a classroom computer, set at whatever size print the student needs
- a Chang Kit, for the student to demonstrate street crossings as he or she writes about them

Preparing the Recipe

Note: This lesson may take several lessons.

1. In the classroom, confirm with the student that he or she still has difficulty identifying the different types of intersections found along a boulevard and hence knowing where to scan at these intersections when crossing.

2. Explain that the student will write a "tongue-in-cheek" fantasy about boulevard intersections to practice using accurate traffic terminology and to review the different traffic patterns and scanning orders for crossing at various boulevard intersections. The student will write the story in the first person.

3. Set the scene for the story. The student is on his or her way to see a science fiction movie and has to cross three plus-shaped intersections while walking parallel to a large boulevard. Ask him or her to think of the name of the movie (and perhaps describe the invented movie briefly) and the names of four streets. The movie theater is on the diagonal corner of the third larger intersection (two large boulevards), and the student will cross the parallel boulevard here. Assist the student (if necessary) to set up the route on the Chang Kit, with a LEGO person near the first intersection and a theater landmark at the third (final) intersection.

4. Continue to outline the story which the student writes in his or her own words: The student walks ——— (the student chooses the direction) until he or she comes to the first intersection, with a small street that he or she must cross. At this point, something strange happens: As the student approaches the curb to cross, there is an earthquake. All the traffic hardware and vehicles sink into a hole. As the student is trying to figure out how to cross, he or she hears a mysterious voice saying, "You have the power to bring back order if you just think. Choose the right hardware, and all will be well."

5. Ask the student what options there are for traffic control (stop signs or traffic lights) and to demonstrate where these options would be placed on the Chang Kit. The intersection returns to normal once the student has placed the correct hardware in the correct place and demonstrated correct scanning while crossing the intersection (the earthquake damage remains if there are any mistakes). If traffic lights are selected, ask the student if there will be pedestrian buttons for crossing the boulevard. The student describes in the story what kind of hardware he or she has chosen for the intersection and how he or she has crossed the intersection, using correct traffic and hardware terminology.

6. In same lesson or the next lesson, the student continues writing the story. He or she is now walking toward the second intersection, another small street that he or she must cross. Again, as the student approaches the intersection, a strange thing happens: There is a tornado, and the traffic hardware and vehicles fly into the air. Again, a voice repeats the same command, and the student must chose the correct hardware and place it correctly on the Chang Kit. If stop signs were selected for the first intersection, then traffic lights must be used for this intersection, and vice versa. The student must also demonstrate the correct scanning order for crossing the intersection and then write all this information in the story.

7. The story continues with the student walking to the third (final) intersection, which consists of two boulevards that he or she must cross.

Once more, a strange thing happens. This time, let the student invent something or suggest a flood, blizzard, hurricane, or other type of disaster. Again, all the traffic hardware and vehicles disappear. Again, a voice is heard, and the correct hardware must be selected and the correct scanning order demonstrated. The student needs to realize that this intersection has to be a fully actuated intersection, since it consists of two big streets (there should be pedestrian buttons at each corner). The student describes the hardware correctly and demonstrates on the Chang Kit how to cross the intersection twice (the theater is on the diagonal corner) and includes this information in the story.

8. After the story is completed, review with the student that story writing is another way of understanding how intersections function, how traffic patterns are organized, and where pedestrians scan as they cross. Review the importance of using correct terms when describing and discussing intersections and traffic patterns.

Recipe Variations

The student can continue using the computer to take notes on topics learned during O&M lessons. Story writing can be used to review or refine knowledge of other orientation skills with which the student has difficulty like compass cardinal directions or the address system.

Rug Squares to Teach Alignment at Different-Shaped Corners

(presented as part of a Residential Street Crossing Unit)

Selecting the Correct Recipe

For middle school- or high school-aged students and/or adult students who are blind; students with additional mild disabilities. This lesson is appropriate for students who have been practicing residential street-crossing skills and have had some difficulty lining up because of the varying degrees of curvature of the corners from which they have been crossing. When the shape of the curb cut is mild and the curb at which the students line up is aligned perpendicularly to them, students will maintain a forward alignment and cross the intersection with no or minimal veering. However, when the students approach a curb with a more severe curvature and the curb is aligned at a diagonal facing, they often have trouble standing still while feeling this unusual alignment with the cane. They usually turn and align to the curb to be perpendicular to it, thereby facing out toward the center of the intersection, rather than toward the desired opposite corner. They will then line up incorrectly and veer into the parallel street as a result. The goal of the lesson is to learn to recognize the differences in curb shapes to enable students to line up correctly.

Ingredients and Equipment

All materials are made ahead of time by the O&M instructor.

- a 24-inch or larger rug square (A), with the top-left corner rounded to represent the corner of a block (a regular curb cut with perpendicular alignment to the pedestrian preparing to cross)

- a 24-inch or larger rug square (B), with the top-right corner cut (a regular curb cut)

- a 24-inch or larger rug square (C), with the top-left corner cut into a large curve (to represent a curb cut with a diagonal alignment to the pedestrian preparing to cross)

- a 24-inch or larger rug square (D), with the top-right corner cut (a diagonal curb cut)

- Optional: tagboard can be taped on to represent parkways and the inner corner area.

Preparing the Recipe

1. While inside, review with the student that lining up has been a problem because of the different ways the curbs have been aligned to the student when he or she has reached the corners ready to the cross the streets. Even though the student has been taught to keep his or her feet still when reaching a curb, he or she has sometimes moved and turned the feet because of the way the curb feels. Explain that rug squares have been cut to represent these different types of corner shapes and that the student will practice lining up while standing on top of these different shapes in the classroom before going outside to practice street crossings.

2. Explain that the student will stand on the rug square as if he or she were traveling counterclockwise, with the front edge of the rug representing the curb to cross and the left side of the rug representing where the parallel street is located. Let the student examine the rug square and note the small rounded corner. Ask the student to remove his or her shoes and stand on top of square A, so his or her feet are hanging over the front edge (the "curb"). In this position, the student can feel the perpendicular edge with his or her feet, like feeling certain curbs with the cane tip that are perpendicular when the student approaches them from traveling along the block. Note that at the real curb, the student notices the alignment with his or her cane, while in the room, the student feels the alignment with his or her feet. This type of curb cut will be called an "easy" corner, because it feels "right" (that is, it is perpendicular to the student) and does not influence the student to realign himself or herself. Explain that when the student has found this type of curb during lessons, he or she has remained still and thus has lined up well enough to cross with little or no veering. Make certain that the student feels the shape of the rug square in front and to the left side, including the small curve at the left corner of the rug square. This curve represents the curve of the real corner that is not in front of the student when he or she approaches the corner but off to the left side. During lessons, because this curve has been off to the side, it has not been noticed by the student's cane while traveling and has not influenced the student's lining-up procedures.

3. Repeat this same procedure with rug square B, noting that it represents lining up to cross a street in the clockwise direction. Again, the corner is an "easy" one, since the curb cut is perpendicular to the student's line of travel and the curve of the corner is off to the side (the right side). Remind the student that these types of corners have not been a problem for lining up during street-crossing lessons outside.

4. Ask the student to sit down and examine squares C and D. Put these shapes next to squares A and B, so the different curvatures of the rug squares can be compared while they are resting on the table. Note that the more severe curvature makes a larger curve at the corner of the rug square, so there is less or no perpendicular area for the student to feel with his or her feet or (at the real curb) with the cane tip.

5. Have the student stand on rug square C with his or her feet hanging over the front edge of the square. The student feels that the edge of the square in front is on an angle, with the left edge much farther back than the right edge (that is, if the student was facing north, the curb would be more of a southwest to northeast alignment than a perpendicular east–west alignment). Explain that this type of curvature, when felt by the cane tip during a lesson, has caused the student to turn his or her feet to the left so the facing would be perpendicular and "feel right." The turning has been the cause of the student's veering when crossing counterclockwise. Assist the student to feel the curve and show him or her how he or she has turned the feet to realign in a perpendicular fashion. Assist the student to realize how he or she is now facing into the parallel street, rather than lining up parallel to it. Repeat the movements of the feet, as necessary, until the student understands what he or she has been doing almost unconsciously at these types of "difficult" corners. The student must maintain the original alignment when reaching the corner even though the cane tip feels the diagonal curvature.

6. Repeat the same procedure with rug square D, a "difficult" corner when crossing clockwise.

7. Take the student to the intersection or area where there are "easy" corners and "difficult" corners, where the student has sometimes veered on the street crossings. Have the student examine the shape of the curbs and compare the "easy" and "difficult" corners. Have the student practice approaching these different types of corners, noting the curvature with the cane tip and keeping the feet still regardless of the shape of the curb. Have the student extend the cane forward to reconfirm his or her line of travel and then cross the street when appropriate.

8. End the lesson by asking the student the purpose of the lesson, what the student did well, and what the student needs to continue to work on. Praise the student for at least one skill demonstrated well during the lesson.

Recipe Variations

Take the student to unfamiliar travel areas to practice these same lining-up skills with "easy" and "difficult" corners. (This is an example of a "scatter" lesson, discussed in Chapter 6.)

Interactive Map Using Lunch Tables to Practice Alignment and Timing for Street Crossings

(presented as part of a Beginning Residential Streets Crossing Unit)

Selecting the Correct Recipe

For elementary school- through high school-aged students who are blind; students with additional mild disabilities. This lesson is appropriate for students who have been practicing basic street-crossing skills at plus-shaped intersections in a residential area using I-shaped routes (not turning before or after the street crossing). The students may not be clear about traffic that turns at the intersection (which lanes the traffic moves along and where these lanes are in relation to the four corners of the intersection). They have practiced moving little cars and LEGO people on the Chang Kit. The goal is to act out how traffic moves through a plus-shaped intersection in order to experience the movement and positioning more fully.

Ingredients and Equipment

- four school lunch tables that are near enough to one another to represent the four blocks of an intersection. (Four desks in an empty classroom can also be used.) The tables are closer along the long side and farther apart along the short sides to form a narrower east-west "street" and a wider north-south "street."

Preparing the Recipe

The lesson must be held when it is quiet and there are no or few students present.

1. Explain to the student that he or she will continue learning about traffic patterns by acting out the way the cars and pedestrians travel in different directions through a plus-shaped residential intersection. It is important to understand exactly where the cars come from and where they are going when crossing intersections. The student will be acting out scenarios similar to the ones he or she set up on the Chang Kit. Explain that this is called an "interactive" model and is another way to help the student understand a concept or skill that has been confusing to him or her.

2. Have the student examine the shapes of the four rectangular tables, travel the shorter north–south "street" and the longer east–west "street" between the four tables, and then stand at the "intersection" area where the corners of the four tables meet. Ask the student to place his or her hands on each of the four corners while standing in the middle of the "intersection." If needed, assist the student to visualize the small intersection where he or she is standing and to understand that this is the place where two streets intersect and where the four different blocks meet. These shapes and relationships have all been examined on the Chang Kit.

3. The student begins by being a pedestrian on the southeast corner facing north. (It is better if the student is actually facing real north.) He or she places one hand on the corner of the table, as if standing on the corner. The O&M specialist acts out the parallel nearside car moving in the same direction from behind the student's left shoulder forward and then driving north ahead of the student. Remind the student that this is the counterclockwise pattern with the parallel street on the student's left side. Car noises can be made, and the student can hold a small stop sign if desired. If there is a stop sign, the O&M specialist has to stop at the "corner" and then proceed north.

4. Repeat this scenario with the O&M specialist approaching the intersection in the same way and then turning left (west) and, the next time, turning right (east). When turning left, make enough sound so the student hears the direction of the movement (forward and then to the left).

5. If the student is still unsure of the traffic pattern, he or she can stand behind the O&M specialist while holding on to the side of the table with his or her right hand. The student will also be a "car" driving north. As the "cars" move forward, the student's right hand will move along the edge of the table past the corner and then reach the farside northeast corner of the "intersection." Repeat this scenario with the two "cars" traveling west and then traveling east from the southeast corner. As the student moves, have him or her reach out and touch the edges of the tables (the "sides" of the "streets") and the various corners of the "intersection" (southeast, southwest, northeast, and northwest).

6. The O&M specialist then stands at the southeast corner as the pedestrian, and the student acts out the movement of the "car" going north and then turning west and east.

7. Repeat steps 3–6 with the student standing at the southwest corner facing north. The student will be listening to and acting out the traffic pattern from a clockwise point of view, with the parallel street on the student's right side. Stop signs can be used for one or both "streets."

8. Review any directions that were confusing. Open the Chang Kit and review the patterns just acted out, if necessary.

9. End the lesson by asking the student the purpose of the lesson, what the student did well, and what the student needs to continue to work on. Praise the student for at least one skill demonstrated well during the lesson.

Recipe Variations

In the next lesson, take the student to the training area and travel a short route leading to the intersection where the student has practiced. Have the student cross all the way around counterclockwise with assistance, referring back to the interactive model and the traffic pattern before each crossing. During the next lesson, repeat the same scenario with the student traveling clockwise.

Mini-Chang Kit to Teach Spatial and Environmental Concepts at Intersections

(presented as part of an Advanced Residential Street Crossing Unit)

Selecting the Correct Recipe

For elementary school- through high school-age students who are blind or have low vision; students with additional mild disabilities. This lesson is appropriate for students who have been learning about traffic patterns on parallel streets, on perpendicular streets, and at plus-shaped intersections. The students will have used the Chang Kit to understand these patterns, in addition to traveling outside and listening to the traffic patterns. They are beginning to learn how to cross streets on I-shaped routes in advanced residential–light business areas but are sometimes confused by turning traffic. The goal of the lesson is to review traffic patterns and terminology using a tactile model or reference while standing at the corner of the intersection and listening to identify the traffic. Although the Chang Kit is too big to hold and use on a lesson outdoors, the mini-Chang Kit is just the right size to take on the lesson.

Ingredients and Equipment

All materials are made ahead of time by the O&M instructor.

- a purchased padded folding 8 x 11-inch notepad that is empty (also called a "bifold," with inside pockets on one side and a place for a notepad on the other side), with black felt or another kind of soft material glued on the entire inside surface

- four small rectangles cut out of yellow tagboard or foam board to represent four blocks, with a small amount of felt or Velcro glued on the back of each corner

- miniature cars that fit on the minkit (the size of the tip of a finger)

Preparing the Recipe

1. Explain that the student will use the mini-Chang Kit, which is just like the bigger one, while standing at the corner of the intersection where he or she crossed during the last lesson. Moving the minicars on the kit as the real cars are passing by will help the student identify the traffic and clarify tactilely where the cars are traveling. Show the mini Chang Kit to the student and help him or her place the four blocks in position, so there is a plus-shaped intersection in the middle of the kit.

2. The student travels a short route counterclockwise along a familiar boulevard to the small traffic light-controlled intersection crossed on the previous lesson. Along the way, review the following terms with the student as the traffic passes by: *parallel near, parallel far, parallel same direction,* and *parallel opposite direction.*

3. At the first corner of the intersection, stop before crossing and listen to the perpendicular traffic. Ask the student to move his or her arm in the direction of the cars as they are heard. Review terms like *perpendicular nearside* and *perpendicular farside* as these traffic patterns occur.

4. Using the mini-Chang Kit, have the student identify the intersection on the kit and point to the corner where he or she is standing. Focusing on the perpendicular traffic, have the student move the minicars in the same direction as the real perpendicular cars. Correct as needed, especially when the perpendicular traffic turns. Ask the student to use correct terminology after the traffic turns (for example, perpendicular farside cars turn left and become parallel to the farside opposite traffic).

5. Focusing on the parallel traffic, have the student move the minicars in the same direction as the real parallel cars. Correct as needed, especially when there is turning traffic (for instance, the parallel nearside same direction traffic turns left and becomes perpendicular to the farside).

6. Ask the student which cars he or she should cross with (parallel nearside same direction) and have the student show you these cars on the mini-Chang Kit. Ask the student to cross to the opposite corner, the second corner, when the parallel nearside surge begins. Walk side by side with the student on the crossing. If the student is tired at this point, take a break and walk, using the sighted guide technique, looking at the businesses on the second corner.

7. Repeat listening to the traffic and using the mini-Chang Kit to verify the traffic patterns, crossing together to the third and then the fourth corner.

8. End the lesson after crossing the fourth corner and completing the route. Ask the student the purpose of the lesson, what the student did well, and what the student needs to continue to work on. Praise the student for at least one skill demonstrated well during the lesson.

Recipe Variations

Use the same lesson format with the student approaching the same intersection from a different route. Cross clockwise, with time out to enter one of the businesses on the second corner of the previous lesson.

8

Working with Others: Collaboration, Professional Development, and Public Relations

CHAPTER PREVIEW

Collaboration
    Collaboration in O&M
    Principles of Effective Collaboration
    Involving Students and Their Families

Maintaining Professional Energy
    Professional Development
    Preventing Burnout

Public Relations
    Generating Administrative Support
    Working in the Community

ALTHOUGH O&M specialists often work one on one with their students, collaborating with others—teachers, other specialists, administrators, individuals from the community, families, and students—to achieve a common goal is both a necessary and beneficial part of their jobs. Effective collaboration often increases opportunities for creative instructional approaches through the sharing of ideas and energy. In addition, participating in professional development activities provides an avenue for reenergizing and expanding teaching repertoires. Finally, taking time to ensure that others clearly understand professional roles through well-thought-out public relations efforts helps to generate the support necessary for continued innovative programming that best meets the needs of students of all ages who are blind or visually impaired. This chapter addresses specific strategies for collaborating with others, creating opportunities for professional development, and promoting a positive image and understanding of the O&M profession.

COLLABORATION

Since the population of individuals who are blind and visually impaired is extremely heterogeneous, their needs for education and rehabilitation cross a wide span of disciplines and expertise. In educational settings, teachers of students with visual impairments and O&M specialists may have caseloads of students ranging from preschool age through high school age. They may serve students who are gifted and talented, as well as those who have mild to severe cognitive disabilities; students who are English speaking and those with limited English proficiency; and students with additional physical disabilities and other health impairments. Similarly, in rehabilitation settings, adults who are blind or visually impaired vary in age, come from culturally and linguistically diverse backgrounds, and may have additional disabilities or health impairments. With this wide range of students, it is unrealistic to assume that these O&M professionals will have all the knowledge and skills needed to serve these students properly without consultation and input from a host of other people, including

- students and family members;
- community members or representatives;
- early interventionists and early childhood educators;
- general and special education teachers;
- physical and adapted physical education specialists;
- occupational and physical therapists;
- audiologists and speech pathologists;
- state or national consultants from departments of education;
- private educational consultants;
- assistive technology specialists;
- school counselors and psychologists;

- school or agency administrators;
- physical facilities and office staff;
- eye care and other medical professionals;
- social workers, nutritionists, and mental health care workers;
- vocational and transition specialists;
- employers and potential employers; and
- other O&M specialists, teachers of students with visual impairments, and rehabilitation counselors and teachers.

To meet the diverse needs of the individuals they serve, O&M specialists and other professionals in the field of visual impairment and blindness have to pursue productive collaborative efforts when the opportunities present themselves. Collective efforts, shared ideas, and team implementation of educational or rehabilitation goals benefit teachers, specialists, families, and students.

Collaboration in O&M

The traditional approach to providing O&M services on a one-to-one basis has led to high-quality, individualized instruction. However, the itinerant and community-based model used by many O&M specialists has not always facilitated collaboration because of the physical isolation of traveling from one school or location to another. Moreover, the itinerant model does not always allow for the extra time needed to establish relationships or pursue collaborative ventures. Providing services across different school districts, areas of a county, or communities also makes it difficult to develop collaborative projects that meet the needs and follow the regulations of multiple entities.

In spite of the inherent challenges to collaboration posed by the itinerant service delivery model, there are many opportunities for O&M specialists to pursue, including these:

- Developing professional development activities or in-service training workshops with colleagues.

- Establishing a positive behavior support plan to address a student's challenging behaviors with the school psychologist and lead teacher.

- Discussing students' progress with family members and other professionals.

- Generating ideas for alternative instructional practices with friends or colleagues.

- Modeling instructional techniques for families or beginning teachers.

- Identifying and solving learning or access problems for students with other teachers, program specialists, and administrators.

- Planning for and implementing assessments for goal development with members of the educational or rehabilitation team.

- Developing goals with students, families, and professionals for the Individualized Family Service Plan (IFSP), IEP, Individualized Transition Plan (ITP), or IWRP.

There are many benefits to such collaborative efforts. Effective teamwork can lead to a greater consistency of approaches for instruction and reinforcement, expanded opportunities for teaching and learning, more sharing of ideas, and increased support for O&M services. Dettmer, Dyck, and Thurston (1999, p. 27) also noted:

> Multiplier effects provide compelling arguments for consultation, collaboration, and teaming. They create benefits beyond the immediate situation involving one student and that student's teachers. For example, through collaboration school personnel are modeling this powerful social tool for their students who are quite likely to experience collaborative climates in their future workplace.

Collaboration does not come without challenges, however. One such challenge is the time required of all the participants. Itinerant O&M specialists, with large caseloads and long driving distances, may have difficulty finding time to collaborate. In addition to scheduling time to collaborate, O&M specialists need to devote time to communicating concerns, identifying problems, sharing ideas, and coordinating collaborative efforts. Making Collaboration a Part of Professional Life presents some suggestions for improving collaboration with others. Furthermore, although there are clearly practical problems to surmount, paying attention to certain principles of collaboration will make the actual process proceed more smoothly and productively.

WORKING WITH OTHERS 331

MAKING COLLABORATION A PART

MAKING COLLABORATION A PART OF PROFESSIONAL LIFE

- Plan set times in your schedule to work with colleagues on collaborative projects.

- Find a physical space that is conducive to working on collaborative projects somewhere at school, the agency center, or even a public location like a restaurant.

- Establish a working communication system (such as a child communication log, professional bulletin board, or e-mail system) with colleagues and families.

- Maintain an open mind when sharing and listening to ideas with others.

- Keep a file of "great ideas" or projects that were discussed but never implemented and review the ideas when you have more time and energy to devote to them.

Principles of Effective Collaboration

The essence of collaboration involves the combined ideas, expertise, experience, and energy of all team members. Each participant has something to contribute that will lead to the accomplishment of the larger goal. Dettmer et al. (1999, p. 7) contended that "the collaborative process is enhanced by diversity among the collaborators—diversity of experience, values, abilities, and interests." Recognizing and valuing differences is the first step toward getting the maximum contribution from each collaborative partner.

Communication, cooperation, and coordination are all essential elements in effective collaboration (Dettmer et al., 1999) as the participants keep open minds and recognize that there is more than one way to achieve a common goal. Through the collaborative process, the participants learn from one another as they listen to others' ideas that may differ from their own.

Communication

Although individual differences enhance the collaborative process, they can also inhibit productive communication. One such difference may be cultural differences in communication styles. For example, individuals from one culture may think it is appropriate to interrupt or talk over one another during group brainstorming, whereas those from another culture may think it is disrespectful to do so. It is important to acknowledge such differences, to learn about each other's cultures through observation and listening, and to develop respect for diversity within the group.

When communicating with collaborative partners, O&M specialists are more effective in expressing their ideas and opinions, enabling others to understand more fully what they are saying and encouraging others to share their ideas, if they avoid using professional jargon, acronyms, and other unfamiliar terms. When new or specialized terminology must be used, O&M specialists can avoid giving misinformation or creating misunderstanding by taking the time to define the words or describe the techniques being introduced. For example, if a cane technique is mentioned in the course of setting goals, the O&M specialist or student can demonstrate it and briefly describe its function. Indeed, all professionals need to be conscientious in not using jargon in communicating with others, both professionals and nonprofessionals, and to use a common language whenever one can be established.

Another important part of communication is being a good listener. The expression of divergent thinking is fostered when all the participants actively listen to each other. Points of confusion, misunderstanding, or disagreement can be more freely and quickly addressed when the team members listen and communicate openly. Nonjudgmental responses to ideas that may be proposed are key to facilitating participation from all team members. Statements, such as "I've never tried that approach—tell me how you do it" or "That's an alternative that I hadn't considered," demonstrate that the participant is listening and open to learning about the approach.

Cooperation

Cooperation—working together—is a key concept of all collaborative efforts. For collaboration to work, the participants need to trust each other and make equal efforts to sustain the team's momentum. When one professional reacts emotionally in attempts to protect traditional roles or territories, the other team members quickly lose interest in devoting the time necessary to develop collaborative projects. Territoriality makes it difficult for people to think of innovative solutions to longstanding problems for cases in which traditional approaches have not been effective. Even when all the participants are enthusiastic about potential collaborative efforts, ideas cannot be fully implemented unless everyone follows through on his or her commitments.

Coordination

Teamwork must be coordinated to be effective. Each participant in the collaborative process must make a meaningful contribution to the desired goal. A clear division of labor must be determined so that all the team members are working with equal effort, and roles and expectations must be clarified.

For example, an IEP team that is planning for a particular student may develop the following goal: "The student will use his cane to travel independently from the homeroom to the language arts class each day." The members must then determine such roles and responsibilities for implementing this goal as the following:

- It will be the role of the O&M specialist to instruct the student in the proper use of the cane and in learning the most efficient route to travel.

- The family and student must assume responsibility for assuring that the child brings his or her cane to school each day.

- The homeroom teacher will check daily to see that the student takes his or her cane when leaving to go to the language arts class.

- The assistant principal will check periodically to see that other students are being respectful of the student while he or she uses the cane in between classes.

- The O&M specialist must also periodically monitor the student to ensure that the student maintains the necessary skills for independent travel along the route.

The benefit of clarifying such roles ahead of time is that expectations are made clearer for the entire team. If the entire team develops an O&M goal, then the achievement of the goal becomes the shared responsibility of many individuals, rather than the sole responsibility of the O&M specialist.

In addition, the clear definition of specialists' roles ensures that the specialists will not infringe on one another and helps general educators, administrators, and family members better understand who is responsible for which service. For example, it is not uncommon for an O&M specialist to come to a general education class to pick up a student for a one-to-one lesson in the community and to have the math teacher ask, "Would you be able to get this quiz put into braille for tomorrow?" This may be an uncomfortable position for an O&M specialist, who then has to decide whether to tell the math teacher that transcribing is not his or her responsibility or to go out of the way to get the quiz to the transcriber or teacher of students with visual impairments. In any case, ignorance of the O&M specialist's role is confusing for the math teacher and ineffective for all the team members. A lot of time and energy can be saved if such roles are clarified at the beginning of the year and reviewed periodically.

Involving Students and Their Families

Successful collaboration is not limited to teamwork among professionals. Involving students and their families as collaborative partners in O&M instruction can be equally rewarding. Family members' involvement in students' learning and educational programming has been shown to enhance student's success in academics and social behavior (Hansen, Himes, & Meier, 1990). Similar positive results could be expected for adults in rehabilitation settings when families are involved in the process. Collaboration has also been shown to increase family empowerment and satisfaction (Hoover-Dempsey & Sandler, 1997). Dettmer et al. (1999) noted that teachers and specialists can gain greater insights into their students' strengths and motivations when families are included in the collaborative process. Families can be powerful advocates for professionals, programming ideas, and schools or agencies. Family partnerships can benefit O&M specialists in many ways, including these:

- When families are encouraged to participate in or observe O&M instruction, the quality of their contributions to assessments and goal setting can be significantly higher.

- Priorities may be more realistic because they are more knowledgeable about the O&M curriculum and their family member's current skills and abilities.

- Increased participation from family members can also increase the likelihood of follow-through at home.

For example, families need to be fully informed about the IEP, ITP, or IWRP process ahead of time by being told who will be at the team meeting, how the meeting will be conducted, and what types of input they may be asked to provide. As families develop greater comfort in participating in the educational or rehabilitation process, they can become more active partners. Developing collaborative partnerships with families goes beyond encouraging participation in educational or rehabilitation programming and extends to shared decision making.

Lynch and Stein (1990) identified barriers to collaboration with families that exist across cultures. These barriers may include work responsibilities, time conflicts, transportation difficulties, and child care issues. Although it may be beneficial to have family members spend time observing O&M lessons, for example, O&M specialists cannot assume that family members will have the time or means to get to a lesson. Perhaps a lesson can be scheduled in the home community at a time when at least one family member is available to observe. Perhaps a videotape can be taken during a few lessons and sent home with the student. If the family does not have access to a VCR, then a clip of the video could be shown at an IEP or IWRP meeting. Professionals need to respect the fact that families have a host of responsibilities to attend to. Encouraging families' participation while accepting individuals' limits of time and energy is important.

Students can also be vital partners in designing O&M programs in different ways. They become collaborative partners when they are given meaningful choices during O&M lessons (such as, "Would you like to get your bus schedule information by phoning the bus company or by searching through the company's web site?"). On a more complex level, students can assume an active role in planning lessons, charting a sequence of lessons, or selecting and previewing the locations of the lessons.

All students should be given the opportunity to participate in setting goals for their IEP, ITP, or IWRP meetings. Young students can be asked in more general terms to identify things that they would like to learn, and older students and adults can assist O&M specialists in actually writing or presenting their O&M goals at the team meeting. In addition to the benefits gained through sharing their ideas with O&M specialists, students may also develop stronger self-advocacy skills by participating in team planning meetings.

MAINTAINING PROFESSIONAL ENERGY

To stimulate creative ideas and maintain their innovative instructional approaches over a sustained period, O&M specialists need to find ways to renew their creative energy and continue their professional growth. Thus, it is important for them to make plans for ongoing professional development.

In addition, many professionals in the human services experience high levels of stress in the course of their jobs. Professionals burdened with challenging caseloads, inadequate time and resources, and limited recognition for hard work and dedication are likely to experience frustration with their job. Dettmer et al. (1999, p. 180) noted that "high lev-

---

 SUSTAINING CREATIVITY

- Take time outside of work to do things that you enjoy or find relaxing.

- Read texts, books, and journal articles to learn about successful techniques and strategies that other O&M specialists are using.

- Attend workshops or in-service programs that are of interest to you, including those that may be appropriate to other disciplines.

- Ask for time to observe colleagues and programs that may be using teaching approaches that are different from yours.

- Find new training areas for instructing students instead of using the same ones over and over.

- Make new versions of useful teaching materials as they get old and used.

- Borrow or adapt successful teaching materials created by other O&M specialists.

- Volunteer to supervise a student teacher or serve as a mentor and learn through observation and sharing what strategies another teacher or other specialists use with particular students.

- Network with other professionals to share ideas regarding teaching strategies and approaches.

- Reward yourself for your personal and professional accomplishments.

els of emotional exhaustion and depersonalization, when accompanied by low feelings of personal accomplishment, signal burnout for teachers, social workers, nurses, and others who serve people's needs." Creating support networks and maintaining other healthy work habits can reduce stress. In addition to the information in the following sections, the ideas listed in Sustaining Creativity will help professionals keep their creative juices flowing and avoid professional burnout.

Professional Development

Completing a university credential, certification, or degree program in a specialized area of visual impairment (O&M, rehabilitation counseling, or teaching) prepares teachers and specialists to provide services to individuals who are blind or visually impaired. However, these training programs are only the first step in what can be a lifelong learning and growth process for each professional.

Developing a plan for professional growth will help O&M specialists expand the realm of skills that can be applied to direct service with students and consultation with other professionals and families. Professional development activities may include

- attendance at in-service programs, workshops, and professional conferences;
- registration for continuing education units at universities or professional workshops;
- enrollment in additional credential, certification, or degree programs;
- reading professional literature;
- conducting in-service programs or workshops;
- collaborating on professional presentations;
- submitting articles for publication in journals or newsletters;
- supervising student teachers or mentoring beginning teachers; and
- teaching courses at community colleges or universities.

These types of activities will not only support professional development related to meeting job responsibilities, but will also be useful for renewing credentials, certifications, and licenses that are important to the profession and maintaining employment. In some employment settings, continuing education credits or university course work are factored into salary increases. Professional development activities, when properly selected, can be energizing and help prepare professionals for the changes and challenges inherent in the O&M professions.

Preventing Burnout

As was mentioned earlier, despite the tremendous satisfaction of working in the helping professions, professionals in the human services face many stresses related to the highly interpersonal nature of their jobs. In addition, itinerant teachers and service providers experience even greater burnout because of factors associated with large caseloads, vast travel areas, multiple supervisors, and less sense of accomplishment (Zabel & Zabel, 1982). Additional factors that may contribute to burnout for O&M specialists may include

- budget cuts and lack of resources for teachers, specialists, staff, and instructional materials;

- public criticisms of teachers and student outcomes;

- abundant state, county, district, or agency regulations and paperwork;

- increased professional responsibilities without compensation;

- angry families or students with aggressive behaviors;

- administrators or supervisors who lack knowledge in the area of visual impairment;

- the lack of recognition or rewards, and

- limited decision-making powers or influence (Dettmer et al., 1999).

Each of these factors may affect individual professionals in different ways, depending on their employment status, attitudes, and dispositions. In some instances, individual practitioners can do little to address the larger issues that cause stress on the job. However, there are immediate things that they can do to change the way they deal with some of this stress, such as managing their time, setting realistic goals, maintaining a healthy lifestyle, and developing support networks. When strategies are effectively used to minimize work stress and maximize work effectiveness, professionals are more able to appreciate the joys of working as part of a vital team that serves individuals with visual impairments and their families.

Managing Time

Working to improve the way they manage their time can help professionals deal more effectively with a multitude of work responsibilities. For example, maintaining a work calendar to keep track of upcoming meetings and students' regular schedules helps professionals prepare to conduct assessments, write reports, and develop goals and objectives for individualized program plans. Making use of planning periods to write lesson plans or keeping up to date with daily progress notes prevents O&M specialists from taking unnecessary work home with them. Technology can be a tool to assist O&M specialists who work on an itinerant basis. For example, if laptop computers are available, O&M specialists can word process between lessons. Cell phones also save time by allowing O&M specialists to speak with others more readily and get help quickly if their cars break down or other emergencies arise. Logging mileage at each stop, rather than trying to reconstruct a month's or year's worth of travel, is also more efficient. Keeping a weekly or daily "to do" list can help professionals organize time and increase a personal sense of accomplishment as items are crossed off the list. When overextended, professionals need to learn to say "no" to things that are not related to the job, do not benefit their students, and are not enjoyable. When appropriate, smaller tasks can be delegated when assistance is available so that adequate attention can be given to those tasks most essential to positive student outcomes.

Setting Realistic Goals

It is often difficult for people to accept that they are unable to accomplish everything asked of them by their employers, students, and families, as well as what they demand of themselves. When work is overwhelming, it is useful to set realistic goals. Students' needs, personal concerns, issues with colleagues, and employers' requests are not always in line with one another and leave the person trying to put out multiple fires. Establishing priorities that one can reasonably expect to meet helps one focus on one's work efforts.

Maintaining a Healthy Lifestyle

Maintaining good nutrition, exercise routines, and sleep habits is important for a healthy lifestyle for all people. A healthy lifestyle is an excellent weapon in combating stress on the job. Adopting such routines is not only beneficial for the individual professional, but also serves as a positive model for colleagues and students alike.

Developing Support Networks

When professionals, especially those who work on an itinerant basis, develop strong support networks, they are more easily able to deal with the myriad of pressures they face at work and not to feel professionally isolated. Support networks can be established at schools or agencies, through professional organizations, or within home communities. In any case, finding a constructive way to release frustrations and maintain a positive outlook is helpful. For example, a group of colleagues may decide to walk together at lunchtime. Exercise is a good way to handle stress and its symptoms, and walking with others may provide a source of emotional support and motivation. Individuals can directly address some of the sources of work-related stress by participating in fundraisers and advocacy campaigns through professional organizations. Such activities can empower them and help them to feel that they can make a contribution and a difference. Families can also be a source of support for many professionals. Social activities, with work colleagues or other friends, can be an effective outlet for stress for many individuals. For example, participating in a "book of the month club" can be a positive social outlet. Regardless of the vehicle or vehicles used, professionals can help to prevent burnout by getting support from others.

PUBLIC RELATIONS

O&M specialists can make an important contribution to the O&M profession and to their work by being aware of the need to develop an effective public relations effort. Fostering positive attitudes toward the profession can lead to invaluable support for O&M programming and the creative efforts of individual O&M specialists.

Many teachers, counselors, therapists, specialists, administrators, potential students, and family members do not fully understand the roles and teaching responsibilities of O&M specialists. O&M specialists can effectively increase their awareness through collaboration and improved communication, explaining students who are blind or visually impaired travel independently and emphasizing the importance of developing body, spatial, and environmental concepts in facilitating independent travel. When questions or concerns arise (for example, Is it safe for students to use their long canes on the playground?), people are more likely to ask relevant questions (like "Why does one student use a long cane for travel and another use a dog guide?") when there is open communication. Increased familiarity with the basic O&M curriculum or principles can lead to improved administrative support, greater instructional follow-through, and lasting partnerships in important advocacy arenas.

On a larger scale, there is much to be done to increase awareness in the community at large of the travel needs and independent capabilities of people who are blind or visually impaired and of the instructional activities of O&M specialists. For example, it is not uncommon to hear stories of a police officer stopping an O&M specialist to question why he or she appears to be following a school-age student who is visually impaired. Similarly, pedestrians, drivers, and store clerks may be confused about why some individuals who use long canes appear to be able to see the pedestrian crosswalk signal.

Efforts to establish positive public relations, whether within a school or agency or the greater community, help to advance awareness and understanding of professional services available to individuals who are blind or visually impaired. Developing an O&M Public Relations Kit lists some suggestions for O&M specialists and other professionals in the field of visual impairment and blindness to help increase awareness of and support for the programs in which they work.

Generating Administrative Support

Whether an O&M program is in a school district or public or private agency, it is essential that the administrator clearly understands the many roles of the O&M specialist. Administrative support can be an essential element of a successful O&M program. Although an administrator can make or break a program, there are ways for an O&M specialist to assume a positive role in supporting and educating the administrator.

At the beginning of the year, it may be helpful to give the supervisor or administrator in the school system a list of students who will be receiving individualized O&M services, so he or she is aware of who will be going off campus for lessons. It may also be beneficial to give the administrator a brief description of the general training areas that may be used, so there is no confusion when the administrator drives by

DEVELOPING AN O&M PUBLIC RELATIONS KIT

- Volunteer to speak at community organizations (such as the Lion's Club or Optimist Club) to increase awareness of your program and the needs of the students with whom you work.

- Speak to high school or college classes about the rewards of working in the field of visual impairment and blindness to increase awareness and to recruit more individuals into the field.

- Invite family members, other professionals, important community representatives, and key administrators to observe O&M lessons or other classes for students who are blind or visually impaired that will best showcase the positive outcomes of O&M instruction.

- Encourage an appropriate company or organization to "adopt" your specialized school, class, or program to generate some financial support for students or special projects that are needed.

- Help to create attractive brochures and web pages that will inform people about your profession by becoming involved in a professional organization.

- Carry a business card or brochure with you during lessons to give to individuals who inquire about your teaching.

an intersection in the middle of the day and sees the O&M specialist working with one or two of the school's students.

Administrators expect O&M specialists to complete all the necessary paperwork before taking students off campus. In some settings, this paperwork may include signed permission slips from parents to take students off campus in the O&M specialist's car. To provide an appropriate rationale for taking students off campus, current IEPs or IWRPs must reflect goals that require lessons in the community. Agency or school campus sign-out procedures need to be consistently adhered to. It is also important to carry appropriate levels of car insurance and professional liability insurance when teaching travel skills. (Professional liability insurance can be purchased through various professional organizations.) Emergency medical contact information can be kept in the trunk of the car for easy access. As was mentioned earlier, O&M specialists who teach in the community need to carry cell phones on lessons in case of emergencies.

On campus, administrators and other school personnel occasionally observe O&M instruction. This can be an opportunity for an O&M specialist to explain briefly what is being taught. As long as doing so does not detract from lessons, students can be encouraged to interact with school personnel at these times, practicing their social skills. Each positive interaction furthers public education efforts.

Professional information brochures can also be sent yearly to administrators, especially to those who are new. Volunteering to create an O&M bulletin board at a school where students with visual impairments are learning to travel independently can also attract interest and inform school personnel, visitors, and families about the scope and practice of O&M instruction.

Public school administrators also learn about the O&M curriculum through participation in IEP meetings. When O&M specialists report on students' progress and develop annual goals together with families and other teachers, they are educating all participants on the IEP team. Administrators are especially appreciative when meetings run smoothly because professionals are properly prepared and communicate effectively with families and other team members. If a disagreement is anticipated, administrators often prefer to hear about the situation before the meeting so that surprises are minimized. In each of these ways, O&M specialists are generating support for their students' achievements and for their instructional programs.

Working in the Community

In much the same way that administrative support can be generated, public relations efforts in the community can be furthered in several ways. O&M lessons in the community often generate interest from passersby, but O&M specialists need to maintain a fine balance between taking time to educate the public and having enough time to instruct their students. An informational brochure can be a handy way to provide information quickly without detracting too much from a student's lesson.

As O&M specialists attempt to simulate greater levels of independence for their students, they may try to pretend that they are not accompanying students during lessons. In these instances, it may be counterproductive to take the time to explain what a student is being taught. At other times, O&M specialists may actually want to introduce themselves to a shop owner or store clerk ahead of time to explain that a student will be traveling to the store that day to practice making a purchase. How the O&M specialist chooses to handle each situation depends on the lesson objectives and the student's abilities.

Students who are blind or visually impaired should be informed of and try to meet expectations for personal appearance and social behaviors when working in the community. Positive impressions help forward the cause of public education.

Both O&M specialists and students can also take the time to learn about the culture or cultures of people in the community in which they will be working to ensure that they maintain appropriate interactions with the people they encounter. A great deal can be learned through observation, but information can also be obtained through reading and attending cultural events in the community. Making an effort to learn about a different culture can also motivate students for independent travel and exploration.

Developing a team approach by collaborating with other professionals, families, and community members enables O&M specialists and their colleagues to provide the highest-quality services to individuals who are blind or visually impaired. Working together with others not only brings fresh and relevant ideas to O&M specialists and professionals in the field of visual impairment but also provides needed support for maintaining a positive outlook while handling the stresses inherent in their jobs. Assuming personal responsibility for professional growth empowers O&M specialists to continue imagining the possibilities for creative and meaningful instructional programming.

References

Anthony, T. (1992). *Inventory of purposeful movement behaviors.* Denver, CO: Colorado Department of Education, Special Education Services.

Anthony, T. (1993). *Early intervention: Orientation and mobility checklist* (rev. ed.). Denver, CO: Colorado Department of Education, Special Education Services Unit.

Bentzen, B. L. (1997). Environmental accessibility. In B. B. Blasch, W. R. Weiner, & R. L. Welsh (Eds.), *Foundations of orientation and mobility* (2nd ed., pp. 317–358). New York: AFB Press.

Blasch, B. B., Wiener, W. R., & Welsh, R. L. (Eds.). (1997). *Foundations of orientation and mobility* (2nd ed.). New York: AFB Press.

Bloom, B., Englehart, M., Furst, E., Hill, W., & Krathwohl, D. (1956). *Taxonomy of educational objectives. Handbook 1: Cognitive domain.* New York: David McKay.

Brown, C., & Bour, B. (1986). Vol. V–K: Movement analysis and curriculum for visually impaired preschoolers. In *A resource manual for the development and evaluation of special programs for exceptional students.* Tallahassee, FL: Educational Materials Distribution Center, Florida Department of Education.

Campbell, B. (1997). The Naturalist Intelligence. The Building Tool Room. http://www.newhorizons.org/article_eightintel.html

Dettmer, P., Dyck, N., & Thurston, L. P. (1999). *Consultation, collaboration, and teamwork for students with special needs* (3rd ed.). Boston: Allyn & Bacon.

Dodson-Burk, B., & Hill, E. W. (1989). *Preschool orientation and mobility screening.* Alexandria, VA: Association for Education and Rehabilitation of the Blind and Visually Impaired.

Fazzi, D. L. (1998). Facilitating independent travel for students who have visual impairments with other disabilities. In S. Z. Sacks & R. K. Silberman (Eds.), *Educating students who have visual impairments with other disabilities* (pp. 441–468). Baltimore, MD: Paul H. Brookes.

Ferrell, K. A. (1996). Your child's development. In M. C. Holbrook (Ed.), *Children with visual impairments: A parent's guide* (pp. 73–96). Bethesda, MD: Woodbine House.

Gardner, H. (1983). *Frames of mind.* New York: Basic Books.

Gardner, H. (1993). *Multiple intelligences: The theory in practice.* New York: Basic Books.

Hansen, J. C., Himes, B. S., & Meier, S. (1990). *Consultation: Concepts and practices.* Englewood Cliffs, NJ: Prentice Hall.

Hill, E. W. (1981). *The Hill performance test of selected positional concepts.* Chicago: Stoelting.

Hill, E. W., & Ponder, P. (1976). *Orientation and mobility techniques: A guide for the practitioner.* New York: American Foundation for the Blind.

Hoover-Dempsey, K., & Sandler, H. (1997). Why do parents become involved in their children's education. *Review of Educational Research, 67* (1), 3–42.

Jacobson, W. H. (1993). *The art and science of teaching orientation and mobility to persons with visual impairments.* New York: AFB Press.

Joffee, E., & Rikhye, C. H. (1991). Orientation and mobility for students with severe visual and multiple impairments: A new perspective. *Journal of Visual Impairment & Blindness, 85,* 211–216.

LaGrow, S., & Weessies, M. J. (1994). *Orientation and mobility: Techniques for independence.* Palmerston North, New Zealand: Dunmore Press.

Long, R. G., & Hill, E. W. (1997). Establishing and maintaining orientation for mobility. In B. B. Blasch, W. R. Wiener, & R. L. Welsh (Eds.), *Foundations of orientation and mobility* (2nd ed., pp. 39–60). New York: AFB Press.

Lynch, E. W., & Stein, R. C. (1990). Parent participation by ethnicity: Comparison of Hispanic, Black, and Anglo families. *Educating exceptional children* (5th ed.). Guilford, CT: Dushkin.

Pogrund, R., Healy, G., Jones, K., Levack, N., Martin-Curry, S., Martinez, C., Marz, J., Roberson-Smith, B., & Vrba, A. (1995a). *Teaching age-appropriate purposeful skills: An orientation & mobility curriculum for students with visual impairments.* Austin, TX: Texas School for the Blind and Visually Impaired.

Pogrund, R., Healy, G., Jones, K., Levack, N., Martin-Curry, S., Martinez, C., Marz, J., Roberson-Smith, B., & Vrba, A. (1995b). Appendix A: Screening instrument. In R. Pogrund, G. Healy, K. Jones, N. Levack, S. Martin-Curry, C. Martinez, J. Marz, B. Roberson-Smith, & A. Vrba, *Teaching age-appropriate purposeful skills: An orientation & mobility curriculum for students with visual impairments* (pp. 195–203). Austin, TX: Texas School for the Blind and Visually Impaired.

Pogrund, R., Healy, G., Jones, K., Levack, N., Martin-Curry, S., Martinez, C., Marz, J., Roberson-Smith, B., & Vrba, A. (1995c). *Teaching age-appropriate purposeful skills: An orientation & mobility curriculum for students with visual impairments: Comprehensive assessment and ongoing evaluation.* Austin, TX: Texas School for the Blind and Visually Impaired.

Recchia, S. L. (1997). Play and concept development in infants and young children with severe visual impairments: A constructivist view. *Journal of Visual Impairment & Blindness, 91* (4), 401–416.

Skellenger, A. C., & Hill, E. W. (1997). The preschool learner. In B. B. Blasch, W. R. Wiener, & R. L. Welsh (Eds.), *Foundations of orientation and mobility* (2nd ed., pp. 407–438). New York: AFB Press.

Warren, D. H. (1984). *Blindness and early childhood development.* (2nd ed., rev.). New York: American Foundation for the Blind.

Zabel, R. H., & Zabel, M. K. (1982). Factors in burnout among teachers of exceptional children. *Exceptional Children, 22*(4), 4–8.

The organizations listed in this section provide a variety of products that will be useful to O&M specialists, but the items mentioned here are those that are specifically referred to in this book. For additional sources of products, materials, and services, see the *AFB Directory of Services for Blind and Visually Impaired Persons in the United States and Canada*, published by the American Foundation for the Blind.

**American Foundation
for the Blind**
AFB Press
11 Penn Plaza
New York, NY 10001
(212) 502-7600 or (800) 232-5463
Fax: (212) 502-7777
E-mail: info@afb.net
http://www.afb.org

Professional books, textbooks, videotapes, pamphlets, journals

**American Printing House
for the Blind**
1839 Frankfort Avenue
P.O. Box 6085
Louisville, KY 40206-0085
(502) 985-2405 or (800) 223-1839
Fax: (502) 899-2274
E-mail: info@aph.org
http://www.aph.org

Educational, technology, low vision products; professional publications and videotapes; tactile graphics tools; Chang tactile diagram kit; portable sound source

**Association for Education
and Rehabilitation of the Blind
and Visually Impaired**
4600 Duke Street, Suite 430
Alexandria, VA 22304
(703) 823-9690
Fax: (703) 823-9695
http://aerbvi.org

Professional publications

Blind Childrens Center
4120 Marathon Street
Los Angeles, CA 90029-3584
(323) 664-2153 or (800) 222-3566 or
(800) 222-3567 in California
Fax: (323) 665-3828

Educational publications in English and Spanish, videotapes

Exceptional Teaching Aids
20102 Woodbine Avenue
Castro Valley, CA 94546-4232
(800) 549-6999
Fax: (510) 582-5911
http://www.exceptionalteaching.com

Educational games, activities, and materials, magnification devices; publications and videotapes; survival signs and flash cards; Wikki Stix; Creative Foam Sheets; Magnetti Spaghetti

Independent Living Aids
27 East Mall
Plainview, NY 11803-4404
(800) 537-2118
http://www.independentliving.com

Watches, magnifiers, household items, sunglasses, adapted games (including jumbo and braille playing cards, bingo, Scrabble, Monopoly, dice, dominoes, checkers, and Connect Four), beeper balls, canes, educational aids, Wikki Stix, Puff Paint, braille compass, cassette players and recorders, computer software and hardware

Journal of Visual Impairment & Blindness
American Foundation for the Blind
11 Penn Plaza
New York, NY 10001
(212) 502-7600 or (800) 232-5463
http://www.afb.org

Professional journal

Lighthouse Enterprises
111 East 59th Street
New York, NY 10022-1202
(800) 829-0500
E-mail: thestore@lighthouse.org
http://lighthouse.org

Professional publications, brochures, fact sheets, multimedia packages, posters, videotapes and audiotapes, vision simulators

Lighthouse Enterprises, Consumer Products Division
36-20 Northern Boulevard
Long Island City, NY 11101
(718) 786-5620 or (800) 829-0500
Fax: (718) 786-0437
http://www.catalogcity.com/lighthouse

Long canes, braille compass, games, measuring tools, wallet, watches, cassettes and tape recorders, household items

LS&S
P.O. Box 673
Northbrook, IL 60065
(847) 498-9777 or (800) 468-4789
Fax: (847) 498-1482
E-mail: vision@lssgroup.com
http://www.lssgroup.com

Long canes, braille products, playing cards, computer software and hardware, household products, watches, magnifiers, cassette players and recorders, sunglasses, money identifier

Repro-tronics
75 Carver Avenue
Westwood, NJ 07675
(201) 722-1880 or (800) 948-8453
Fax: (201) 722-1881

Tactile image enhancer

RE:view
Heldref Publications
1319 Eighteenth Street, NW
Washington, DC 20036-1802
(202) 296-6267 or (800) 365-9753
Fax: (202) 296-5149 or (202) 293-6130
http://www.heldref.org

Professional journal published by the Association for Education and Rehabilitation of the Blind and Visually Impaired

Stoelting Company
620 Wheat Lane
Wood Dale, IL 60191
(630) 860-9700
Fax: (630) 860-9775
http://www.stoelting.com/tests/index.htm

Hill Performance Test of Selected
Positional Concepts

**Texas School for the Blind
and Visually Impaired**
1100 West 45th Street
Austin, TX 78756-3494
(512) 206-9240
http://www.tsbvi.edu/publications/

Professional publications, assessments,
curricula, videotapes

Vision Associates
7512 Dr. Phillips Boulevard, Suite 50-316
Orlando, FL 32819
(407) 352-1200
http://www.visionkits.com

Vision assessment kits and materials,
books and materials, infant development
materials

Index of Activities

This index lists concepts and skills discussed in this book and the activities that are suggested to address them.

address system concepts
  Address Bingo, Chapter 2, Appendix
    2B; Chapter 3
  address grid, Chapter 5, Appendix 5A
  Address Rap, Chapter 2, Appendix 2B;
    Chapter 5, Appendix 5A
  corkboard map with activity cards,
    Chapter 7, Appendix 7A
  hopscotch, Chapter 3
  How to Find a Specific Destination
    form, Chapter 5, Appendix 5A
  interactive model, Chapter 2,
    Appendix 2A; Chapter 3; Chapter 5;
    Chapter 5, Appendix 5A
  O&M recipe box, Chapter 5; Chapter 5,
    Appendix 5A
  O&M scrapbook, Chapter 5, Appendix
    5A
  quiz, Chapter 2, Appendix 2B
  unit on Learning the Address System,
    Chapter 2, Appendix 2B

alignment at corners
  role-playing, Chapter 3

body awareness concepts
  "Guess Who?" game, Chapter 5,
    Appendix 5A
  hopscotch, Chapter 3
  human guide races, Chapter 3
  games and manipulatives, Chapter 3;
    Chapter 4

  O&M recipe box, Chapter 5, Appendix
    5A
  Red Light, Green Light, Chapter 3

bus travel skills
  bus information forms, Chapter 5,
    Appendix 5A
  bus travel trivia, Chapter 5, Appendix
    5A
  How to Find a Specific Destination
    form, Chapter 5, Appendix 5A
  O&M journal, Chapter 5
  O&M recipe box, Chapter 5, Appendix
    5A
  role-playing, Chapter 3

cane skills
  grip cane and wrist practice, Chapter 5,
    Appendix 5A
  rhymes and poems, Chapter 5,
    Appendix 5A
  role-playing, Chapter 3
  temporary tangent mini-unit on
    residential travel focusing on fences,
    Chapter 2
  treasure hunt, Chapter 5

cardinal direction concepts
  How to Find a Specific Destination
    form, Chapter 5, Appendix 5A
  interactive model, Chapter 5,
    Chapter 7, Appendix 7A

cardinal direction concepts *(continued)*
    O&M recipe box, Chapter 5, Appendix
        5A
    Red Light, Green Light, Chapter 3

communication skills
    board games and manipulatives,
        Chapter 3
    How to Find a Specific Destination
        form, Chapter 5, Appendix 5A
    mobility "rap" session, Chapter 3,
        Chapter 5
    O&M journal, Chapter 5
    planning a lunch outing, Chapter 2,
        Appendix 2B
    role-playing, Chapter 3
    tape-recording a class presentation,
        Chapter 5

directionality concepts
    human-guide races, Chapter 3

environmental concepts
    Book in a Bag, Chapter 5, Appendix 5A
    create crossword puzzles, Chapter 5
    curiosity cards, Chapter 3
    How to Find a Specific Destination
        form, Chapter 5, Appendix 5A
    I Spy, Chapter 3
    In My Suitcase, Chapter 3
    light business travel area discovery
        learning, Chapter 3
    Mini-Chang Kit, Chapter 7, Appendix
        7A
    Mobility Adventures with Sherlock
        Holmes, Chapter 5, Appendix 5A
    O&M bulletin board, Chapter 4,
        Appendix 4A
    O&M recipe box, Chapter 2; Chapter 5;
        Chapter 5, Appendix 5A
    O&M scrapbook, Chapter 5, Appendix
        5A
    O&M spelling bee, Chapter 5
    Parallel Nearside Song, Chapter 5,
        Appendix 5A

planning a dream vacation, Chapter 3
pictures of traffic light housings,
    Chapter 5, Appendix 5A
role-playing, Chapter 3
scout pouch, Chapter 3; Chapter 4,
    Appendix 4A; Chapter 5
sequence maps of a highway system,
    Chapter 7, Appendix 7A
treasure or scavenger hunt, Chapter 3,
    Chapter 5

fence concept
    temporary tangent mini-unit on
        residential travel, Chapter 2

fine motor skills
    board games and manipulatives,
        Chapter 3
    grip cane and wrist practice, Chapter 5,
        Appendix 5A

gross motor skills
    adapted dances, Chapter 4
    games and manipulatives, Chapter 3
    grip cane and wrist practice, Chapter 5,
        Appendix 5A
    human guide races, Chapter 3
    rug squares for lining up at different
        corners, Chapter 7, Appendix 7A
    stair travel warm-ups, Chapter 5,
        Appendix 5A

information-gathering skills
    How to Find a Specific Destination
        form, Chapter 5, Appendix 5A
    Intersection Analysis form, Chapter 5,
        Appendix 5A
    Learning About a Neighborhood form,
        Chapter 6
    Mobility Adventures with Sherlock
        Holmes, Chapter 5, Appendix 5A
    O&M recipe box, Chapter 5; Chapter 5,
        Appendix 5A
    treasure or scavenger hunt, Chapter 3;
        Chapter 5; Chapter 5, Appendix 5A

intersection analysis concepts
  "And How Do You Cross?" Game,
    Chapter 5, Appendix 5A
  Crossing at the "T" poem, Chapter 5
  danger point and traffic pattern
    quizzes, Chapter 5, Appendix 5A
  fantasy story, Chapter 7, Appendix 7A
  interactive model, Chapter 5,
    Appendix 5A; Chapter 7, Appendix
    7A
  Intersection Analysis form, Chapter 5,
    Appendix 5A
  O&M recipe box, Chapter 5, Appendix
    5A
  Parallel Nearside Song, Chapter 5,
    Appendix 5A
  pictures of traffic light housings,
    Chapter 5, Appendix 5A

intersection analysis skills
  "And How Do You Cross?" Game,
    Chapter 5, Appendix 5A
  danger point and traffic pattern
    quizzes, Chapter 5, Appendix 5A
  Intersection Analysis form, Chapter 5,
    Appendix 5A
  pictures of traffic light housings,
    Chapter 5, Appendix 5A

landmark concepts
  calendar box, Chapter 5
  class presentation, Chapter 4,
    Appendix 4A
  interactive model, Chapter 5
  landmark recipe box, Chapter 2,
    Chapter 5
  O&M recipe box, Chapter 5, Appendix
    5A
  scout pouch, Chapter 3; Chapter 4,
    Appendix 4A; Chapter 5
  temporary tangent mini-unit on
    residential travel, Chapter 2

landmark skills
  calendar box, Chapter 5

How to Find a Specific Destination,
    Chapter 5, Appendix 5A
  I spy, Chapter 3
  landmark recipe box, Chapter 2,
    Chapter 5
  object cues, Chapter 5
  role-playing, Chapter 3
  scout pouch, Chapter 3; Chapter 4,
    Appendix 4A; Chapter 5
  shuffle map, Chapter 7
  treasure hunt, Chapter 5

laterality concepts
  games and manipulatives, Chapter 4
  role-playing, Chapter 3
  treasure hunt, Chapter 5

listening skills
  I Spy, Chapter 3
  identifying tape-recorded natural and
    man-made sounds, Chapter 5,
    Appendix 5A
  In My Suitcase, Chapter 3
  Red Light, Green Light, Chapter 3
  tape-recorded auditory cues, Chapter
    5; Chapter 5, Appendix 5A
  tape-recorded description of rote route,
    Chapter 7
  tape-recorded list of items to purchase,
    Chapter 5
  Telephone or Whisper Down the Lane,
    Chapter 3; Chapter 5
  treasure hunt, Chapter 5

mapmaking
  acetate overlay maps, Chapter 7,
    Appendix 7A
  add-on map with paper cutouts
    (pop-up maps), Chapter 7,
    Appendix 7A
  class presentation, Chapter 4,
    Appendix 4A
  edible map, Chapter 4, Appendix 4A;
    Chapter 6
  map series, Chapter 7

mapmaking (*continued*)
  scout pouch, Chapter 3; Chapter 4,
    Appendix 4A; Chapter 5
  shuffle map, Chapter 7
  student-made maps, Chapter 7
  student-shared maps, Chapter 7
  tactile landmarks to glue on map,
    Chapter 7
  treasure or scavenger hunt, Chapter 3
  unit on mapmaking, Chapter 2;
    Chapter 4, Appendix 4A

map-utilization skills
  Book in a Bag, Chapter 5, Appendix 5A
  calendar box, Chapter 5
  class presentation, Chapter 4,
    Appendix 4A
  edible map, Chapter 4, Appendix 4A;
    Chapter 7
  I Spy, Chapter 3
  map series, Chapter 7
  role-playing, Chapter 3
  scout pouch, Chapter 3; Chapter 4,
    Appendix 4A; Chapter 5
  shuffle map, Chapter 7
  student-made maps, Chapter 7
  student-shared maps, Chapter 7
  tape-recorded description of rote route,
    Chapter 7
  unit on mapmaking, Chapter 2,
    Appendix 2B; Chapter 4, Appendix 4A

memory skills
  In My Suitcase, Chapter 3

monocular skills
  I Spy, Chapter 3
  In My Suitcase, Chapter 3
  Mobility Adventures with Sherlock
    Holmes, Chapter 5, Appendix 5A
  Monocular cheers and chants,
    Chapter 5, Appendix 5A
  monocular quiz, Chapter 5, Appendix
    5A
  temporary tangent mini-unit on
    residential travel, Chapter 2

treasure hunt, Chapter 5
unit on learning the address system,
  Chapter 2, Appendix 2B
Visual Scanning study sheet, Chapter 2
word search, Chapter 5

organizational skills
  How to Find a Specific Destination
    form, Chapter 5, Appendix 5A
  student portfolio, Chapter 3, Chapter 5

questioning skills
  curiosity cards, Chapter 3
  How to Find a Specific Destination
    form, Chapter 5, Appendix 5A

residential block concepts
  Book in a Bag, Chapter 5, Appendix 5A
  class presentation, Chapter 4,
    Appendix 4A
  edible map, Chapter 4, Appendix 4A;
    Chapter 7
  interactive model, Chapter 5; Chapter
    7, Appendix 7A
  Mobility Adventures with Sherlock
    Holmes, Chapter 5, Appendix 5A
  O&M scrapbook, Chapter 5, Appendix
    5A
  portable tactile diagrams of residential
    grassy strips, Chapter 7, Appendix
    7A
  rug squares for lining up at different
    corners, Chapter 7, Appendix 7A
  scout pouch, Chapter 3; Chapter 4,
    Appendix 4A; Chapter 5
  treasure hunt, Chapter 5
  unit on mapmaking, Chapter 4,
    Appendix 4A

route design, planning, and travel
  board games and manipulatives,
    Chapter 3
  career cards, Chapter 6
  full-body checkers, Chapter 3
  How to Find a Specific Destination
    form, Chapter 5, Appendix 5A

landmark recipe box, Chapter 2, Chapter 5
O&M recipe box, Chapter 5
O&M scrapbook, Chapter 5, Appendix 5A
object cues, Chapter 7; Chapter 7, Appendix 7A
planning a field trip, Chapter 5
planning a lunch outing, Chapter 2, Appendix 2B
role-playing, Chapter 3, Chapter 5
shuffle map, Chapter 7
treasure hunt, Chapter 5
verbal map, Chapter 7
writing a short story or skit, Chapter 5

route-shape concepts
interactive model, Chapter 5
O&M recipe box, Chapter 2; Chapter 5, Appendix 5A
scout pouch, Chapter 3; Chapter 4, Appendix 4A; Chapter 5
treasure hunt, Chapter 5
unit on mapmaking, Chapter 4, Appendix 4A

search skills
How to Find a Specific Destination form, Chapter 5, Appendix 5A
Mobility Adventures with Sherlock Holmes, Chapter 5, Appendix 5A
treasure or scavenger hunt, Chapter 3, Chapter 5

spatial concepts
board games and manipulatives, Chapter 3
calendar box, Chapter 5
cardboard shoe organizer, Chapter 4
full-body checkers, Chapter 3
How to Find a Specific Destination form, Chapter 5, Appendix 5A
interactive model, Chapter 5
mini-Chang Kit, Chapter 7; Chapter 7, Appendix 7A
O&M spelling bee, Chapter 5

Parallel Nearside Song, Chapter 5, Appendix 5A
treasure or scavenger hunt, Chapter 3, Chapter 5
Visual Scanning study sheet, Chapter 2

stair travel skills
stair travel warm-ups, Chapter 5, Appendix 5A

street-crossing skills
color gels for scanning at streets, Chapter 7, Appendix 7A
danger point and traffic pattern quizzes, Chapter 5, Appendix 5A
interactive model, Chapter 7, Appendix 7A
Intersection Analysis form, Chapter 5, Appendix 5A
pictures of traffic light housing, Chapter 5, Appendix 5A
rug squares for lining up at different corners, Chapter 7, Appendix 7A
temporary tangent mini-unit on residential travel, Chapter 2

time-distance concepts
human guide races, Chapter 3

trailing skills
feather duster, Chapter 5

visual skills
color gels for scanning at streets, Chapter 7, Appendix 7A
"Guess Who?" game, Chapter 5, Appendix 5A
I Spy, Chapter 3
In My Suitcase, Chapter 3
Mobility Adventures with Sherlock Holmes, Chapter 5, Appendix 5A
treasure or scavenger hunt, Chapter 3, Chapter 5
Visual Skills Scanning study sheet, Chapter 2

A

Abstract understanding, of concepts, 98, 99

Academic achievement, assessment of, 13–14

Acquired vision loss, people with
assessment questions for, 27–28
necessity of training for, 8

Action games, 77

Adaptive functioning, assessment of, 13–14

Adding-on based on route shape
add-on map, lesson with, 293–297
with Ls, 251–253
training environment for, 251–252

Address Bingo, 78, 79

Address system
address grid, 202–203
bodily-kinesthetic approach for teaching of, 211–213
lesson plan, 57–64
musical approach to teaching of, 196
spatial approach to teaching of, 202–203
visual-tactile map lesson, 301–306

Administration, and public relations, 341–343

Adults
assessment interview questions, 27–28
and concept instruction, 108
learning formats of, 180
learning styles, determination of, 159–160
and role-playing, 82
strengths/weaknesses, identification of, 162

Age of students
and content of lessons, 179–180
See also Adults; Children

Alternative instructional units, 46–53
collaborative approach to, 53
examples of use, 46–49
feature unit, 48–49
generating ideas for, 49, 52
study sheet, example of, 50–51
temporary tangent mini-unit, 47–48

APH Tactile Graphics Kit, 268, 273

Aptitude test, related to multiple intelligences, 161

Arc width, meaning of, 5

Assessment interview questions
for adults with acquired vision loss, 27–28
for cognitive level assessment, 17–18
correct form for questions, 18–20
for diabetic clients, 28
for family members, 11, 26–27
for referral source, 11–12
for school-age students, 11, 20, 25

Assessment of students, 6–22
assessment tools for, 14–15
for concept understanding.
See Conceptual knowledge, assessment of
environment for, 15, 16–17
for environmental concepts, 20
individualized approach to, 6–8
interview of family/professionals, 11–12
interviews in, 9, 11–12
multiple intelligences, strength/weaknesses assessment, 161–163

Assessment of students (continued)
  natural observation in, 15
  O&M assessment plan, sample form,
    10, 31
  as ongoing process, 21–22
  planning stage, 8–9
  review of student records/files, 12–14
  steps in, 9
  travel activities during, 17–18, 20–21
Assessment tools
  bibliography of tools/instruments,
    30
  selection of appropriate tool, 14–15
Atlas Speaks, 268
Audible toys, 265
Auditory identification, naturalist
  approach to teaching, 224
Auditory maps, 195–196, 277–278
Automobile, storage of materials in, 291

B
Blocks in neighborhood
  bodily-kinesthetic approach for
    teaching of, 213–215
  rug block activity, 214–215
  See also Residential areas; Training
    environments; Travel environments
Bloom's taxonomy of learning, 17–18
Board games, 76–77
  skills related to specific games, 77
Bodily-kinesthetic intelligence, 146–150
  learning activities geared to, 164–165,
    167–168, 206–217
  skills/competencies related to, 171
  teacher strengths related to, 167–168
  teaching strategies related to, 146–148
Body concepts, assessment of, 103–104
Body image, 92–93
Book in a Bag, 191–194
Burnout, prevention and O&M specialist,
  338–339
Bus routes, 6
Bus travel
  interpersonal approaches to teaching
    of, 219–220

intrapersonal approaches to teaching
    of, 223
  routes, 6
By demand routes. See Student-traveled
  routes

C
Campus environment, 237, 239–240
  campus orientation/cane skills lesson
    plan, 149
  environmental features of, 239
Cane skills
  bodily-kinesthetic approach for
    teaching of, 215–217
  constant contact, 5–6
  constant contact method, 5–6
  lesson plan, 149
  linguistic approach to teaching of,
    186–188
  logical-mathematical approach to
    teaching of, 199
Cards with cues
  landmarks on, 277–280
  shuffle maps, 270–273
Chang Kit, 74, 268
  assessment of spatial concepts, 105
  mini version, 275, 324–326
  use in lesson about traffic patterns,
    324–326
  uses of, 275
Children
  assessment interview, 11, 20, 25
  concept development of, 97–98
  concept instruction, 107–108, 109–110
  learning formats of, 180
  natural observation of, 15
  and role-playing, 80–81
  strengths/weaknesses, identification
    of, 161–162
Closed-circuit television (CCTV), for
  map-making, 272–273
Closing of lessons, 40
Cognitive mapping, 263–264
  nature of, 263
  usefulness in O&M skills, 263–264

Collaborative approach
  to alternative instructional units, 53
  benefits of, 330
  challenges related to, 330
  and communication, 331–332
  concept instruction, 110–111, 118
  and cooperation, 332–333
  coordination of activities, 333–334
  family involvement, 334–335
  professionals to collaborate with,
    328–329
  roles and responsibilities in, 333–334
  situations for use in O&M services,
    329–330
  student swap, 175, 177
Communication
  with collaborative partners, 331–332
  language, uses of, 136–137
Communication methods, of people with
    multiple disabilities, 181–182
Community, and public relations, 343–344
Compass cardinal directions
  to maintain directionality, 95–96
  teaching about with interactive map,
    297–299
Computers
  computer games, 77
  for verbal maps, 275–276
Concept development
  body image, 92–93
  challenges for people who are blind,
    99–103
  conceptual understanding, categories
    of, 98
  directionality, 95
  distance concepts, 96
  environmental concepts, 96
  laterality, 95
  and learning, 91–92
  measurement concepts, 96
  spatial concepts, 93–95
  time concepts, 95
Concept formation
  abstract understanding of concepts, 98,
    99

concrete understanding of concepts, 98
  developmental aspects, 97–98
  functional understanding of concepts,
    98
  and whole-to-part learning, 100
Concepts, elements of, 92
Concepts, instruction in, 107–123
  and adults, 108
  and children, 107–108, 109–110
  collaborative approaches, 110–111, 118
  concept class group, 118
  concrete experiences, value of, 112–113
  concrete experiences in, 112–113,
    122–123
  in context of mobility activity, 117–118,
    120
  daily routine, integration of concepts,
    121, 122
  and dual disabilities, persons with,
    121–123
  and early interaction of children,
    109–110
  environmental terms, teaching of, 112
  family in, 109–110
  group activities, 116
  instructional strategies in, 108–109
  instructional unit example, 124–131
  instructional unit teaching, 118–120
  learning activities, 114
  linguistic approach to teaching of,
    188–194
  one-to-one instruction, 115
  sensory overload, avoiding, 113
  skills and concepts, integration of,
    113–114
  spatial terms, teaching of, 111–112
  structure of lessons, 107
Conceptual knowledge, assessment of,
    102–107
  body concepts, 103–104
  environmental concepts, 106–107
  scope of assessment, 102
  spatial concepts, 104–106
  verbalisms in, 103
Concrete understanding, of concepts, 98

Constant contact, meaning of, 5–6
Creativity of student, encouragement of, 70–72
Critical skills approach, 43–46
    combined with traditional sequence model, 46
    environment for teaching, 44
    situations for use of, 45
    and splinter skills, 44–45
    compared to traditional sequence approach, 45
Crossing street. *See* Intersections; Traffic patterns
Cultural factors
    culturally relevant assessment, 17
    exposure to different cultures, 179
    and O&M lesson content, 178–179
Curbs, learning about different shapes lesson, 318–321
Curiosity of student, stimulating, methods for, 71–72
Curricular units (O&M), skills/concepts related to, 4

D
Daily routine
    concept instruction in, 121, 123
    as environment for teaching, 87–88
Danger points, logical-mathematical approach to teaching of, 202
Decision-making
    maps as aid, 266
    student participation in, 72–73
Department store, as training environment, 253–255
Destination
    destination form, 198
    logical-mathematical approach to teaching of, 197–198
Diabetic clients, interview questions for, 28
Dino Park Tycoon, 77
Directionality, 95
    cardinal compass directions for, 95–96
Discount store, as training environment, 253–255

Discovery learning, 68, 70
    lesson plan, example of, 69
Distance concepts
    challenges for people who are blind, 99–100
    and route planning, 96
Dual disabilities. *See* Multiple disabilities, people with
Dual disabilities, people with
    assessment questions for, 29
    assessment review of, 12–13
    scheduling lessons for, 87–88

E
Electronic equipment, tools for O&M, 265, 272–273
Enablers, 23
Environment and assessment, 15, 16–17
    cultural relevance of, 17
    for environmental concepts, 20
    for experiences versus inexperienced traveler, 15, 16–17
Environment for teaching
    critical skills approach, 44
    environmental concept learning, 96
    location of lessons, 36–37, 44
    natural routine approach, 87–88
    off-campus travel with peer, 84
Environment for travel. *See* Travel environment
Environmental concepts, 96
    assessment of, 20, 106–107
    Chang Kit lesson, 324–326
    environmental terms, in concept instruction, 112
    logical-mathematical approach to teaching of, 200–201
Experiential learning, meaning of, 266

F
Family
    and assessment process, 11, 26–27
    barriers to working with, 335
    as collaborative partner, 334–335
    and concept development, 109–110

Feature units, 48–49
Field trips, 85–86
    learning activities during, 86
Functional understanding, of concepts, 98

G
Games and activities approach, 74–80
    action games, 77
    board games, 76–77
    computer games, 77
    group games, 78
    movement-related games, 78, 80
    turn taking, 75–76
Gender, and O&M lesson content, 177–178
Global positioning systems, 268
Goal-setting, (O&M) specialist, 339
Goals and objectives for students, 33–34
    in lesson plans, 36
    long-term goals, 33
    wording for, 33, 36
Group activities, 82–87
    concepts, instruction in, 116
    discussions, 86–87
    field trips, 85–86
    formation of groups, 82–83
    group games, 83
    interactive models, 83–84
    mini-lessons, 84–85
Group games, 78, 83

H
Hands-on learning, in concept instruction, 112–113
Highway system, lesson on, 299–301
Hill Performance Test of Selected Positional Concepts, 103
Hot pen, 274

I
Incidental learning, challenges for people who are blind, 101
Individualized Educational Program (IEP)
    assessment review of, 14

goals and objectives in, 33–34
Individualized Written Rehabilitation Program (IWRP)
    assessment review of, 14
    goals and objectives in, 33–34
Indoor training areas, 233–234
    environmental features of, 234, 258
Infants, concept development of, 97
Instructional materials
    Chang Kit, 105, 275
    electronic equipment, 265
    including in lesson plans, 37
    portability and durability of, 287–288
    storage of, 290–291
    tactile diagrams, 264
    See also Manipulatives; Maps; Models
Instructional strategies
    for concept instruction, 108–109
    games and activities approach, 74–80
    group activities, 82–87
    natural routine approach, 87–88
    prompts, use of, 89
    reverse chaining, 88–89
    role-playing, 80–82
    shaping, 89–90
    students' initiatives approach, 66–74
    task analysis, 88
Instructional units, 41–53
    combining approaches, 46
    concepts, instruction in, 118–120, 124–131
    critical skills approach, 43–46
    learning address system, sample unit, 55–64
    purpose of, 41
    traditional sequence approach, 42–43
    unit quiz, 61
    See also Alternative units
Integrated teaching approach, layering lessons, 38–40
Intelligence theories, multiple intelligences. See Multiple intelligences theory
Interactive models, 276–277
    construction of, 277

Interactive models (*continued*)
   group activity, 83–84
   teaching about compass cardinal
      directions with, 297–299
Interactive skills, interpersonal approach
   to teaching of, 217
Interpersonal intelligence, 150–152
   learning activities geared to, 166–167,
      168, 217–220
   skills/competencies related to, 171
   teacher strengths related to, 168
   teaching strategies related to, 150–152
Intersections
   Chang Kit lesson, 324–326
   crossing safely lesson plan, 35
   grassy strips found at corners lesson,
      312–315
   interpersonal approaches to teaching
      of, 219
   intersection analysis form, 218
   intrapersonal approaches to teaching
      of, 221
   movement of traffic through plus-
      shaped intersection lesson, 321–324
   shapes of, 237
Interviews. *See* Assessment interview
   questions
Intrapersonal intelligence, 152–153,
   155–156
   learning activities geared to, 166–167,
      168, 221–223
   skills/competencies related to, 171
   teacher strengths related to, 168
   teaching strategies related to, 152–153,
      155–156
Introduction to lessons, 37–38

K
Keller, Helen, 181

L
L-shaped routes, 251–253
Landmarks
   cards with cues, 277–278

remembering with object cues lesson,
   306–308
   shuffle maps, 270, 272
Language, uses of, 136–137
Laterality, and, 95
Layering lessons, 38–40
Learning activities
   bodily-kinesthetic intelligence based
      activities, 164–165, 167–168, 206–217
   concepts, instruction in, 114
   interpersonal intelligence based
      activities, 166–167, 168, 217–220
   linguistic intelligence based activities,
      164–165, 185–193
   logical-mathematical intelligence based
      activities, 164–165, 197–202
   musical intelligence based activities,
      164–165, 194–196
   naturalistic intelligence based
      activities, 166–167, 168, 223–224
   spatial intelligence based activities,
      164–165, 167, 202–206
   See also Instructional strategies; Lesson
      plan examples
Learning formats, age-specific, 180
Learning moment, teaching for, 67–68,
   117
Learning styles
   definition of, 134
   determining style, for adults, 159–160
   matched to teaching styles, 134, 169,
      172–177
   and multiple intelligences concept,
      159–160, 172–177
Learning taxonomy, Bloom's, 17–18
Lesson plan examples
   crossing safely at residential
      intersections, 35
   developing basic cane skills/campus
      orientation, 149
   developing travel skills for light
      business areas, 69
   improving orientation skills, 176
   improving semi-independent travel
      skills, 183

learning address system, 57–64
understanding left and right, 119
understanding residential blocks
concepts, 125–131
Lesson plans, 34–40
closing of lesson, 40
completed plan form, sample of, 35
goals and objectives for, 36
instructional materials in, 37
introduction to the lesson, 37–38
learning address system, examples of,
57–64
lesson location specified in, 36–37
light business travel, example of, 69
method of teaching, 38–40
post-lesson teacher written notes, 40
Light business areas
developing travel skills lesson plan, 69
environmental elements of, 235
as training area, 235–237
Linguistic intelligence, 136–139
learning activities geared to, 164–165,
185–193
skills/competencies related to, 170
teacher strengths related to, 166
teaching strategies related to, 137–139
Location of lessons. See Training
environments
Logical-mathematical intelligence,
142–144
learning activities geared to, 164–165,
197–202
skills/competencies related to, 170
teacher strengths related to, 166–167
teaching strategies related to, 142–144,
176
Low vision devices, assessment review
of, 12

M
Mall. *See* Shopping mall
Manipulatives
definition of, 265
uses in O&M curriculum, 265–267
Map-making, 284–286

CCTV, use of, 272–273
as group activity, 84
interactive models, 276–277
materials for, 289
musical approach to teaching of,
195–196
of tactile maps, 273, 275
teaching approaches to, 285–286
teaching sequence for, 285
tips for construction of, 288
of verbal maps, 275–276
of visual maps, 268–273
Map-reading
and experiential learning, 266
as motivational activity, 266
Map-related lessons. *See* Orientation
lessons, Mobility lessons
Map skills, 280–286
environment for, 281
introduction of maps, 280–281
linguistic approach to teaching of,
191–194
pre-made maps, use of, 284
premap skills, 282
sequence for teaching of, 269, 281–284
simple-to-complex teaching approach,
283–284
teaching style and student modes of
learning, 262–263
Maps, 267–280
definition of, 264
edible maps, 268
enlargement of, 270–271, 272
interactive models, 276–277
for people with multiple disabilities,
277–280
perceptual mode targeted by, 269
pop-ups on, 269–270
shuffle maps, 270
tactile maps, 273–275
use in lessons, examples of, 270
uses in O&M curriculum, 265–267
verbal maps, 275–276
visual maps, 268–273
Measurement concepts, 96

Method of teaching, in lesson plan, 38–40

Mini-lessons, group lessons, 84–85

Mobility lessons, interpersonal approach to, 220

Mobility lessons, with maps, 308–326
  learning about grassy strips at intersection corners, 312–315
  learning about movement of traffic through plus-shaped intersection, 321–324
  learning about scanning patters used in crossing intersections, 308–311
  learning to recognize different curb shapes, 318–321
  reviewing traffic patterns at intersections, 316–318
  reviewing traffic patterns while listening, 324–326

Models
  definition of, 264
  interactive models, 276–277
  uses in O&M curriculum, 265–267
  See also Maps

Monocular skills
  intrapersonal approaches to teaching of, 221–223
  logical-mathematical approach to teaching of, 200–201
  musical approach to teaching of, 194–195

Movement
  games/activities for, 77–78, 80, 164–165
  intelligence in. *See* Bodily-kinesthetic intelligence

Multiple disabilities, people with
  assessment questions for, 29
  assessment review of, 12–13
  communication methods of, 181–182
  concept instruction for, 121–123
  maps and manipulatives, use of, 277–280
  multiple intelligences theory applied to teaching/learning, 181–182, 184
  and O&M curriculum, 181–182
  scheduling lessons for, 87–88

training environments for, 258–260

Multiple Intelligences Inventory, 161, 225–230

Multiple intelligences theory, 134–158
  aptitude test related to, 161, 225–230
  bodily-kinesthetic intelligence, 146–150
  hobbies/interests related to, 160
  interpersonal intelligence, 150–152
  intrapersonal intelligence, 152–153, 155–156
  linguistic intelligence, 136–139
  logical-mathematical intelligence, 142–144
  musical intelligence, 139–142
  naturalistic intelligence, 156–158
  spatial intelligence, 144–146
  and teaching. *See* Multiple intelligences theory, O&M application of
  See also individual types of intelligence

Multiple intelligences theory, O&M application of
  learning formats, 180
  learning styles, 159–160
  learning styles/teaching styles compatibility, 159–160, 169, 172–177
  multiple disabilities, people with, 181–182, 184
  O&M curriculum, 169, 177–182
  O&M skills and competencies in, 170–171
  student assessment, 161–163
  teacher self-assessment, 159–161
  teaching styles, 163, 166–168

Musical intelligence, 139–142
  learning activities geared to, 84, 164–165, 194–196
  skills/competencies related to, 170
  teacher strengths related to, 166
  teaching strategies related to, 139–142, 176

N

Natural observation
  guidelines for, 16
  in student assessment, 15–16

Natural routine approach, 87–88
Naturalistic intelligence, 156–158
    learning activities geared to, 166–167,
        168, 223–224
    skills/competencies related to, 171
    teacher strengths related to, 168
    teaching strategies related to, 156–158
Neighborhood Map Making Machine, 77
Note-taking
    equipment for students, 74
    post-lesson evaluative notes, 40

O
O&M Recipe Box, 188–191
Observation. See Natural observation
Orientation lessons, with maps, 293–308
    teaching about address system,
        301–306
    teaching about community relationship
        to highway system, 295–297
    teaching about highway system using
        map sequence format, 299–301
    teaching beginning map concepts,
        293–295
    teaching compass cardinal directions,
        297–299
    teaching use of object cues to
        remember landmarks, 306–308
Orientation and mobility (O&M)
    curriculum
    and age of students, 179–180
    cultural factors, 178–179
    gender considerations, 177–178
    keeping up to date with, 5
    and multiple intelligences theory, 169
    and people with multiple disabilities,
        181–182
    requisite knowledge, 5–7
    sources of information about, 5
Orientation and mobility (O&M)
    specialists
    burnout, prevention of, 338–339
    goal-setting, 339
    and healthy lifestyle, 339–340
    professional development, 337–338

and public relations, 340–344
support networks, types of, 340
sustaining creativity by, 336
time management, 339

P
Part-to-whole learning, and people who
    are blind, 100–101
Pedometer, 265
Peer tutoring, off-campus travel, 84
Perimeter (block) organizer, training
    environment, 247, 248–250
Physical prompts, 89, 182
Plus-shaped organizer, training
    environment, 246–247
Polycentric frame of reference, 95
Pop-ups, on visual maps, 269–270
Portfolios, contents of, 73–74
Professional development, O&M
    specialist, 337–338
Prompts, physical and verbal, 89, 182
Public relations, 340–344
    administrative support for, 341–343
    and community, 343–344
    importance of, 340–341
    public relations kit, 342

R
Raised-line maps, 273–275
    construction of, 273
Raised-shape maps, 273–275
    construction of, 275
Records of students, information
    contained in, 12–14
Reinforcement, in shaping, 89–90
Residential areas
    bodily-kinesthetic approach for
        teaching about blocks, 213–215
    crossing safely lesson plan, 35
    environmental elements of, 234
    training areas, 234–235
    See also Blocks in neighborhood
Reverse chaining, 88–89
Role-playing, 80–82
    for adults, 82

Role-playing *(continued)*
  ideas for roles, 80–82
  for older students, 81
  for young students, 80–81
Routes by demand. See Student-traveled
  routes
Routines. *See* Daily routine
Rug block activity, 214–215
Rural areas, training environment for, 243

S
Scanning patterns, for crossing
  intersections lesson, 308–311
Scatter-shape organizer, training
  environment, 247, 250–251
Scout pouch, equipment for, 74, 75
Sensory integration, challenges for people
  who are blind, 100–101
Sensory overload, 113
Sequential learning, instructional
  approach to, 42–43
Shaping, 89–90
Shopping mall
  basic layout, 257
  as training environment, 256–258
Shopping plaza, as training environment,
  253–255
Shuffle maps, 270, 272
Singing, 84
Social elements, of travel environment,
  23–24
Spatial concepts, 93–95
  assessment of, 104–106
  Chang Kit lesson, 105, 324–326
  and cognitive mapping, 263–264
  levels of understanding, 104
  logical-mathematical approach for
    teaching of, 199–201
  spatial approach for recognition of,
    205–206
  spatial terms, in concept instruction,
    111–112, 169
Spatial intelligence, 144–146
  learning activities geared to, 164–165,
    167, 202–206

skills/competencies related to, 170
teacher strengths related to, 167
teaching strategies related to, 144–146
Splinter skills, 44–45
  improvement of, 45
  nature of, 44
Stair travel, bodily-kinesthetic approach
  for teaching of, 206–211
StreetFinder program, 77
Strip organizer, training environment,
  247, 250
Student participation
  in decision-making, 72–73
  encouragement of participation, 74
  group discussions, 86–87
  in lessons/meetings, 73–74
Student swap, 175, 177
Student-traveled routes, 67, 237, 239–240
  campus environment, 237, 239–240
Students' initiatives approach, 66–74
  discovery learning in, 68, 70
  encouraging curiosity/creativity, 70–72
  portfolios in, 73–74
  and reluctant students, 74
  shared decision-making in, 72–73
  teaching at the learning moment, 67–68
  teaching requested routes in, 67
Study sheet, for alternative unit, 50–51
Sullivan, Anne, 181
Supermarket
  basic layout, 256
  environmental features of, 255
  as training environment, 253–255

T
Tactile diagrams
  definition of, 264
  shape of grassy strips at intersections
    lesson, 312–315
Tactile image enhancer, for map-making,
  268, 273, 289
Tactile maps, 273–275
  construction of, 273–275
  raised-shape maps, 274–275
Tape recorders, 265

auditory maps, 195–196, 279
raised-line maps, 273, 274
Task analysis, 88
Teacher self-assessment, 159–161
aptitude test, 161
educational experiences in, 159–160
hobby/interest identification in, 160
Teachers
bodily-kinesthetic intelligence of, 167–168
interpersonal intelligence of, 168
intrapersonal intelligence of, 168
linguistic intelligence of, 166
logical-mathematical intelligence of, 166–167
musical intelligence of, 169
naturalistic intelligence of, 168
self-assessment, 159–161
spatial intelligence of, 167
styles of teaching. *See* Teaching styles
See also Orientation and mobility (O&M) specialists
Teaching Age-Appropriate Purposeful Skills (TAPS), 14
Teaching materials. *See* Instructional materials
Teaching styles
map skills, and student modes of learning, 262–263
matched to learning styles, 134, 169, 172–177
and multiple intelligences theory, 163, 166–168
Temporary tangent mini-units, 47
Thermoform paper/machines, 268, 273
Time concepts, 95
Time management, O&M specialist, 339
Traditional sequence approach, 42–43
combined with critical skills approach, 46
situations for use of, 45
Traffic light housing
spatial approach for recognition of, 203–205
types of, 204

Traffic patterns
logical-mathematical approach to teaching of, 202
musical approach to teaching of, 194
review of traffic patterns at intersections lesson, 315–318
scanning patterns and crossing lesson, 308–311
Training environments
adding-on based on route shape, 251–252
critical skills approach to, 44
crowding/traffic factors, 23
destinations, examples of, 245
and environmental concept learning, 96
imperfect environments, 240–241
indoor training areas, 233–234
L-shaped routes, 251–253
light business travel areas, 235–237
linguistic approach to teaching about, 188–191
map for O&M specialist, 244
natural routine approach to, 87–88
naturalist approach to teaching of, 223–224
off-campus travel with peer, 84
perimeter (block) organizer, 248–250
for persons with multiple disabilities, 258–260
physical characteristics of, 22
plus-shaped organizer, 246–247
pre-lesson site selection, 36–37, 44, 232–233, 243–246
residential training areas, 234–235
scatter-shape organizer, 250–251
shopping mall, 256–257
small shopping plaza, 253–255
social aspects of, 23–24
strip organizer, 250
student requested routes, 67
student-traveled routes, 237, 239–240
supermarket/department store/discount store, 255
training area, map of, 244

Training environments *(continued)*
    unfamiliar environments, 241–243
Treasure Hunt, 199–201
Turn-taking, teaching activities for, 75–76

U
Unfamiliar environments, 241–243
    environmental features, 243

V
Verbal maps, 276–277
    types of, 276
Verbal prompts, 89
Verbalisms, nature of, 103
VisuAide, 268

Visual clutter, 268
Visual functioning, assessment of, 12
Visual input and learning, challenges for
    people who are blind, 99
Visual maps, 268–273
    construction of, 268–273
Visualization, and cognitive mapping,
    263–264

W
Walkie-talkies, 265
Weekly planning. *See* Lesson plans
Whole-to-part learning, challenges for
    people who are blind, 100–101
Wikki Stix, 273